AUTOBIOGRAPHY OF
A CHINESE WOMAN

ALSO BY BUWEI YANG CHAO

HOW TO COOK AND EAT IN CHINESE

AUTOBIOGRAPHY OF A CHINESE WOMAN

Buwei Yang Chao

PUT INTO ENGLISH BY HER HUSBAND

Yuenren Chao

ILLUSTRATED

Original publication 1947

All rights reserved. This book, or parts thereof, must not be reproduced in any form without permission.

Designed by Robert Josephy

TO THE MEMORY OF "AUNTIE"
WHO GAVE ME ME

FOREWORD

SINCE my wife has the last word, I shall have the foreword. This is a book about a personality. My wife is interested in personalities; therefore she will tell about the person. I am interested in books; therefore I shall tell about the book.

My wife began her autobiography in 1913. She began writing it as a novel, but soon decided that real events were more exciting than imagined ones and that a simple story would be a more satisfactory form of writing than a literary composition. But in those days, when an archaic, literary style was the only proper thing, she lacked a suitable medium in which to tell the story of the woman she is, and she stopped her writing before she went very far with it.

Those who have followed the cultural trends in China will remember that writing in a classical form of Chinese was not a passing fashion of an age, but the universal practice of twenty centuries. It still is among some newspaper correspondents, many scholars, and all officials and business men. Until Hu Shih's Literary Revolution of 1917, everybody wrote in the classical language as a matter of course. Even familiar letters were written in that form. What that revolution did was to make writing in the vernacular respectable. In the field of biography, Hu Shih set the example by writing the story of Li Ch'ao,[1] a quite unknown girl, who has since become famous at

---

[1] Hu Shih, *Wentr'un* (Collected Works), first series, Vol. 4, pp. 1077-94, Shanghai, 1919. A significant feature of that biography is that all the direct quotations from letters are, of necessity, still in the classical style.

Harvard University and Radcliffe College by being part of the required reading in "Chinese 3." Then he wrote his *Self-Portrait at Forty*, Shanghai, 1933, also in the colloquial language.

My wife, however, has not tried to write like Hu Shih. Like most vanguards of revolutions, Hu Shih writes his colloquial as a scholar thoroughly versed in the classical tradition. Her debt to Hu Shih lies rather in that, because of the revolution, she can now take courage in writing as she talks without having to feel apologetic about it. She can now even feel fashionable about it.

Nor has she tried to write in the pure Mandarin of Peiping, as I am in the habit of doing. Writing in a pure dialect may be of scientific interest, in that it gives an authentic record of a speech community. But she is primarily concerned with telling about herself, and, since she does not speak any pure dialect, whether of Peiping or of Nanking, she writes only as she talks in real life. She aims at no particular style, except in so far as the style is the woman.

It is one thing to have a language to write a book in and another thing to write it. It was only eight months ago that she really got started—

No, Yuenren, you are all mixed up. You started with the *English* version eight months ago. I started with my Chinese a year ago—

You are right, Yunch'ing, you started a year ago. Well, one day, while my wife was visiting New York, Pearl Buck suggested to her the idea of writing a short—

You are wrong there again, Yuenren. I did not see Pearl Buck on that occasion. It was Mrs. Lin Yutang who told me that Pearl Buck had asked her if she might—

But, darling, is this your foreword or mine? If you keep interrupting—

Why not make it both yours and mine?—

That's an idea, too. Suppose you go on from here, Yun ch'ing!—

All right, I will. Well, Mrs. Lin told me that she might perhaps be able to write a short biography of me, possibly in the form of an article. She had known me for twenty-five years, and all she needed would be some details about my younger days.

I told my husband about it and added that, since I had started my own story many years ago, I had better finish it myself.

"I have written your biography already," he said.

"When? Where?" I said. "You have never told me about it."

"No, I haven't. I started writing it nineteen years ago."

He showed me a manuscript of forty pages of closely written Chinese. It was too long for an article and too short for a book. It was not for publication anyway. He had kept it for a surprise gift someday, perhaps for our silver wedding. But now that I was going to write the thing myself, he decided it was time to show me his manuscript.

I found that what he had written was me all right. The life he wrote lived like me and felt like me. But the language was in pure Mandarin, which I do not speak. And, for the parts before we met each other, he often got personalities and order of events quite mixed up. I said I had better edit it a little.

"But no," he said, "I think it will be much nicer if you start it afresh and write it as a book-length autobiography."

The final impetus to writing came from Pearl Buck and Richard J. Walsh. One night, at a dinner party, they told me that, when my cookbook was first published, a critic from Baltimore had exclaimed: "Well, this woman ought to write a book!" When I said: "All right, I am going to write an autobiography," they said:

"Good, you write it and we'll print it."

All that remained, then, was for the Asia Press or the John Day Company to have a few hundred thousand Chinese types ready. Since they had none, we agreed that it would be much simpler to have the whole thing translated into English. At this, everybody around the dinner table looked at Yuenren, and here is the result of that look.

The present book is not one of those "as told to so-and-so" stories, since I had it down in writing. Nor is it quite an English translation of a Chinese book, since the Chinese has not yet been published. When I do publish the Chinese, it will not be the same book, either. For, to a Chinese reader, there would be no point in telling what weddings and funerals are like in China, while, on the other hand, a "ticket" from a traffic officer would take a lot of explaining before he understands that it is not a policeman's invitation to go to the theater. So, although this book was written in Chinese, it was written for readers of English.

But my husband has not always been a well-behaved translator. While he tries to render my simple Chinese into Basic English, he constantly lapses into his academic style of involved qualifications. Now, I want to make it clear once for all that, in the Chinese language, there is no such thing as a relative clause, the use of which I have never quite mastered. And he likes to indulge in verbal paradoxes. I think life is complicated enough without relative clauses and strange enough without playing on words. I have tried to catch him doing these things and registered my protests in the form of footnotes, but I won't guarantee that I have not let some slip by.

His translations of the dialogues are usually better than his renderings of my reflections. My general reflections are few and direct. If some may seem deep and abstract, then he is making more of a philosopher of me than I really am. I am good at remembering what people have said. Something like one-tenth of the direct quotations were the exact words, about two-tenths almost the exact words, and the rest should be understood as "words to that effect." The English for the dialogues—what I can understand of it—seems to be quite accurate.

In a number of places, my husband has changed things around, so that the outcome of an incident will be delayed until the end—

That, my dear, is called "fictional technique"—

But this is no fiction! I still like the straightforward way better and have insisted, in many cases, on keeping the announcement of the outcome at the beginning of a story. I believe in keeping the reader informed.

I can summarize my feelings about this English version of my autobiography by comparing it with a portrait of a Chinese woman in oil painting. An oil painting looks inescapably foreign to a Chinese eye. But if I have to be done in oil on canvas, I think this picture is about as near a likeness of me as I can get—next to the original in colors on Chinese silk—

Thank you, my dear—

But I still prefer silk.

Buwei Yang Chao
Yuenren Chao

Cambridge, Massachusetts

CONTENTS

1 ABOUT MYSELF 3

Part I "BOYHOOD" 7

  2 MY PARENTAGE AND ENGAGEMENT 9

  3 AN EXCITING YEAR 15

  4 THE YAMEN IN CANTON 19

  5 EARLY CRISES 25

  6 SCHOOL AT HOME 31

  7 DOINGS OF LITTLE MASTER THREE 37

  8 THE YOUNG REVOLUTIONIST 41

  9 NEW HOUSE ON YENLING HSIANG 49

  10 GROWING UP TO BE LITTLE MISS THREE 53

Part II GIRLHOOD 61

  11 LIFE WITH UNCLE AT WUCHANG 63

  12 LIFE WITH FATHER AT TAYEH 69

  13 MY FIRST MODERN SCHOOL 73

  14 CALAMITY AND FORTUNE 79

  15 WRITING TO MY FIANCÉ FROM McTYEIRE SCHOOL 85

  16 MY GRANDFATHER 93

  17 OCTOBER 8 AND OCTOBER 10, 1911 101

  18 SITTING OUT THE REVOLUTION 107

  19 HOW I GOT MY NAME "BUWEI" 115

Part III THE YOUNG WOMAN 121

  20 PRINCIPAL YANG BUWEI 123

  21 CHASING GHOSTS AND SUPERVISING EXECUTIONS 129

  22 RETURN OF THE NATIVE TO ANHWEI 137

- 23 THE SECOND REVOLUTION 143
- 24 GOING TO TOKYO IN A RICKSHA 149
- 25 GETTING A SCHOLARSHIP 153
- 26 STUDYING MEDICINE 159
- 27 THE TWENTY-ONE DEMANDS AND SINO-JAPANESE FRIENDSHIP 163
- 28 GRADUATION AND RETURN 167
- 29 THE FILIAL DAUGHTER 173
- 30 MY HOSPITAL IN PEIPING 177
- 31 PLANS AND INTERRUPTIONS 183

Part IV AND THE YOUNG MAN 187
- 32 CHAO YUENREN SAUNTERS IN 189
- 33 A "BYSTANDER'S" POINT OF VIEW 193
- 34 THE REPATRIATION OF AN EXPATRIATE 201
- 35 PLANS FOR LIVING 205
- 36 "NEW-STYLE WEDDING OF NEW-STYLE PEOPLE". 213
- 37 HONEYMOON POSTPONED 217
- 38 IN AMERICA 221
- 39 THE SMALL FAMILY 225
- 40 IRIS AND NOVA 229
- 41 THE EUROPEAN PLAN 235
- 42 HURRIED TOURS 239
- 43 LEISURELY TOURS 243

Part V "PEACEFUL" YEARS 247
- 44 PROFESSOR'S WIFE 249
- 45 TRIPS TO "THE SOUTH" 255
- 46 THE NATIONALIST REVOLUTION 261
- 47 VISITS TO CANTON AND SHANGHAI 265
- 48 LENSEY IN A LONG HOUSE 271

49 BELLA IN A BIG HOUSE 277
50 SECOND SOJOURN IN AMERICA 281
51 A "PERMANENT" HOME IN NANKING 287
52 A REALISTIC VIEW OF THINGS 295

Part VI WAR YEARS.. 301

53 REFUGEES TO CHANGSHA AND KUNMING 303
54 LIVING AT 6,000 FEET ABOVE SEA LEVEL 309
55 A YEAR OF HAWAIIAN SUMMER 315
56 "YOU'VE COME A LONG WAY" 323
57 NEW HAVEN, CONNECTICUT 329
58 LOOKING AT YESTERDAY 337
59 TROUBLES AND COMPLAINTS IN CAMBRIDGE, MASSACHUSETTS... 339
60 WAR AND COOKING 345
61 V-J DAY 351

APPENDICES 355

APPENDIX I NOTES ON CHINESE NAMES AND TERMS OF ADDRESS 357
APPENDIX II MY GENEALOGICAL TREE 359
APPENDIX III GLOSSARY 362
APPENDIX IV Map of Nanking.. 364
APPENDIX V Map of China 365

1. Buwei Yang Chao
(Courtesy of Joseph A. Stone, New Haven, Conn.)

2. Grandfather (seated) and Big Uncle in England

3. Father

4. Mother, Sixth Brother, and Myself in My First Girl's Dress (see pp: 58-59)

5. Sixth Brother, Mother, and Myself Ready for My First Modern School

*6. For the First Time in My Life,
My Self Was My Own (see p. 91)*

7. My Grandfather (Chapter 16)

8. Principal Yang Buwei (Chapter 20)

9. With Three Professors and Another Student

10. "I Hate to Wear Japanese Clothes" (borrowed from the nurse standing behind me)

11. Dr. Yang Buwei

12. My Family

1. Niece Lucy
2. Myself
3. Nephew
4. Nephew
5. Nephew
6. Cousine Chinghua
7. Cousine Lang
8. ?
9. Third Sister-in-Law
10. Yüsheng's first wife
11. Second Sister-in-Law
12. Auntie (seated)
13. Second Brother
14. Aunt Lang (seated) Cousine Lang's mother
15. First Sister-in-Law
16. Sixth Brother
17. Mr. Chu
18. Cousin (my ex-fiancé's brother)
19. Third Brother

13. *"And the Young Man" (Part IV)*

14. *"New-Style Wedding of New-Style People"*
(see p.215)

15. *A Roof Garden Party in Peiping, with Bertrand Russell, Dora Black, and E. S. Bennett*

16. *"Regarde-là, Nova!" dit Iris —St. Aubin, France, 1925*

17. *The Banyan Tree in Canton, 1928*

*18. My Rose Garden in Lanchia Huang,
Nanking, 1936*

*19. "Sit Back a Little!"
—Yellow Mountains*

*20. "Lady, You Are the First Woman to
Have Crossed the Perch's Back"
—Yellow Mountains*

21. Bella and Lensey (at left) Looking at the First Bomb Crater in Changsha

22. Boating at 6,000 Feet above Sea Level—Kunming

23. Umbrella in Hand, I Welcomed the Students Who Had Marched 1,000 Miles from Changsha to 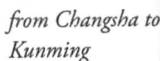 Kunming

24. "Thou shalt Not Covet Thy Neighbor's Mangoes"
Bella and Lensey in Honolulu

25. "Z-Blah Ngécou-ngé-cou," whatever that means. (It means, "This way to the hotdog stand in the San Francisco fair; that way to the hotdog stand in the New York fair."—Bella)

26. *Our Family, June 1, 1946: P'eiyung, Nova, Bella, Lensey, Iris, Hsuehhuang, Buuvei, Yuenren. (Courtesy of Purdy Photographers, Boston, Mass.)*

AUTOBIOGRAPHY OF
A CHINESE WOMAN

1

ABOUT MYSELF

I AM A TYPICAL Chinese woman. I grew up in a big family of four generations living in the same house. I was taught to read and write at home. I learned later to cook and sew. I am married, as most other Chinese women are. I have much power in the family, but let my husband decide on the important things, which are few and far between. I have four children, a very typical number for a Chinese woman to have. I love my children, but hate outward shows of solicitude. I am very much attached to my relatives and friends and put personal loyalty high on my scale of values.

I am also a typical *woman*. I have such an amount of vanity as becomes my sex. I like some jewelry and a lot of good clothes. I compare my daughters' pretty looks with mine at their age with satisfaction; I compare my parties with those of Mrs. Chang Three and Mrs. Lee Four; I compare my husband's station with those of his friends. Though I do not keep a diary, I write an autobiography.

I am a woman with an unusual experience. I had four parents. I broke my engagement at a time when engagements were never broken. I was principal of a school before I went to college. I joined revolutions and took refuge from wars. I healed grownups and brought a few hundred children into the world. When I was married, I was married without a wedding.

I have traveled in twelve provinces and three continents. I have lived six years in Japan and thirteen years in the United States. Speaking broken English and reading very little English, I have become a popular consultant on things American for my Chinese friends and on things Chinese for my American friends.

But, above all, I am myself and not somebody else. I am five feet one and not five feet four, though I wouldn't mind if I were. I was once ninety pounds and wished I were a hundred twenty; now I am a hundred thirty-five pounds and still wish the same. I have a fair complexion and go easy on my makeup. Though I used to wear Western clothes, and was the first woman to bob my hair in my community, I dress conservatively. A straight dark-green Manchu gown, with black trimmings, is my favorite. For it just about takes off those fifteen pounds I don't need and adds those three inches I do. I eat what I like.

I have the voice of a second alto. When I say "Hello" over the telephone and the other party says, "May I speak to *Mrs.* Chao?" I say, "This *is* Mrs. Chao." My voice carries well. When I argue with someone, and our reasons are equally good, I usually win.

I love poetry. I knew the *Three Hundred Poems of the T'angs* by heart; I still can recite from memory Po Chü-i's 120-line *Song of Everlasting Regret*. I devour novels, the longer the better. I like drama and music, but do not sing. I don't appreciate pure science, but believe in science for the welfare of man, and have practiced it. I am not naturally language-conscious; I never heard of Spoonerisms until my third daughter Lensey started collecting them.

I am a city girl, but I like the country. I like to raise chickens and geese. I like to get up early and water my flower-beds. Above all, I like the open air.

I like openness in everything. I like open issues openly discussed. Wherever I find ways that are dark and tricks that are mean, I always confront person with person and word with word. I never speak ill of a person but that I will tell the same thing in his face. Because I do speak ill of persons, it sometimes troubles me not to find a chance to tell him before someone else tells him in garbled words.

I like to move; I like to act. When I first met my American educated husband, a typical contemplative Oriental, before I ever set foot on America, he said that I was a typical American. I want to do things just for the fun of doing them. There is too much to do in the world to sit around and waste your time.

I have a quick temper. I am contrary and stubborn. If you play rough, I can play rougher; if you are reasonable, I will beat you in reasonableness. I am on the side of the weak and humble. If I see a wrong, I cannot look on but must meddle with what is none of my business.

People often pay me the doubtful compliment of saying that I am not like a woman. Maybe there is something in that statement. Whatever the explanation, it is true that I am as good a mixer among men as among women, or better.

This, then, is the Chinese woman whose story I am about to tell. You may find that some of the things said above may contradict some of the others—that makes them all the truer. If I have not succeeded in being a perfectly coherent, rational personality, a true description of me cannot of course be a coherent, consistent description. But, anyway, all this is only what I think I am—no, not even that, it is only what I now think I am. If you want to know what I really am, you should read the story of my life. Here it is.

Part I
"BOYHOOD"

2

MY PARENTAGE AND ENGAGEMENT

I WAS BORN in 1889 in a 128-room house on Huap'ailou in Nanking. Huap'ailou of those days was not the wide boulevard of the 1930's where, as a housewife, I did my shopping among the neon signs in blue and orange characters, but a narrow street, on which two sedan chairs would have to slow down in order to pass without sideswiping each other. It was one of the busiest centers of a bustling city, where bakers sent off puffs of odor from sesame biscuits and puffed fritters, venders sang out their ware, water carriers warned off pedestrians, and parents of good families told their children to stay away from the front door, instead of watching the world go by.

The Huap'ailou house was the first of the two places where my family from my great-grandmother down lived during my childhood. As we were a big family of thirty-four, with twenty-seven servants, we needed all the one hundred twenty-eight rooms, all on one ground floor, grouped around a number of courtyards, and covering a lot of ground.

Before I was born, a lot of arguments had been going on about me. In the first place, my parents were to be my uncle and aunt, and my uncle and aunt were to be my parents. In the second place, I was engaged before I was born. I was to be my cousin's wife or husband, according as I was going to be girl or boy and he or she was going to be a boy or a girl—provided, of course, that we were not both boys or both girls. Now I am going to explain things a little. I had better.

First about my parentage. My grandfather's eldest son had nine children; his second son had none. So he adopted his brother's ninth child. And that was me. To be sure, I was plainly informed, as early as I could understand things, that I was adopted by my uncle and aunt from my parents. But, since I was adopted before I was born and had always called them "Big Uncle," "Auntie," "Father," and "Mother," it was—and still is—more natural for me to say that I was adopted by my parents from my uncle and aunt. With this qualification, however. I was nursed by "Auntie," my real mother, and always felt a special attachment to her. Of my four parents, my favorite parents were "Auntie" and "Father."

Now I must tell about my engagement before telling further about birth, since it happened before my birth. My grandfather's eldest daughter was married to the Ch'engs of Anhwei. They were then living in Yangchow, which was two days' sailing across the river from Nanking. It was her habit to return to Nanking every time she was with child, and stay until about one month before her time. She had been herself a very spoiled child. She was unhappy with Uncle Ch'eng. She did not like to live all the time with a great many Ch'engs around her. It was much nicer to live with a lot of Yangs. They were not only her own people, they were expected to treat her and hers with special honor. This was the fourth time she came back with child—with my fiancé in fact—bringing along three children, her own servants, and two additional servants to each child, and the chief burden of attending to her and her retinue fell on the sisters-in-law, that is, on "Auntie" and "Mother." In China, a married daughter coming home is king. And whenever king arrived in our home, things usually happened.

"Mother" had a special grudge against Aunt Ch'eng. They had been married in the same year. But while Aunt Ch'eng gave birth to one child after another, my "mother" never gave birth to a child throughout her life. Now it was a common belief that if two members of the family married during the same year, the one married first would get away with all the good luck. This was my "mother's" constant complaint—against my grandmother for her partiality in letting Aunt Ch'eng get married first and against my "father" for yielding in such matters. Since he was her elder brother, why hadn't he stood for his rights? Now she was back again, bringing more good luck for herself and more troubles for the sisters-in-law.

"Auntie" bore all this very well. For one thing, she already had eight children and a ninth one to spare. In the second place, she had the sweetest temper. But "Mother" took it hard and often cried when she told us years afterwards about those miserable days.

Grandmother saw all this very clearly. She was getting along in years. She was sure that after she died, her favorite daughter would not be invited back home so often by the sisters-in-law. So she thought of a plan. I was then already more in evidence than my cousin, as I was four months older than he. Pointing to what was obviously him through Aunt Ch'eng and at what was still more obviously me through "Auntie," Grandmother said:

"Why don't we Yangs and Ch'engs strengthen our ties further by adding match on match? Let us have these two grandchildren betrothed to each other, so long as one is a boy and the other is a girl."

Of course nothing would have happened if both children had been boys or girls. But Grandmother had another idea about me. She had been very unhappy over Grandfather's refusal to enter public life, thus frustrating her desire to become a lady of rank. The more so, because his refusal had been due to disappointment in a romance with another girl. So she laid down the rule, uncommon for that time, that no man in the family was allowed to marry a concubine, not even for the all-important reason of continuity of male lineage. If anyone had no son, he should adopt one from a different branch of the family.

Now my "Mother" had been married for six without a child. So Grandmother decided, as if by way of an afterthought, that if both children turned out to be of the same sex, so that the match would be called off, then there should be an adoption or something. It had nothing to do with her plan to keep Aunt Ch'eng closer home, but, at an age when she felt the world was slipping away from her, she would like to do something with somebody. If it was not one thing, it was another. She did both the one thing and the other, and both things have shaped my life fundamentally.

So at the first double-hour, on the third day of the eleventh month of the 25th year of the Kuang-hsü era (1875-1908), with everything prepared for my arrival, I was born. In simpler English, I was born on November 25, 1889.

The year 1889 was about as good as any to be born in if I had had my choice. At that time, Nanking had recovered a little of its former prosperity after the ravages of the T'aip'ing up rising (1850-64). The first Sino-Japanese War was not yet fought. The monarchy was declining, but not tottering. Dr. Sun Yatsen was still to organize his Revolutionary Party. In 1889, my grandfather and father "were abroad, bringing China's greetings to Paris on the completion of the Eiffel Tower at the opening of the World Exposition—I am eight months younger than the Eiffel Tower.

Four nights before my birth, "Auntie" had dreamed that an old woman gave her a double-blossomed orchid branch. When she woke up, she thought she was going to have twin girls, and told "Mother" that she would give one girl to her for daughter and the other to Aunt Ch'eng for daughter-in-law, as promised. Four days after, it became evident to everybody that I was one girl and not two. But "Mother" was very happy just the same, and said:

"Then I want to adopt all of her, since she is only one."

She was worried, however, over the possibility that Aunt Ch'eng's child would turn out to be a boy, in which case I should automatically be his fiancée, as ordered by Grandmother, and "Mother" would not like it at all.

"Auntie," bless her soul, said nothing. In her heart, she could reconcile herself neither with the adoption nor with the match. She was sure that her newborn child would have nothing to look forward to but a temperamental mother and a capricious mother-in-law. But being as she was, all she did was to cry to herself. She nursed me and gave me my pet name of Lansien, "Orchid Fairy," from her dream of orchids.

"Mother," being more demonstrative, sighed aloud day in and day out, praying that Aunt Ch'eng would give birth to a girl to put an end to her worries.

After four months, word came from Yangchow that Aunt Ch'eng had given birth to a boy, and I was more engaged than ever.

3

AN EXCITING YEAR

MY FIRST YEAR was the most exciting year of my life. I do not remember any details about it, but it must have been wonderful. In that one year, I learned more than I did in all the subsequent fifty-odd years put together. I learned very quickly that people were not me, though it surprised me for quite a while that my toes were not somebody else. Then I learned that things were neither me nor people, though it was sometimes hard to draw the line. I found that I could control the movements of what was me with a peculiar sense of freedom, and I have loved and wanted to keep that freedom ever since.

In that same year, I grew to more than twice my weight. I did not, however, keep on doubling my weight from year to year. Later, I was even so underweight at times that I was nick named "Lamppost." But "Auntie's" own nursing gave me a good start on the road to a life of health. Spells of serious and even dangerous illness I did have, but I was never frail or sickly.

On my first birthday, I performed the customary act of "grasping the first year." The custom is like this. When a child is one year old, he is dressed in nice birthday clothes, and a specified array of sundry things is laid out in an arc, each article serving as a symbol of a future profession or a type of life. The child is placed in the center of the arc and, according as he first grasps a book, an abacus, a vanity box, or something else, he will later lead a life of learning and letters, of trade and business, of love and romance, or what not. Each article has a fixed conventional interpretation.

On this my first birthday, the first thing I reached for was a footrule. Unfortunately, I have forgotten what it meant. Did it mean that I was going to lead a life as straight as a ruler? Or that I was later to measure pulses and temperatures?

Soon after this, Grandfather and "Father" returned home from abroad. They loved me at first sight and went about at once settling my affairs. There was no question about my adoption. As for my engagement, neither Grandfather nor "Father" was keen for the match, but they had no good reason to oppose it. What tipped the balance was something about which Grandfather specially wanted to appease Grandmother.

It was this. When Grandfather and "Father" returned from abroad with Envoy Liu Chih-t'ien, to whom they had been councillor and attaché in the joint Legation at London and Paris, Liu had already been appointed Governor of Kwangtung and had appointed my "Father" to be Chief Comptroller in the Governor's yamen. On the voyage home, "Father" had asked Grandfather for permission to take his family along to Canton, the usual rule being that a daughter-in-law had to remain home to attend to the mother-in-law's wants. So this time, in order to get Grandmother's consent to releasing her second daughter-in law from duties at home, Grandfather agreed both to the adoption and to the engagement.

But another kink appeared in the plans for my trip to Canton. Good-natured and obedient as she was, "Auntie" objected strongly that her baby, soon to be taken away from her for good, should be weaned so early. To wean a child soon after she was only one year old, it was unheard of! So Grandmother got busy engaging a wet nurse for me. She changed my name from Lansien to Ch'uanti, or Ch'uan'er, which means "bring along little brother," a lucky name commonly given to a first-born girl. She tried to comfort "Auntie" by telling her that she could have me back again any time "Mother" should give birth to a child.

Shortly before our departure for the South, Grandfather decided to take a photograph of the whole family while everybody was at home. Photography was then a great novelty. Grandfather was the earliest to have brought photographic equipment to China on any considerable scale, and it was he who supplied the old Pao Chi Studio of Shanghai with their first cameras. It was a great event for the family. There was much arranging and posing and changing around, and I was the greatest problem of all, as I usually was in matters concerning the whole family. You couldn't take snapshots in those days, when everything had to be on slow-acting wet plates and the lens had to be uncovered and covered by taking the cap off and putting it on again by hand. When at last everybody was made to look nice and smile and hold their breath at the same time—there were twenty people in that picture—I would start to wiggle and squirm, until some brother or sister of mine got out of place or looked in the wrong direction again. In this way I spoiled several valuable plates in succession. Finally, Grandmother got exasperated and said:

"Let us take the photograph without the baby. She's only a girl. What difference does a girl more or a girl less make?"

Then both my mothers put their hearts and heads together. They stood me on a quickly provided tea table near the center background, held me tightly between themselves and thus saved for me the first photograph ever taken of me. I turned out to be the most expressive person in the picture.

Saved? Yes. It was in our house for some twenty years, until destroyed by fire during the 1911 Revolution.

My trip to Canton was the first of a life of travels. I still consider Nanking my home, but I lived there for only nineteen years, spread over a period of several decades. The rest of the time, I was either in other provinces, or in Japan, or in Europe, or in America. In this first trip, I was still too young to remember anything about it. I must have taken a river steamship down the Yangtze from Nanking to Shanghai; I must have stayed in a Chinese-style hotel in Shanghai; I must have taken a coast wise steamship from Shanghai to Canton; I must have been a constant source of trouble and happiness to my now thoroughly adopted parents. From now on, I will take the quotes off Father and Mother.

4

THE YAMEN IN CANTON

THE UNIQUE THING about my two years' stay in Canton was that it was the beginning of my remembered life. There were no "must have been's" about the Governor's yamen. I remember the place and I remember things about the place. Our family occupied the western courtyard, which we entered from a western gate of a central courtyard inside the second main hall. Our courtyard—think of it as a big flat apartment—had a width of five rooms, each two rooms deep, and had wings on both sides of the courtyard. My room was a backroom of my mother's. Every morning, Huang Ma, the maid who took care of me, would carry me on her back and make a tour of the garden or the second main hall to play. Huang Ma was a Yangchow maid my father had brought along from Nanking. That was why I started my talking life in a sort of Southern Mandarin dialect instead of Cantonese. What happened to that wet nurse whom Grandmother had taken so much trouble to find for me? Well, for some reason I do not remember, I did not like her milk, so I started to feed myself without her. I do not even remember whether she went with us to Canton.

I had no playmates, and children of that time did not have to have toys. While Huang Ma carried me from one courtyard to another, I would jump, or jerk on her back, tickle her neck, and take off the holding cover on her hairdo, so that her hair would fall all apart—wouldn't you have done the same thing when the temptation was so handy? But Huang Ma did not enjoy the fun so well as I. She would give notice to Mother, who would then give me a mild scolding and her a big raise. As I could not understand how expensively my fun was costing the family, I kept up my fun and Huang Ma's wages.

In Canton I had my first glimpse of the grim sides of life. During the Empire, when an official held court to try criminals, corporal punishment was the usual thing. Important cases would come up to the provincial yamen. When I heard sounds of pleading and wailing, I would steer Huang Ma in the direction of the sound, and, in order to keep her hairdo intact, she usually obliged. From a vantage point off one side of the screen behind the governor's seat, I could see everything that was going on. I was told that they were bad men being spanked. But I did not like it. When Father learned where Huang Ma had been taking me, he reprimanded her severely, and so we stayed away from court hearings. But after a few days I clamored again to see what I hated to see and yet wanted to see.

There was much social life in a yamen. Even a small district yamen would house many offices and the families of the magistrates and his chief associates. In a governor's yamen, it was of course on a much larger scale. Afternoons, Mother often went to the main courtyard to play cards with the Lius. It was probably the game of "ten-points," played with thin, long cards, with circles, bamboos, and characters, being the nineteenth century version of modern mahjong. Sometimes Mother played so long that I had already gone to bed when she returned to our western courtyard.

I also remember much feasting going on. I saw gift bearers bringing in complete banquets, sometimes including whole roast pigs. But more than half of the time, banquets were brought in without anybody eating anything. For they were gifts from job seekers and visiting officials asking for favors, and it was the duty of my father as business director to dispose of the gifts for the Governor. Usually a gift from one party would be given to another in return for a previous gift, thus relieving the Governor of favors owed. When too many banquets came in, we had to eat some of them or turn over some of them to the servants. Just the same, our cook submitted a bill regularly for the day's provisions bought.

Performances of plays were also a legitimate form of gift to an official, especially on festival days or birthdays of members of the official family. When plays were given, I would sit astride the shoulder of a manservant in order to be high enough to see the stage. At one of such performances, a lady guest, who had been watching my fidgety behavior during a nice aria, said to my mother:

"Madame Yang, doesn't this young gentleman of yours seem to be something of a wild boy?"

Whereupon I confirmed her view by uttering such a big yell that all the audience turned around and tsk-tsked me and said: "Naughty boy, naughty boy!"

For I had been dressed as a boy and never bothered much as to whether I was a boy or a girl until much later.

Childhood scenes like those flash on and off quite unrelated, sometimes as if they belonged to somebody else or to some of my dreams. Like dreams, they lose much of their favor when told in words. To read me, you would really have to be me. Thus passed my two years in Canton, with few incidents to tell, but with a characteristically two-years-in-Canton favor. I wish I could share it with you, but I don't know how.

One landmark I remembered very clearly. It was the big banyan tree in our western courtyard. During those two years, I don't know how many times I climbed in and out the hanging roots. On my second visit to Canton, thirty-eight years later, when the yamen was no more, and the place had become the Chungshan Park, the banyan tree still stood there in all grandeur.

One day there was a great commotion. Firecrackers went off, horns were sounding and, through the noise, I could discern also the sound of grown-up people crying from the central courtyard. Everybody was rushing about. My father was so busy that for three days he did not come back to his room, nor stop to talk or play with me when home, as he had used to. Nobody bothered about telling me what had happened. But finally it dawned upon me that the Governor had died.

Quite a number of such days of confusion had passed when one day I heard that we were going to pack up for returning to Nanking. Back to Nanking! The Nanking where I was told I was born, the Nanking I had seen, if I could not remember it. In the freshness of childhood, I was as elated then over the prospect of going back to Nanking as I am now over the same prospect as I listen to the news of V-J Day in King's Cottage, Greensboro, Vermont. I jumped and hurrahed and got into everybody's way, trying to help them pack up.

But I soon found out that I was in the wrong mood. Nobody smiled or laughed. Nobody wore beautiful clothes any more. Nobody wore beautiful flowers, nor gathered bouquets to put in the vases. All the men and women wore white gowns of cotton, matched by white caps or bonnets of the same material on their heads. All over the yamen, gates and pailous were erected, covered with decorations made of white, blue, and yellow cloth. The whole place blossomed with a strange kind of gaiety. During one of the now rarer occasions when my father had a few moments with me I said:

"Daddy, what are they building those pavilions for? And why don't they put some red and green things on them? They would look so much prettier."

"You ignorant child!" said Father. "This is a funeral and you have to use white for funerals. You use red only on birthdays and at weddings, you see?"

Thus began, as far as I can remember, the first of a series of casual instructions which I always enjoyed when Father had time to talk to me. I enjoyed it because he was always very patient in explaining things and rarely answered with anything more severe than a "You ignorant child!" He even allowed answering back and arguing with him, which Big Uncle, my actual father, never permitted. When, on the day of the formal mourning, I saw the coffin of the deceased in a colossal bright red satin cover, embroidered in brilliant gold, carried by a gang of sixty-four bearers, I was puzzled again.

"Daddy," I said, "you said you couldn't use red during mourning. But that's red."

"What I meant," Father said, "was that the mourners must use white, but the deceased doesn't wear mourning for himself, you see?"

I did not see. But very often I merely enjoyed being given an answer when I asked a question, and if I liked the sound of it, I just said, "I see."

My trip back to Nanking was made in a warship called "Hai-something" —I don't remember the whole name. The chief passengers were the Lius, whom my father was taking care of.

The Yangs and the Lius have kept up their friendship. But since the passing a few years ago of the last of the Liu ladies, there is no more living member of the Liu family who can tell about the yamen and the banyan trees of Canton.

5

EARLY CRISES

I WAS VERY HAPPY about returning to my grandfather's home in Nanking. For one thing, I could now make frequent visits to the courtyard of my Big Uncle and Auntie, my actual parents. Another thing I was very happy about was that I not only had companions to play with, but could also talk with them in my dialect. For, as I told you, I never learned the Cantonese dialect while in Canton and could not talk with anyone there outside a very limited circle. Now I could run around everywhere and feel at home even when I got scolded. I can tell you from experience that it is pleasanter to be scolded in a language that you understand than to be spoken to in a language that you don't understand.

Soon after I returned home, I came very near losing it. My father had had a new blue sedan chair made. This was the same as buying a new-model expensive car would be these days, and gave rise to rumors that he had made a lot of money in Canton, especially as he often rode in the new chair to call on the Lius. One day, when my father had been to the Lius for some time, a servant came to our house saying that the ladies of the Lius missed Little Master Three—so called because I was Big Uncle's third daughter and was always dressed as a boy—and had sent him with a hired sedan chair to take me there. That is to say, the family car being in use, they had sent a servant with a taxi. So Big Sister and Second Sister[1] dolled me up

---

[1] These were my wife's actual sisters. In the Chinese language, relatives of the same generation are addressed or spoken of as follows:
    ko-ko   elder brother or male cousin,
    ti-ti   younger brother or male cousin,
    chieh-chieh elder sister or female cousin,

and sent me off in the hired chair with Huang Ma. Now it happens that I like to have everything in the open, as I have told you before. So, on this occasion, when the screen of the sedan chair was let down in front of me, I would try to roll it up. The servant, who was walking beside the chair, would let it down again, and I would object strenuously and try to roll it up again as soon as it was down. It was obviously very difficult for the chair bearers to go very fast with such a lively load on their shoulders. Just before making a turn near Pigeon Bridge, I saw, during one of those moments when I had the upper hand in the fight over the screen, that it was our family chair coming from the opposite direction. So I shouted:

"Daddy, is that you, Daddy?"

"Why, it's Ch'uan'er!" Father said. "Where in the world are *you* going?"

At this, my bearers suddenly double-timed their steps. I shouted and stamped my feet and got down on the floor of my chair with my legs dangling outside. It was dangerous business, even though it was not a real taxi. By this time my father had also stopped his chair, and when he turned around and walked to my chair, a crowd had gathered and joined us in wondering what had happened. Then we realized that the chair bearers were gone. The "servant," too, had disappeared.

As soon as we were home, Father sent to inquire about the invitation from the Lius and was informed that they had never sent for me. He reported the happenings to the district sheriff, but after several months' investigation, they could not find out who the "servant" or the bearers were. After this incident, my grandfather ordered that no children should be allowed to go out bedecked all over with

---

mei-mei   younger sister or female cousin.
Consequently adoption of a brother's child will make no difference in the child's way of addressing his brothers and sisters or his cousins. For simplicity, *Ta Chieh* and *Er Chieh* in the Chinese text are translated here as "Big Sister" and "Second Sister."—Y.R.C.

jewelry. It was wrong, he reasoned, to put temptation before people who could either do good or do evil.

I had my first serious illness when I was about four, as a result of which I almost became a pockmarked person. Before vaccination became common in China, it was assumed that smallpox was something every child had to get over with, like the way chicken pox and measles were later regarded. When smallpox broke out in the neighborhood, Mother felt that it was unavoidably coming to me, especially as I liked to go out a great lot. It was supposed to lighten the attack if it was "planted" into a child by blowing an activating powder into the child's nose before infection came in unknown ways. Nonetheless, I had very high fever and serious eruptions all over. During my delirium, eight people watched me day and night, and the whole family observed religious vegetarianism for fourteen days. Finally, the fever subsided and, after a convalescence lasting half a year, I was able to walk again. But Mother was still despondent.

"With a pockmarked mother-in-law and a pockmarked husband, must I now have a pockmarked daughter too?"

My second and third elder brothers; the only other children born of Big Uncle and Auntie besides myself who are still living, saw a chance to win back some of their lost battles of words with me. Third Brother is quite a stammerer. (Of course I am writing this at a safe distance from him, half a world away in Chungking, and both of us half a century more grown up.) Whenever he was short of logic, he would wind up with a taunt about my face.

"Y-you po-po-po-pockmarked girl! N-nobody will w-want you any more. Who will m-marry a girl like you? Your fiancé will be-break his en-g-en-g-g-g-G-G—he won't marry you any more."

"Aw, what do I care," I said. "Didn't Grandpa want Grandma? Didn't Mother want Father? Why shouldn't anybody want me? If Cousin Ch'eng doesn't want me, I haven't been wanting him in the first place. Of course I am going to have someone better."

My logic did not appear very strong even to myself at the time. But Third Brother's advantage over me lasted only a short while. Before many months had elapsed, Mother was completely happy again. Years afterwards, I had to prove to Yuenren that he had married a pockmarked wife by pointing out to him where exactly the three marks were located.

Mother's peace of mind did not last long, however. The next year a white spot appeared in my left eye. It grew bigger and bigger. Soon I could not see through my right eye either. In three months I lost all vision except a blur around the edges of the obstructed field. Neither old-style doctors nor Western doctors were able to do anything for me. Even secret hearsay formulas were tried. They dropped honey with ground ivory into my eyes and fed me with pig's liver, stewed with a kind of pearl grass, which made me hate liver ever since. They burned incense and made vows to temples. On the twentieth of each lunar month, Auntie and Mother would observe an Eyesight Fast by going vegetarian. They had a theory that it was the effect of the smallpox, and felt remorseful for having prayed for saving their mutual daughter's face at the cost of her sight. How much more important it was for her to see than to be seen! This went on for eight or nine months without anybody being able to do anything about it. And Father was away that year.

One day Old Ts'ai, the gateman, told Mother that at a street bazaar at Ta-hsing Kung (later a part of Chungshan Road), there was a medicine man from Shantung who had a sign about curing eye diseases, and wondered whether Madame wouldn't give this man a try. Mother was sure that modern-minded Grandfather would disapprove. But this was my last chance. Better not say anything about it. Anyway there was no harm to go and see. We could still decide about it when we saw the man. So she took Huang Ma and me to the medicine man from Shantung at his street-corner stand. The man stuck a needle into each of my temples and let out two tiny cups of blood. As far as I can recall, it did not seem to hurt. He gave me a pack of herbs to make an infusion to drink. A month after, I was again able to see.

When they went to Ta-hsing Kung to reward the man, the stand was no more. My family was sure that it must have been a saint sent by Buddha in answer to their prayers. In fulfillment of their promises, Mother and Auntie offered incense and presented embroidered red-satin hangings to temple after temple. From that time to the end of their days, they kept their Eyesight Fast on the twentieth of every lunar month. They enjoined me to continue its observation after them. But as I have never been able to remember dates on the lunar calendar since China adopted the Gregorian calendar in 1912, I don't know when is the twentieth of the lunar month and so have never continued the Eyesight Fast. Is that why I have been having eye trouble lately? My doctor in Cambridge, Massachusetts, recommends liver. It is a small world.

How my eyes did get well is still a puzzle to me. Would they have got well anyway if I had not gone to the medicine man? When I took my medical course years later, I never came across any case of cataract being treated by letting blood. At any rate, I got very poor marks in ophthalmology.

6

SCHOOL AT HOME

CHILDREN IN OUR FAMILY began school at five years of age. Boys and girls were taught together until they were twelve, after which the girls retreated to the interior courtyards, to continue their education in less academic subjects. Because of illness, I did not go to school until I was six. School then meant studying under private teachers engaged to teach at home. Institutions of instruction open to the public were not common until much later.

There were two teachers in our family. One of them taught Big Brother, Second Brother, and two male distant cousins, who were staying with us. The other taught Third Brother and me, and Fourth Cousin (son of Fifth Uncle). Our first reader was the *Three-Word Classic*, a thirteenth-century rhymed reader for children, starting with human nature being good and going on through an outline of Chinese history to everything else about the world. I was the only girl in the school, and was given a *Women's Classic* for supplementary reading. I hated it, because its chief theme was to make a woman know her place of unimportance. As this was a book of no recognized standing, I was permitted to go unprepared with it most of the time.

School hours were from nine to twelve, and again from one to six. But all the pupils of the same teacher had to stay in school if one of them could not finish the day's assignment at the dismissal hour. As Fourth Cousin was younger and slower, I often scolded him bitterly for being the cause of my having to stay after school. This usually made him cry and slowed down his work still further. For my part, I usually finished my lesson in half of the assigned hours. So I had to find enough mischiefs to keep myself occupied the rest of the time.

Our classroom was in a courtyard just outside of Great-grandma's. Outside of the lunch hour, we were permitted to leave the classroom four times a day. Since I was a girl, I had to go inside to Great-grandma's room, while the boys could find any place in the outside courtyard that was convenient. My trips to Great-grandma's courtyard gave me wonderful opportunities. What wouldn't a great-grandma do to spoil a great-grandchild? She would give me little chores to do, or even errands to run, so that I could visit the other courtyards too. On one of such occasions, Teacher sent word complaining that I was overstretching my four daily trips. Thereupon Great-grandma came out herself and, wielding her staff in the face of the teacher, told him that it was his duty to teach the children how to serve their elders. Not daring to answer back, my teacher appealed to Grandfather. Grandfather, the great liberal, said:

"Young man, don't drive your pupils too hard. If you do, you will spoil their taste for books and learning. Besides, if the girl has finished her work, why can't she go and play?"

Still not satisfied with the verdict, our conscientious teacher appealed to one generation further down, his generation. The fathers being out during the day, he had to send in the appeal to the mothers, by messenger, as it would not have been proper for a man to speak to womenfolk of the same age group who were not his relatives. The message got garbled on the way and, by the time it reached the inner courtyards, possibly through another audio-stage of amplification when it passed the input-output channels[1] of the maidservants, the story of one student's truancy had grown to a strike by the whole class. All the mothers called in all the members of the class for a spanking. Auntie spanked *her* son: Third Brother. Fifth Aunt spanked *her* son: Fourth Cousin. But my mother let me, the real offender, go unpunished, as she was sensitive about my being her adopted child. Besides, she thought it was not so important for a girl

---

[1] Not responsible for forced analogies added by the translator!—B.Y.C.

to study anyway. Third Brother was stammering too badly to be able to explain the situation. Fourth Cousin, on his part, thought that he was being justly spanked for holding up the class by being too slow, and made me feel bad about his receiving the punishment in such good grace.

The news of the development angered Great-grandma. She went out of one courtyard and into another scolding the teacher.

"What is a teacher being fed[2] for? To punish the children because *he* doesn't know how to teach? And, besides, how dare a young man have messages sent into the inside courtyards? What are our morals coming to?"

Grandfather also blamed the teacher for making so much fuss about such a small matter. The teacher was discouraged and wanted to leave. To avoid the trouble of getting another teacher, who might not be any better, Mother tried to amend matters by getting somebody to apologize to him. No properly qualified person was willing, and she could not go herself, of course. Finally, she got Old Ts'ai to put on his half-length "riding coat" over his gown and he went to perform a full kowtow and made a formal apology to our teacher. He knew, of course, that Old Ts'ai was only the gateman. But a full kowtow from anyone in such gentlemanly dress and manners was enough to restore his self-respect, and so he was able to remain with dignity.

Our mothers, however, had to kowtow to Great-grandma. The theory was that, if for any reason a senior member of the family was angered or made unhappy, it was due to lack of filial piety on the part of the children, especially the daughters-in-law and granddaughters-in-law.

---

[2] The word *chiung*^{1}, which was actually used, was even stronger. It is a dialect word of Shihtai, Anhwei, of unknown etymology, meaning "to keep as domestic animals."—Y.R.C.

After this incident, the rule was changed, so that each pupil was assigned as much work as he or I could finish by six o'clock, and not before.

In China, New Year holidays lasted from five days for stores to nearly a month for schools. There was no conception of a summer vacation until new-style schools were inaugurated. Grandfather ruled however that there should be no school for the day whenever the thermometer, one of those new-fangled things he had brought from England, reached 90 degrees Fahrenheit. The thermometer was hung on the shady side of a column at the corner of the porch. So the three of us in our class agreed on a plan. When we went out on our regulation trips, we would take turns in taking down the thermometer and holding it in the sun for a minute or two. After giving the thermometer three such treatments in close succession, the last one coming in would bring it in to show our teacher that it was hot enough to dismiss school. Soon Teacher began to wonder why Nanking had such a series of hot spells. So he took the thermometer in and put it on his desk. After that, the heat waves became less frequent.

I was not a quite reverent follower of the sages, and got into trouble once by questioning their authority. When I read that Confucius would not eat meat that was not cut in regular shapes, I said:

"What a wasteful man Confucius was! If only regular cuts are fit to eat, what's going to be done with the corners and things?"

This brought a severe reprimand and a threat of beating from Big Uncle and Father. How dare I criticize the Great Sage!

A favorite game of school children of our age was to parodize our lessons. When we were taught the *Hundred Family Surnames*, a Sung dynasty rhymed reader (actually containing 438 surnames), we would add interpolations like these:

"Chao, Ch'ien, Sun, Li,
Teacher's too poor to buy *mi* (rice).

>Chou, Wu, Cheng, Wang,
>Teacher has no *ch'uang* (bed).
>Feng, Ch'en, Ch'u, Wei,
>Teacher has no *pei* (bedding).
>Chiang, Shen, Han, Yang,
>Teacher is afraid of my *Shih-niang* (Teacher's wife)."

In this manner, I acquired my classical education at home. I do not know whether I learned more from my teacher or from my grandfather and father. Probably the former provided the occasion and material and the latter gave me light and incentive. Between chores from Great-grandma and the hot spells, real or artificial, I managed to learn by heart, in unparodized form, *The Great Learning, The Doctrine of the Mean, Confucius' Analects, Mencius, Book of Odes,* parts of *Tso's Chronicles, Three Hundred Poems of the T'angs,* some of the T'ang essays, and, from hearing my big sisters reading aloud, snatches of the *Diamond Sutra* and other Buddhist scriptures. I was permitted to read "idle books," as novels were then called, but they were not considered educative—all right for womenfolk.

One thing in which I feel I have never quite graduated is calligraphy. My father used to say that a person's handwriting was his intellectual physiognomy. Fine ideas presented in a poor hand were under as great a disadvantage as a fine personality behind an underprivileged face. But I did not listen to his advice. Today I annoy and amuse my friends by filling my letters with illegible and even made-up characters.

7

DOINGS OF LITTLE MASTER THREE

AS I HAVE told you, I have often been complimented for not being like a woman. I feel as natural in the company of men as in the company of women, if not more so. For to be called "Little Master Three" and to be dressed as "Little Master Three" also made me feel and behave as "Little Master Three." I was privileged to do things which none of my sisters or female cousins would dream of doing.

Winters, I would go out in the early morning and sneak into the bedrooms of men guests in the outer courtyards and stick snow balls at their feet inside their nice and warm quilts. One of my victims was Uncle Li, sworn brother of Big Uncle. He was then living with us as Big Uncle's secretary-interpreter when Big Uncle supervised the construction of forts of Nanking on Lion Hill and Mufu Hill with the aid of German technicians. Big Brother, Third Brother, and I were great friends with Uncle Li. Every morning before school, Huang Ma would take me out to buy three hot sesame biscuits, Uncle Li's favorite breakfast food. One morning, after I gave him the biscuits, he closed the door, told me to put out my hand, and gave me five whacks with a ruler.

"You know what you have done?"

"I don't know," I said, "How can I know if you don't tell me?"

"You must have put a whole snowman my bed. How could I sleep with half of my bed wet?"

"What proof have you that it was snow?" I demanded. "Maybe it was this, this, this, this, this!" as I spanked him five times with his ruler. "There! That'll make you a good boy!" and I opened the door and ran away before he could catch me.

"Ch'uanti," he shouted after me, "if you want to be naughty, you should at least be honest about it. No good arguing against reason!"

"You can't convict a person without evidence," I shouted back, and, gauging the distance that was separating me from him, I added, "You are lucky that I did do it this time," and quickened my steps.

"Wait a minute, Ch'uanti," he said, evidently pleased with my confession. "When you are married, I am going to tell this story to your husband."

Later, he said to my father:

"Second Brother, I see that you have adopted a 'son' all right. Better teach her well, otherwise she not only would not make a peaceful daughter-in-law in the home, but might also make trouble in society."

Several years after Li Yuanhung retired from serving two terms as the second president of China, I visited him at his Tientsin residence. The first thing he said to me was:

"Are you still as naughty as before, Ch'uanti?"

A vitally important part of my male attire was that I never had my feet bound. Foot-binding was relatively less universal in the lower Yangtze valley, where women often had to work in ankle-deep water in the rice fields. But for a family of our standing, it took a revolutionary like my grandfather to connive at failure to observe foot-binding. My father, feeling that he was adopting a "son," was also willing to let my feet go where they wanted. This irked Aunt Ch'eng, my prospective mother-in-law.

"What kind of a looking bride will that girl turn out to be, with a pair of webby feet thumping along in front of the red skirt! When she arrives at our house, how will the servants be able to tell whether it's the bride or a newly bought slave girl?"

This made me hate her and started my thoughts of getting out of the whole arrangement.

Big Brother made up a jingle about my feet:

> "Boy of a girl,
> With great big feet,
> With face unwashed,
> She goes outdoors for things to eat,
> And coming home,
> She argues and debates with heat."

My unlimited range of activities once almost cost me my life. At the back of our house, there was a vegetable garden and a stable in which Big Uncle kept two horses, one white and one grey, for riding to the forts he was working on. One day the groom was washing and combing one of the horses and, as I was admiring the smoothened, shiny tail, he said Little Master Three could have some of the horse's tail for a fly swatter. He would get me a pair of scissors to cut with as soon as he was through with the grooming. Being, as usual, too impatient to wait, I started to pull some of the hair from the horse's tail. With what seemed a thunderbolt of a hoof, it floored me, with a big bruise on my chest. After first aid was applied, it did not seem to bother me when the bruise disappeared. Two years after that, I had spells of low fever. They told me that it was due to injury to the lungs. The fever disappeared after half a year. I do not remember how I got well; it left no after-effect of any kind.

My life as a boy reached full manhood when I went pleasure boating on the Ch'inhuai River inside Nanking city with Fifth Uncle and elder brothers, engaging singsong girls, one girl to each gentleman. According to our family standards of the time, it was wrong to stay with the singsong girls overnight, but it was respectable practice to send for the same girls when you were in a restaurant or a houseboat. When they came, they did not join you at the table, but sat behind their respective patrons to drink, banter, or sing. After an hour or two, you dismissed them with two to five dollars, depending upon their popularity. It was a tame affair compared with what goes on at a modern night club. But I was very proud to be old enough to go bad by having a twelve-year-old singsong girl (older than I was) to sit with me and eat melon seeds at the bow of the boat, while Fifth Uncle and elder brothers drank noisily inside with older girls. I often boast of this to my husband, who has never called in a singsong girl in his life, not to say to go to one—at least not to say to me.

I regret the passing of the gay life on the Ch'inghuai River. From the Six Dynasties down to recent times, poets sang of it. My family took part in it. Colored lanterns, with dancing reflections in the water, shining from the tea houses, restaurants, and singsong-girl houses, flanking the meandering stream, are no longer lighted. Melodious voices and flutes, echoing between the banks and the boats, are silent. Cannot life be gay without commercialized love? At this transitional stage, when the New Life Movement is trying to stamp out old evils and when free men and women of a new generation are still learning to feel natural in each other's company, we should perhaps try to be patient while unseen stage hands are shifting the scenes in the drama of China. They will come around to the Ch'inghuai River in time.

8

THE YOUNG REVOLUTIONIST

I AM NOT a member of Kuomintang, but my family got quite mixed up with the revolutionists, and I joined the T'ungmeng Hui, predecessor of Kuomintang, when I was old enough. My grandfather was not much of a loyal subject of the Ch'ing dynasty. Besides his disappointment in love I spoke of, his radical ideas must have been part of the reason why he avoided official life after his return from abroad.

One summer evening, when I was about seven, my grandfather and my father were having a lively discussion about constitutional government in Great Britain, while I was loitering around, or rather swinging on, one of the latticed doors opening into the courtyard. I neither understood nor was interested in much of what they were saying, until I heard them talk about people's rights and systems of voting. I hated to be always told things and thought it nice for everybody to have the right to say what they thought and decide things for themselves.

"What are people's rights '?" I asked. "Am I going to be people some time?"

"Don't interrupt," Father said sternly, "when big persons are talking. Where are your manners?"

Then he showed a faint smile, by which I knew he meant: "I will tell you all about it later."

He had to make concessions to traditional manners, under which he had been brought up, but actually both Grandfather and he encouraged the children, to the point of spoiling them, to ask questions and answer back. That is probably why I have never learned to observe the-chair-recognizes-so-and-so style of social conversation, as commonly followed by cultivated people in the West. By the time it is my floor, I usually have forgotten what I wanted to say. Besides, how else can you stop a bore?

But to come back. Grandfather, seeing that Father's rebuke was obviously perfunctory, said to me:

"Come. I will tell you about it now. Although Great Britain has a king, it has a constitution. You don't know what a constitution is? Well, to put it simply, a constitution is a system of first rules which everybody in the country must obey, including the king. According to the British constitution, the people have the right to choose by vote their representatives to form their government, and their representatives in the government vote on laws and decisions on what is best for the people. If the government is bad, the people can vote to change it."

"Have you the right to vote now, Grandpa?" I asked. "Can you vote to change the government?"

"Sh!" said two of my cousins who were also standing by. "You mustn't say that. You might get beheaded for such talk!"

I could not understand why anyone should be beheaded for carrying on such perfectly sensible discussions. But Grandfather said:

"This has gone far enough. Someday your generation will understand, I hope."

And we dispersed in a hush-hush atmosphere, which seemed to me strangely inappropriate.

That night, I asked Father again about people's rights, especially as to whether a person had the right to decide about his own affairs. He explained to me that, before accepting the responsibility of deciding things for oneself and for society, one had to study the classics in order to know the past and go to modern schools in order to know the present, and that in foreign countries one had to become of age before one could exercise one's full rights. Then, with a deep sigh, he added:

"But I am afraid your case is very difficult. It's a pity."

I wanted to ask him what he meant by that, but Mother became very angry and warned Father not to indulge further in such dangerous talk, otherwise I might tell all the neighbors about what was going on in the house and get everybody into trouble.

From that time on, I started to make a list of things which I would be able to decide for myself as soon as I should be of age, which was still more than a dozen years away. Such as: stay up as late as I wanted to, swing on the lattice door, quit practicing calligraphy, go out where I wanted to and return when I wanted to, and—let me see—and why not break not break my engagement with Cousin Ch'eng and marry whom I wanted to? So that was put down on my schedule.

One thing about me that seemed incongruous with my assertive and revolutionary tendencies was my fear of ghosts. Our whole family, at least all the menfolk, were rationalists. Although Grandfather was the leading lay Buddhist of the day, he was more of a "unitarian" than a "fundamentalist" in belief, and his chief work in Buddhism was that of textual criticism and interpretation in philological or in rationalistic terms. The result of this was that I had a much higher regard for Buddhism than did the other young modernists of my age. We believed in Heaven, we believed in remembering and sacrificing to our deceased ancestors "as if they were there," as Confucius put it. All of us children loved ghost stories, but ghosts didn't really exist, of course. Nevertheless, I was awfully afraid of them. At the end of a day of brave words and brave action, when vegetable oil lamps with grass-pith wicks began to flicker and cast big, waving shadows on the walls all around, then I would have to find grown-up persons to give support to my back.

One winter day, when I was talking loudly with Grandfather about the nonexistence of ghosts, Second Brother, who was always jealous of my privileged position with Grandfather, interrupted me and said:

"You said you don't believe in ghosts. All right, I dare you to walk alone in the night. I will bet you a whole leg of fresh salted duck if you dare to walk alone in darkness from the last inside courtyard to the back of the outside reception hall."

The famous Nanking duck was a strong attraction. But it was the question of maintaining face in front of Grandfather that was decisive.

"I accept the challenge," I said.

Grandfather tried to find a way out for me by warning me that I might stumble in the dark, but I said it was all right.

"Tonight," Second Brother said, "shall we say at First Watch?"

"All right, First Watch, at the last stroke of eight o'clock." I enunciated the last few words very clearly, as if the new phraseology related to the foreign timepiece Grandfather had brought back would help charm away the old-fashioned ghosts.

When the time came, and it was dark and cold, Second Brother and Third Brother went with me to the last inside court yard, while Fifth Uncle waited at the finishing line behind the outermost reception hall.

Third Brother was helpful. He told me to rub my brow upwards three times, so as to produce thirty feet of spiritual flames to scare away the ghosts—not that they existed, but just to be prepared in case they changed their minds about it.

"Upwards, not downwards, mind you!"

I did not like the waiting at all. I felt something creeping at my back. But I had to act the unconcerned.

"Dong, dong, dong, dong, dong, dong, dong, dong!" went Grandfather's grandfather's clock.

At Third Brother's "One, two, three!" I started to run—out of one courtyard into another, each time going through a deep, hall-like central room. There were only seven courtyards to pass, but that night they seemed to be interminable. I was sure I was being followed, not by my brothers, since it was a rustling sort of sound right close behind me. The faster I ran, the closer it seemed to get—now actually crackling on my back! I did not say "Eek!" or anything like that, but kept right on, with both hands and both elbows over my head, forgetting that I might be obstructing my own spiritual flames.

Finally, panting and perspiring all over, I saw the dark form of Fifth Uncle emerge gradually in front of the—well, it must have been the fourteenth courtyard now. In a few moments my brothers also arrived.

"You win," they said, and broke into inordinate laughter. "What's so funny about my winning the bet?" I wondered. Then more rustling behind me. I quickly turned around—a thing I had not dared to do while I was running—and found a big dried lotus leaf tied to my pigtail. But I was too tired from the running to fight with them that night. The boys got a scolding from Auntie and Mother. They could have frightened me crazy, they said. But actually they cured me of[1] being afraid of ghosts.

During those years, the last years of the century, the dangerous thoughts in our family began to take less academic forms. In 1896, two years after China suffered a great defeat from Japan, when forward-thinking people in China began to experiment on new ways of government and education, a School of Current Affairs was established at Changsha by the provincial government of Hunan. Hsiung Hsiling was supervisor—as a principal was then called—and my father was business director and teacher of surveying. After a brief but intense activity of two years, the school was closed by the authorities for teaching revolutionary ideas, and the supervisor was put in

---

[1] ?—Y.R.C.

prison. Father was out of a job and returned to Nanking, bringing with him a bad record in the eyes of the authorities.

One summer evening, when I was about nine, Grandfather and Fifth Uncle rushed excitedly to various courtyards and told our mothers to take all the children to two neighboring rice stores through our back door and to stay there until further word. Soldiers were coming soon to surround and search our house for propaganda literature. As the local garrison commander was known to our family, he had sent word in advance so that anything embarrassing could be put away in time. When after many hours we were told to go home, I found everybody still talking in subdued tones. They had heard a report that Big Uncle had been arrested while in Tientsin, because of his association with T'an Szut'ung. When it was learned that T'an was executed, consternation reigned in our house.

I must explain that T'an Szut'ung was executed by the Empress Dowager in the coup d'état of 1898. Today, the reformist loyalists led by K'ang Yuwei, Liang Ch'ihch'ao, T'an Szut'ung, and others, seem pretty old-fashioned. Their aim was to help the emperor Tetsung, popularly known by his era name Kuang-hsü, seize power from the Empress Dowager, in order to introduce progressive measures, working ultimately to a constitutional monarchy. Plans went awry and, with the help of Prince Tuan, the Empress Dowager shut up the Emperor on the Yingt'ai Island in the "North Sea" inside Peking and executed six of the leaders, including T'an. K'ang and Liang escaped to Japan. Thus ended the reformist movement.

Now, T'an Szut'ung was my grandfather's pupil in Buddhism and a friend of our family. Big Uncle had accompanied him to Peking. The night before his arrest, T'an already got wind that things were going all wrong. He warned Big Uncle to run for it first.

But, in our Nanking home, agony grew daily as the family waited for the news, not knowing when it would come and what it would be when it came. It would not do to write or telegraph; we just had to wait. For me, bad-tempered, autocratic Big Uncle became the nicest father. If I could see him only once more to tell him how badly I had always behaved towards him!

Two weeks passed.

   *   *   *   *   *   *

"My son," said Grandfather, after the excitement and tearful rejoicing had subsided enough for one person to talk at a time, "I have a job for you. have bought three and half acres of ground on Yenling Hsiang. Would you like to supervise the construction of our family's new residence?"

He knew that Big Uncle would not and could not stay quietly at home, and yet for the time being he had better not take any public job. So he let him apply his skill as a builder of fortresses to the building of a house.

9

NEW HOUSE ON YENLING HSIANG

YENLING HSIANG means much to me now, because the house is still standing. Damages from a small fire during the Japanese occupation of Nanking (1937-45) have been repaired. With about the same number of rooms over a much larger lot, it is even more of a sprawling affair than our first house. The southern fence wall is so long that the street changes its name from Yangkung Well to Kungchia Bridge. There is a pond at the southwestern corner, with fish big enough to make liars of us, who catch them for supper. The main courtyards are grouped in center-back. The main door opens eastward at No. 49 Yenling Hsiang, which is a secondary street one block—if you can speak of blocks in Chinese cities—west of Huap'ailou. But formerly it was the main macadamized highway leading from Hsiakuan, Nanking's port, four miles away. At the upper right-hand corner of the entrance, there is a sign "Ch'ihchow Yang's Residence," Ch'ihchow being the prefecture in Anhwei to which our original district Shihtai belonged. Across the top is another sign "The Chinling Buddhist Press." For, along with his family, Grandfather moved to the new place also the establishment for printing the *Tripitaka* and other Buddhist works he was editing. The wood blocks for printing occupy a whole courtyard of rooms. Little spiritual foxes, beings intermediate between gods and devils, haunt the courtyards and bring you nightmares by lying on your chest during your sleep, especially since the house became old.

But it was a brand-new house when we moved into it in the summer of 1899. In fact we could not wait for the lacquer and paint to dry, that is, Great-grandma could not wait. She was very sick that summer and wanted to die in her new house. On a very hot summer day, she was carried on a reclining chair, or bed, through a tour of the nice new courtyards. She was satisfied and happy. Three weeks later, she passed on. Her life had spanned almost exactly the length of the nineteenth century.

There were the usual elaborate forms of mourning in the household. An altar in front of the coffin was set up in a central hall. Mourning at home was divided, as usual, into seven times seven, or forty-nine days. This time I understood why everybody wore coarse white cloth. Choruses of Buddhist monks said all-day and all-night masses every seven days. Relatives and guests came at all hours of the day to kowtow to the altar and give condolences to the family. The family, especially the women, had to cry whenever a guest kowtowed, as it would mean bad luck to him to be received in silence. As my grandmother had died before my great-grandmother, the duty of greeting by crying fell on my mother and aunts. There were six granddaughters-in-law of the deceased to divide the crying schedule into three shifts. Once, while Fifth Aunt was eating her lunch, one of us youngsters said:

"Hurry up, Fifth Aunt! Here are some guests. It's your turn."

Running over from the west courtyard in her fluttering white gown, she started to cry, with a morsel of rice still in her mouth.

"Swallow your rice before you cry," I said, as I stood beside the entrance to the main courtyard.

Thereupon she broke into uncontrollable laughter. Fortunately it was not real guests that were coming in. Brothers and cousins had put on gowns two sizes bigger than their own to stage-set the whole thing. For this, Big Uncle locked us all up for a whole day without food. Otherwise, the funeral was a great success, as Mencius put it, in the passage about proper forms of mourning

In China, when a person lives to a very old age (my great grandmother was ninety-eight), the funeral takes on the color of festivities. While our family wore white, guests presented us with draperies of red silk instead of the usual blue cotton. This made the decorations in the reception halls gay with colors of life. To us children, the period of mourning meant also an unscheduled long vacation from school.

When I was nine, my mother was still childless. That summer, Fifth Aunt gave birth to a boy. As she already had a boy, the boy was adopted by my father and mother as son. I called him Sixth Brother, being the sixth grandson in the family. Because of Great-grandmother's death, no celebration of birth or adoption was held until my birthday in the autumn.

It my ninth birthday, and I was ten years old by Chinese reckoning. I did not know why they gave me such a big party. Why did I have so many new clothes? Why were there more guests than ever? Why were there so many grown-up guests at a child's birthday?

So Mother explained to me that, because I was engaged, it was not likely that I would have my next big ten-year birthday at home. She said that, unlike the women of Western countries Father told her about, who were free to go about choosing their own mates, Chinese women had to obey the word of their elders to determine their future for them and that, though she was opposed to the match, Grandmother's orders had to be obeyed.

She wished that I would be more cooperative in ameliorating matters by learning more of the arts of women, in order to be an acceptable daughter-in law. Looking at the way Auntie, Big Sister, and Father, and especially Grandfather, were spoiling me, she could not share Father's confidence in my ultimately growing to be a sensible person. She thought it a waste of money for Father to give me an education instead of concentrating on educating the real son adopted, that is, Sixth Brother.

She did not say all this during that one day, but enough of it in that depressing tone to spoil my birthday for me. I tried to argue back as usual. But the pressure of *mores*, especially in the form of such lively and festive celebrations, was so overwhelming that even I felt helpless at the time. I suppose I would have succumbed if it had been my wedding. My first big birthday was not a happy birthday to me.

10

GROWING UP TO BE LITTLE MISS THREE

I DO NOT believe in behaviorism. I practice it. If consciousness means talking to oneself about oneself, then I must have vegetated—or "animated"—for years before I attained consciousness. As Little Master Three, I had no clear idea as to what it was to be a woman. My remoteness from women's affairs could be seen from my surprise when I heard that needles had holes in them. Stirring crises there had been, both emotional and physical, as I have told you, but they had all seemed to be part of the events of the family, rather than inside myself. Even after I began to think that I was thinking about myself, my thoughts about me continued to consist largely of echoes of words of Mother, Father, Grandfather, Big Uncle, Auntie, sisters and brothers, Huang Ma, etc., etc., talking about "Lansien," "Ch'uanti," or "Little Master Three." When I thought about myself, there was little of "I" or "me" about it.

But as I grew past my tenth birthday, I learned to behave and to make my own rules of behavior and my plans for behaving. National events, sicknesses, family crises—they seemed to affect me more now than before, at least differently from before.

One day, in the spring of 1900, I noticed that Grandfather was unusually angry.

"What a time for such nonsense!" he said gravely: "Never heard of people with such responsibilities trusting affairs of the state to such an ignorant, superstitious lot of bandits! 'When the nation totters, monsters rule.' How true are the words of *Tso's Chronicles*!"

He was referring to the acts of the Empress Dowager and Prince Tuan in giving imperial sanction to the Boxers to exterminate all foreign devils in the country. Armies of eight countries were converging on Peking. The court was fleeing to Shansi.

Down in Nanking, we got only the tail of the storm. From our house, messengers were dispatched to the crowded telegraph office to tell Big Uncle to hurry home from Tientsin and Father to turn back on his way to Wuchang. We did not see any of the Boxers. But just to be safe, Mother put us to bed in the early afternoon every day to keep us away from any evil spirit that might fly over to the Yangtze region. The servants put more trust than we did in the devil-killing powers of the Boxers and their affiliates "the Red Lantern Shines" and "the Cult of the White Lotus," but they were afraid of them just the same. If any of the occult spirits should stray our way, they could be struck down with the lid of a commode. For quite a while, therefore, the maidservants were unusually diligent in keeping the commodes clean, so that they would have the lids ready if they saw any red lanterns or white lotuses floating by.

It was the 15th of the seventh moon, the Chinese All Soul's Night, when sacrificial alms were given hungry ghosts and lotus candles were floated on ponds and long lines of incense were planted on the ground to help the ghosts see. Not being satisfied with the special eggplant cakes eaten on this festival day and other things, Fifth Uncle and brothers proposed to buy a roast duck—of equal if not greater fame than Nanking's fresh-salted duck. The news was bad, they reasoned, and we might not have another chance for a good feast in Nanking before the Mid-autumn Festival a month hence, you know.

My fever could not have been from eating unclean duck bought from outside, since the incubation time should have taken several days, and it started the very next day after the festival. After two relapses, caused once by eating water caltrops and again by eating rice-four dumplings, my fever was running into its third month, and, when intestinal hemorrhage developed, my family got thoroughly alarmed. Because of the Boxer uprising, all Western doctors had left Nanking and we had to go to old-style medicine, in which the treatment of typhoid fever had had a history of eighteen hundred years. My father consulted the doctor on the use of the sulphur drug—not sulfa drug—and concentrate of animal glue, the former a Chinese typhoid specific and the latter something to help coagulation of the blood. These were extreme measures. Besides being dangerous, the sulphur drug was supposed to have the aftereffect of a bad temper. Aunt Ch'eng objected to the drug, because it would give her a bad-tempered daughter-in-law. This angered Father.

"My dear sister," he said, "the child's life is the only thing that matters. If you don't like the temper, I will keep the child at home. You can call me disobedient to our mother if you like. But I will not permit you to put your daughter-in-law's sweet temper before my child's life."

So he allowed the doctor to give me the maximum dose. I was in a delirium. Seven or eight members of the family kept continuous vigil for five days and five nights and did not go to sleep until they were sure that I had passed the crisis. When I finally got up, after being bed-ridden for the whole autumn and winter, and started to have my hair unsnarled, my pigtail came off in one piece. My present head of hair is a heavier crop, which started to grow anew after that illness.

When I learned, during my convalescence, about the argument over the sulphur drug between Father and Aunt Ch'eng, I was sure I would never want to be a member of the Ch'eng family.

I missed school for seven months. Both Father and Mother thought that I had grown enough to be taught as a grown-up child. They differed a great deal, however, in their emphasis. For Mother, the sooner I became conscious of being a girl the better. It was then that I started all the relatives laughing when I thought it strange that every needle had a hole in it. Whenever one of their girls was poor at sewing and embroidery, they would say:

"You are another Ch'uanti."

My father, on the other hand, had other ideas. While he did not encourage any break with the Ch'engs, he was not unaware of the growing likelihood of such an eventuality. Both Grandfather and Father often talked about the freedom enjoyed by women in England—that was still before the days of Mrs. Pankhurst and the suffragettes. I asked why our womenfolk shouldn't start changing things ourselves by going out and meeting and speaking to men of our class and why our sisters and aunts couldn't take jobs outside. Somebody had to make a start some time. But Father reasoned that it was no good to make a bad name for ourselves without helping the cause any. There were too few of us.

It seemed all right to him, however, that if anything should happen between the Yangs and the Ch'engs—marriage was always conceived in terms of families rather than individuals—it would be all right for the girl to go into teaching. He had seen women teachers in England and when and if occasion should arise for me, the times might have advanced far enough for a woman of good family to teach school. As he was out of a job, at the time, he started to give me some instruction in a few modern subjects. He taught me English, paper-and-pencil arithmetic, as well as the usual arithmetic by abacus, and even a few sentences of French and German. But in his pronunciation, the three foreign languages seemed to sound all alike. As soon as I learned to count in English, I said I had "two m-ma," that is, two mamas. This was disrespectful, especially to Mother, and I was promptly shushed.

You know the common weakness of children. The more you treat them as adults, the more they have to live up to their reputation. I never felt so proud as when Grandfather nicknamed me "Little Fairy Fair," on account of my insistence on dividing things fairly.

In the summer of 1901, Grandfather proposed to divide his property among his children—no, I was too young to help him in that. Rather, it was an occasion for me to learn. In China, the head of a family holds all its property and all the earnings of grown-up children. He apportions the pooled income to various branches of the family according to need. Division of property and income usually does not occur until after the death of the head of the house, and even then it is considered brotherly not to divide the family too promptly. But Grandfather had plans he wanted to see carried out during his lifetime. He had willed the house to the Buddhist Press, with the condition that he and his descendants could live indefinitely in the courtyards not already assigned to use for the Press. He divided his own farm ownings and savings in cash, out of which he had been supplementing the income of the family, among his three sons then living, Big Uncle, Father, and Fifth Uncle, with the injunction that they should subsidize the Press when they got well established themselves. From now on he retired as the head of the household and was theoretically being supported by his sons.

I was still too young to understand about the property side of it, but it was fun to watch the masons and carpenters remodel the row of seven big grass-fuel stoves into three separate parts and build three supplementary coal ranges with bricks and mortar. Our original chef was assigned to serve the Press people. We three new small families each employed a new cook. The first morning for marketing, the three sisters-in-law, Auntie, Mother, and Fifth Aunt held a conference and told their cooks to buy exactly the same things. Auntie had been at it for thirty years and all of them were used to keeping house together. When the dishes were cooked, each "household" served a portion to Grandfather.

"Isn't this nice?" he said. "Formerly, I had only one portion, now I have three portions of everything."

After disposing of the important transactions concerning property, Grandfather took out a great array of crockery, silver, glasses, bric-a-brac, blankets, which he had bought from abroad, and silk and formal robes he had not worn for years.

"Little Fairy Fair," he said to me, "you divide these things among the three houses!"

I had divided cakes and fruits and even dishes of food, but this was frightening. Fortunately, they were used to me already. I had always advocated proportional representation. Of the people in the three households, ours were the least numerous, as the only children in it were Sixth Brother and me, the two adopted children. Besides, Father was earning more money than Big Uncle or Fifth Uncle. Therefore I had always assigned the smallest share to ourselves. For this, Mother called me "big gun," that is, a thoughtless person. Her logic was that since we had half as many children, each child should get twice as much of everything as any of the other children.

After the family was formally divided, Grandfather told each of his sons that whoever was able to support his family while working outside would be permitted to take his family along. Big Uncle was then in charge of the Wuchang Arsenal, and since Auntie had toiled at home for thirty years, she had the best right to go out for a change. This meant taking with them Big and Second Sisters, and Big, Second, and Third Brothers. Because Second Sister had been attending to Grandfather about his personal wants, Big Uncle was going to leave her behind, but Grandfather would not have it. Instead, he called Cousine[1] Lang, Auntie's own niece, to come to our family and take care of him. I was very sad because my (actual) brothers and my very motherly Big and Second Sisters were going so far away—400 miles up the river was then a great distance. Just before sailing, when I was trying to be brave and noisily cheerful, sisters whispered into my ears:

"Little Third Sister, you shall come to visit us in Hupeh at Big Brother's wedding."

I was already quite a big girl in 1901. I was almost as tall I am now, which is not tall. But as I lacked the enhancement of the weight which I have since acquired during the following forty-odd years, I appeared very tall and thin, and was nick named "Lamp-post." I grew more awkward in the attire and under the title of "Little Master

---

[1] See Glossary.

Three." And I was conscious that I was a woman when I found that I could not romp as well on some days as on others. Father was supervising the Iron Mines at Tayeh—he was always supervising things. One day, Mother got a letter from him saying that I was too big to continue studying in the same school with the boys and that I had better begin to wear women's clothes. Auntie, who had Wuchang, Hupeh, sent me two very beautiful dresses made of grass linen, for which that region was famous. Big Sister also often advised me to change into women's dresses. So, on the 21st day of the seventh moon, I remember it was the day of Big Brother's formal engagement, "Little Master Three" became "Little Miss Three."

Part II
GIRLHOOD

11

LIFE WITH UNCLE AT WUCHANG

THE OCCASION of my going to Wuchang, capital of Hupeh province, was to attend the wedding of Big Brother Marriage in China, as I have told you, was between families rather than between individuals. Big Brother was engaged to the Hsüs of Nanking. So all the Hsüs went to Wuchang—the bride's widowed mother, a younger sister, and the bride herself—all went to live with Big Uncle's family. It was the custom for the bridegroom to welcome the bride in person. So Big Brother had to come down to Nanking to bring the party to Wuchang, four hundred miles up the Yangtze River.

This was my first big travel since I began to notice and remember things. I was fascinated by the sand bars with waving reeds on them, just like big, long steamships sailing by on the river. The Little Orphan Hill, with what seemed to be toy temples and houses on it, rose straight up in midstream like dream scenes—or had I seen it before in paintings? I thoroughly enjoyed seeing so much water and running about in such a big ship, not realizing that I was later to become such a poor sailor on the sea.

Big Uncle ordered an elaborate wedding for Big Brother. I had been at wedding parties in Nanking, but this was the first wedding in my immediate family and the one at which I had the greatest opportunity to do my mischievous pranks. In fact, as soon as I had called "Big Uncle" and "Auntie" (greeting relative older than oneself consisted of simply addressing him respectfully), Second Sister and Third Brother greeted me in a chorus:

"Is our dear little [nuisance mischief] here again?"

The Hsüs had to stay at a hotel, as the girl could not stay in the house of her betrothed unless she was one of those "reared daughters-in-law," brought up in the future husband's family because of poverty. It was true that the Hsüs were going to live with Big Uncle's family after the wedding. But propriety required that they set up a bride's household before the wedding.

Wedding day was five days after our arrival. We were eager to watch the bride's sedan chair arrive at the front gate. Someone was saying something to the unseen bride inside the heavily draped sedan chair. I could not hear, amidst the music and other festive noises, what they were saying, but they told me that it was to warn the bride that it was time to stop crying.

The rule was that a bride was supposed to start crying aloud as soon as she was carried (by her father or big brother) into the bridal chair and to continue crying until just before entering her husband's house, or, as we say in Chinese, her mother-in law's house. The front door was closed for a few moments before the bridal chair was admitted to teach the bride her first lesson in patience. When the chair was set down in the main reception hall, the bearers and all servants retired. Bridesmaids of perfect happiness were chosen to lift the curtain and assist the bride out of the chair.

What is a lady of perfect happiness? Well, both her parents are living, she has a husband and children. Isn't that perfect happiness?

There was a whirlwind of ceremonies, most of which consisted of the bridal pair kowtowing to the altar, to their elders, and to other relatives, while the mistress of ceremonies had lucky phraseology for every movement she told the bride or the bridegroom to make.

As Big Uncle had a large family, it was fatiguing enough for the bride to get down upon her knees and get up again all the time. But Third Brother and I added to her burden by getting to the head of the reception line, after having met her to kowtow at the end of the line—something like having two pictures of oneself taken by catching a revolving camera at both ends. But we did worse than twice. It was permissible for anyone to take the initiative in kowtowing to the bride, who would then have to return the kowtow. As there were several of us children to take turns at it, we could have made ourselves quite mean with our trickery if Big Uncle had not stopped us in time.

The most exciting thing about an old-fashioned Chinese wedding was the unveiling of the bride, since usually she had never been seen by anyone of her husband's family. This was what made the long-drawn ceremony filled with such exciting suspense. Since I had already seen my sister-in-law, the unveiling was an anticlimax to me, but not to Big Brother. Didn't he go to welcome her in person and bring her and her family along? He did, but, during the whole trip from Nanking to Hankow and crossing to Wuchang in a junk, he managed, as propriety required, never to come face to face with his fiancée. He saved for himself the experience of seeing his bride for the first time on the night of the wedding. It was a matter of course.

Big Brother was Big Uncle's favorite son. So Sister-in-law felt very important. So did her mother and sister. The usual story of daughters-in-law being badly treated by mothers-in-law was reversed. For the first time in thirty years, Auntie was really in anger. The crisis came in connection with a theater party, and I got my first experience of a serious quarrel.

There was a series of plays given outside the Grass Lake Gate of the city wall. One show was specially given for the families of the officers of the arsenal who were working under Big Uncle. One night he detailed four guards to accompany members of the household to the show. For some reason or other, only three of us went—Sister-in-law's younger sister Miss Hsü, Third Brother, and myself. At the opening of the show, a masked character danced once around the stage to present the good luck of official promotion, at which box holders were expected to tip the actors. There were only three of us children in our box, and none of us understood anything about what to do at a theater. One of the guards said to me jokingly:

"Miss Three, this is specially in your honor, why don't you bestow something?"

I was somewhat flustered and said that I did not have my purse with me.

"Give them a gold ring," the guard said.

Before I could reply, off came a ring from the Hsü girl's finger.

"Take this," she said to the guard, "and give it to the troupers!"

"What a generous young lady you are!" I said. "He's only joking. You don't really need to give them that. Guard, will you pay them two dollars for me? Mr. Yang will return you the money tomorrow."

I was only trying to be polite, as it was always polite to fight over being hostess. But this angered the Hsü girl.

"You, pretending to be hostess!" she said. "You have been adopted out. You are only a niece of the house now. What sort of a hostess is that?"

I was so taken aback that I almost cried. When Third Brother took my side, she few into a rage and we had to leave without seeing the show.

Big Uncle decided that the daughter-in-law and relatives had been spoiled beyond reason. He ordered, through his son, a full apology from the bride. She appeared in full formal dress, in dark red coat and long red skirt, and begged everybody's pardon for her sister's behavior. This time it was we who had to return the kowtow.

During my fifteen months' stay in Wuchang, I continued school under the tutorship of an old scholar, Mr. Ch'en Hsi'an, who later became one of the trustees of the Chinling Buddhist Press. Mr. Ch'en was a Hupeh man and was the origin of a few Hupehisms still left in my speech. For example, I still say, when I am careless, *chü yü tz'u nei* instead of *chu ju tz'u lei* for "and so forth." Then I become self-conscious and overcorrect myself by saying *tsou chü* instead of the correct *tsou chii*. That is, when I want to say: "Move your rook!" what I am actually saying is, to my husband's ear, "Move your pig!"

Wuchang has atrocious summers. While you can count on cool summer nights in Peiping and hope for them in Nanking, you get cool summer nights in Wuchang only by staying away. I used to wonder why people should ever like to sit and lounge about in the dingy streets and lanes and feed the mosquitoes. As I grew older, I realized that people were where they were because they would be worse off where they weren't. For even spacious rooms in big houses were steaming hot throughout the summer. This was the way I went through my long siege of malaria in Wuchang. I still say that I was never weak and sickly, but only had big sieges of illness. For, between the malaria attacks, I ran about and studied and played as a well did not take to my bed until I had to, when the attacks were actually on. However, several months of this did not improve my health, and Third Brother and others continued to call me "Lamp-post.

12

LIFE WITH FATHER AT TAYEH

I DID NOT return to Nanking from Wuchang, but went to Tayeh, some fifty miles to the southeast, to live with Father and Mother. The Tayeh mines, as you know, have been the main source of iron for the Hanyang Iron Works. Father was then assistant manager of the iron mines at Tayeh. He was also organizing a stock company for opening a small coal mine there. Uncle Ch'eng, my fiancé's father, had returned from Yangchow and bought a large estate near our house in Nanking. When he heard of the new enterprise, he mortgaged his property and moved his whole family to Tayeh to join Father's business. Father had not been on the best of terms with the Ch'engs. But since I was ultimately to be theirs and since Cousin was studying well, he, my father, might as well be cooperative and improve my possible future—in case.

We lived in a big house on the top of a hill. A western courtyard of ten rooms was assigned to the Ch'engs. Business was very successful from the beginning, and Aunt Ch'eng proposed that we should be wed. I was then fifteen, not an unusual age for a girl to be married at. But Father was opposed to it. He said it was not that he would go back on his word about the engagement, nor wanted to be new-fashioned, but that, even according to old standards, it was legitimate to demand that the son-in-law should have his education completed and become independent before marriage. If Aunt Ch'eng would not continue Cousin's education, he would send him to Lunghua Academy himself and support him until graduation.

"Ask Erman himself," said Aunt Ch'eng. "If he will wait, I will."

So they sent for my cousin. He lived down the hill with other workers in the office, because it would not be easy for us to avoid each other if we stayed in the same house. I had seen and spoken to him as a cousin, but as we grew up, the correct thing to do was to meet as little as possible. Yet I was vitally interested in what he had to say and wanted to hear it for myself. So I pretended not to notice what they were doing and remained in the room. Mother motioned me, with her mouth, to go into the inner room. But Father understood my intention and was in favor of my being present at their talk. So they compromised by letting me sit in a chair astride the inside doorway.

As soon as my cousin entered, Aunt Ch'eng said to him: "Would you rather be married in our hands, or would you rather listen to Second Uncle's idea to go and study now and take care of your own wedding later?"

"The best thing for you," Father said, without waiting for his reply, "is to become independent first, and then get married and set up house for yourself. You know your mother and your cousin will never get along."

Now, this was downright heresy.

"What is a girl married for, anyway? To serve her mother-in-law and rear children for the family, of course! To set up house apart, why, it's unheard of!"

Before Aunt Ch'eng had time to say any of such words aloud, my cousin said bravely: "I will follow everything that Second Uncle commands. If I cannot become independent, I shall never marry."

Father was pleased. Even Mother smiled broadly at her son-in-being. But Aunt Ch'eng was greatly annoyed. "Isn't that fine now," she said. "Instead of getting a daughter-in-law, I have sold out a son! Have you ever heard of anything like that!"

"Let's not worry about the children's affairs," Uncle Ch'eng said. "I shall be happy so long as Second Uncle won't cause the nephew to make such sacrifice in vain."

This closing speech of Uncle Ch'eng's brought me safely over the immediate crisis, but at the same time it added another bar to any possible breaking of the engagement. Must not cause him to make such sacrifice in vain!

After Father returned to his room, I said: "This must not be the end. Would you allow it, Father, if I did something later?"

"If it's about regretting the engagement," Mother said, "I won't permit the subject to be brought up again. Since your cousin is such a fine boy, he certainly fits the title of 'half-son' in our family."

Later, Father said to me: "Let's not talk about it anymore. 'The sky may hold unpredictable winds and clouds.' You just keep quiet for a few years. Even girls in the foreign countries cannot decide their own affairs until they are of age. I have told Juiching to go to Lunghua Academy. You should also settle down to your studies. And when China starts to give women a general education, you may perhaps become a teacher. You know, Ch'uan'er, I think the country is due for some revolutionary changes."

After a few days, Uncle Ch'eng proposed to have a big engagement ceremony, now that the wedding was indefinitely postponed. Father agreed. Now, a formal engagement was a formidable affair. The boy's family had to present, by a long procession of bearers, so many pieces of jewelry, so many silks and satins, literally loads of tea, fruit, cake, flowers, etc., etc. In return, the girl's family had to present the four treasures of scholars—ink slabs, writing brushes, ink sticks, and books silks, and other valuables. For families of our standing, it would have to be a matter of quite a few thousand dollars, and a dollar was no small matter in the 1900's. I said to Father privately: "Why waste such a lot of money on such useless things? Besides, I am sure they will ultimately turn out to be meaningless. Why not save all this money for me to enter a missionary school and prepare to study abroad?"

"China opens modern schools for girls," Father replied, "I shall send you to one, but not to missionary schools. Nobody of good family goes to a missionary school."

I passed my engagement day like any festival day. I talked loudly and joined lights over fruits and nuts. I meant to tell them by my behavior that I regarded the whole thing as somebody else's affair with which I had nothing to do. Apparently they did not or would not understand me. They just remarked that I was too much used to being a boy.

That was in the spring of 1904. In the winter, Grandfather was seriously ill. Big Uncle dispatched Auntie and Big and Second Sisters from Wuchang back to Nanking to attend to Grandfather. I wanted to go, too. But Father told me to wait. If news from Nanking did not improve we should all go home together. After half a month word came that Grandfather was well again. So we remained in Tayeh.

The next year, Big Sister wrote to Father saying that a middle school for girls was going to be opened in Nanking. Chou Yüshan had been appointed Viceroy of Liang Kiang, that is, governor of Kiangsu, Anhwei, and Kiangsi. He often came to our house, and Grandfather persuaded him to establish a school for girls. They were just looking for a schoolhouse. Would I like to apply for entrance? For Big Sister was very anxious that I should be the first person in our family to enter a modern school. After reading the letter, Father asked me what I thought of it. I promptly replied that I would apply. Mother tried to stop me, but Father overruled her.

Six days after Sister's letter came, Father sent me on my way to Nanking, escorted by a cousin on Mother's side and a man servant, taking along five hundred dollars for tuition and expenses. On my departure, Aunt Ch'eng called after me: "Don't forget to fill in engaged on your application blank!"

"All right, First Aunt," I laughed as I shouted back, "I might as well fill in 'married'!"

13

MY FIRST MODERN SCHOOL

WHEN I ARRIVED at Nanking after a three-day voyage, I heard that Big Sister had already applied on my behalf for entrance to Lüning School. Grandfather informed me that my name was Yunch'ing, which means "person with rhyme." So, over the signature of "Yang Yunch'ing," I took my entrance examination. The subject for composition was "The Importance of Education for Women." Like everybody else, I started the enumeration of such eternal truths as "The women of today are the mothers of the future people of the country." After putting down this sentence, I kept biting the upper end of my writing brush and blaming myself for not having listened to Father's advice to study hard and practice my calligraphy. After an indecisive struggle, I produced an essay of a hundred-odd words. I was disappointed for a brief moment to find myself admitted into Class B instead of Class A, but to enter a brand-new modern school, that was the chief thing.

On the day of the opening of the school, the street was filled with green-covered sedan chairs, some with large red awnings or parasols. Governor Chou Yüshan, honorary principal of the school, arrived with his family and conducted the opening ceremonies. Shen Shihjan was assistant principal, who actually ran the school. Of the teachers, Mrs. Huang and Miss Sun of McTyeire School of Shanghai came to teach English, Miss Chang of the Nanking Presbyterian Hospital taught mathematics, the wife of Chang Poheng taught Chinese. There were altogether twenty or thirty teachers.

Auntie and Big Sister thought I had better be a day-student, as the school was only half a *li* from home, and I might find living in school too hard. But I said that it was all right and reminded them of the proverb: "Only through the hardest of hardships, can one become a man above men."

I felt like a bird released from the cage, darting in and out, buying this and arranging that, in preparation for moving into the dormitory. There were five in a room. My roommates were Chang something, Hsü something, Lin Kuanhung, and Ts'ai Suchüan. They were two pairs of cousins and all belonged to Class A. I was an odd number in an odd class and felt rather embarrassed about it. But they were all very nice to me, especially Kuanhung and Suchüan, or Margaret, as she was sometimes called. Later she changed her foreign name to Christina, under which she is known by her American friends. Kuanhung's elder brother Pingnan was Third Brother's schoolmate. The Lins descended from the national hero Lin Tse-hsü, of Opium War fame. Whenever you meet a Lin from Foochow, it is almost a form of greeting to ask: "Are you a descendant of Lin Tse-hsü?"

One thing I could not understand about my upper-class girls was why they were always studying hard all evening until very late. One thing they could not understand about me was why I was always running around from one place to another instead of studying. I found that it was pencil-and-paper arithmetic that was troubling them most. What difficult assignments they must be having, I thought. One night, I overheard Suchüan and Kuanhung arguing about the order of a series of operations. I don't remember exactly what, but the problem looked something like:

$$17 \times 25 - 3 \div 49 + 1$$

They argued whether the operations should be done in the order in which they occurred, or whether certain operations should be done before others.

"Let me look at your work sheet, Kuanhung," I said. "Why, it's the same problem as the one I had in class today! And this, and this, too! How come? Your class has the same set of problems as my class!"

Thus I learned that the only difference between the classes was on the basis of Chinese, all the other subjects being the same for all classes. It happened that Father had already taught me the same textbooks in arithmetic they were using in school, a set of three books called *Pisuan Shu-hsueh* or "Arithmetic by Pencil Calculations." So I was always able to finish my exercises in class, while our teacher was explaining them to us, instead of having to bring them out for homework. Moreover, because Grandfather had brought a lot of material from abroad for the making of celestial and terrestrial globes and all members of the family took part in this family industry, geography came easy to me, as an old friend. Before I realized it, I was doing a flourishing business of explaining to my roommates and other schoolmates that multiplications and divisions should be done before additions and subtractions,[1] that latitudes ran right and left but were reckoned up and down, while longitudes ran up and down but were reckoned right and left. News of my activities reached the teachers. Before the end of the first week, I was promoted to Class A.

While studying in Lüning School, I was offered a chance to go to America as one of the so-called indemnity-fund students. You remember the 1900 Boxer uprising I spoke of, which resulted in the occupation of Peking by the armies of eight countries? In the settlement, China was to pay an indemnity of 450 million taels,[2] a fabulous sum of money in those days, long before people talked in terms of billions. Of this amount, about 24 million dollars in American money was to go to the United States. After the actual damages to Americans were more accurately figured out, it was found that the amount was actually twice as much as necessary. On the initiative of John Hay and Elihu Root, it was decided to return the excess amount to China, with the understanding that the money was to be used for

---

[1] I wish I had met you then, Yunch'ing, for I was using the same three textbooks at the same time in Soochow and nobody told me about this rule.—Y.R.C.

[2] One tael was roughly half a dollar in American money.

sending Chinese students to study in America. Thus were founded the American indemnity-fund scholarships.

For the first two years (1909 and 1910), before a preparatory school was established, students to be sent abroad were selected by competitive examinations open to the whole country. Since, however, girls had not had the same opportunity to go to modern schools to compete with the boys on an equal footing, they were selected without examination from various schools, priority being given to schools run by the Chinese. Six girls were chosen, and among them were the top three girls from our school, Lin Kuanhung, Ts'ai Suchian, and myself. Kuanhung did not want to go, because she felt she did not know enough English. Suchüan wanted to stick to her. I did want to go, but Grandfather said that it was no use going to a country without a knowledge of the language and that I could wait a year or two, as there would be scholarships every year starting from 1909. So none of us went. Actually I waited twelve years before I went to America for the first time. If I had known that in the 1910 class of students sent to America I was ultimately to marry one of them, I would have—well, like all historical if's, one if involves so many other if's that it ceases to make sense.

Unlike the attraction that it is nowadays, going abroad was going away from home and country to the strange and unknown. Now that that question was brushed aside, we three returned to our happy life at Lüning School. I took up piano lessons. Whenever there was a meeting or something, Kuanhung was usually the main speaker, Suchüan would recite a poem or tell a story in English, and mine was the inevitable piano solo. Now, don't you laugh at me, Iris! You may call your mother unmusical if you like. It is true that I cannot carry a tune very steadily, but it was a full six-page Mozart's something or other that I played to a very appreciative audience. My fellow students knew that a piece of classical music was something that you never got tired of hearing tired of hearing over and over again.

I was proud of my accomplishments. But Aunt Ch'eng was ashamed of me. "I don't want to have for daughter-in-law a woman who sells songs." For that was a term only a little more decorous than "singsong girl." When Father wrote to me about it from Tayeh, I was so angry that I looked for more things to do that would meet with Aunt Ch'eng's disapproval.

Hitherto I had avoided meeting any boys who were not my relatives. There was no such thing as one-to-one dating—not for decades yet. Brothers and other members of the immediate family were the only men allowed to see the girls or take them out. I did not even go out when Third Brother and Kuanhung's brother Pingnan and Suchüan's brothers came to take us out together. But, after I heard about my being "a woman who sells songs," I promptly accepted all invitations to the parties. Seven or eight of us would go to Yuehsheng Company at the Four Elephants Bridge (Street) to eat *ta-ts'ai*, or foreign dinners, after which we would go into the houses of our schoolmates and their brothers to play. Those parties were very unorthodox for the times, though they were pretty well chaperoned.

Our house was quite a center of attraction for my schoolmates and their brothers. We played the new-fangled game of tennis. We played chess under an arbor between two big willows. We fished from the pond. We took photographs and developed them ourselves, since there was no place to send them to. Somebody brought a phonograph into our house, not one of those cylindrical things, heard through a sort of stethoscope at the temple fairs for two coppers a song, but a real His Master's Voice machine, with horn and all, which everybody could listen to at the same time. Occasionally, Grandfather would join our party and tell stories about foreign countries or explain the principles of some of the scientific gadgets we were playing with. The boys met almost every day. We girls joined them weekends.

When Aunt Ch'eng heard of what was going on, she got busy and sent my cousin to Nanking to enter the Huiwen Academy and instructed him to join our parties as much as he could. I did not avoid him, as it would have been proper and natural for a girl in my position to do, but continued to be as active in the group as ever. He was full of fun, but somehow was always afraid of me. So they teased him by parodying the nursery rhyme about the little mouse. Whenever they saw him, they would sing:

This teasing went on with my implicit approval. It compensated for my inferiority complex in not being a free person like most of my schoolmates.

"Little mouse Climbs up the lamp, Stealing oil, Can't get down, 'Squeak, squeak, squeak!' Calls 'ma-ma.' When he hears, 'Pus-sy's here!' Ku-lu ku-lu ku-lu ku-lu tum-bles down!"

Those were the happiest school days I ever had, not because I am looking back from this distance through a time-filter, but because I told myself I was happy and everybody else told me so. I was successful in my studies, I had friends to play with. I was pampered by friends and family in every way. I thought nobody in any school, nobody in the world, could be as happy as I.

But a Chinese proverb says: "At the extreme end of happiness comes grief."

14

CALAMITY AND FORTUNE

ALL WAS WELL at Big Uncle's household after the departure of the in-laws on Big Brother's side—until Big Uncle was promoted to be Supervisor of the Saddle Mountain Coal Mines in Hupeh. For a man of his standing at his age, it was not at all unusual to take in a concubine. But Grandmother had ordered to the contrary. Big Uncle tried to get around the order by telling Auntie to make the suggestion to Grandfather as her own idea of being virtuous. For not to be jealous was the height of virtue. But Auntie refused.

"At my age," she was fifty-six when she said this, "of course I no longer care if you do take a concubine. But if you want me to say it's my idea, I am not that insane. What are you going to say about Mother's command? And besides, how can you support two married sons with five grandchildren, and then support a concubine?"

Big Uncle's excuse was that, since Grandfather was getting old and needed attention, Auntie and the children should return to Nanking. Who then would attend to him at Saddle Mountain? Finally, at Big Brother's suggestion, part of the family went with Big Uncle and the rest, including Auntie, went to Nanking

Big Brother had not been happy with his too eventful marriage. His lungs had not been in good condition for some time. Having to see Auntie go back to Nanking under the circumstances worried him a lot. Five months after moving to Saddle Mountain, he died of consumption. His four-year-old daughter caught it and died soon after. After this, the whole family except Big Uncle returned to Nanking. But the disease continued to spread. One after another, Big Brother's remaining three children caught it and died. Then, what seemed to be absolutely impossible to happen, Big Sister and Second Sister also passed away. They had been too careless of themselves while attending the sick.

If you have never had a sister eighteen years bigger than yourself who was both a sister and mother to you in every way, you couldn't appreciate what it meant to me to lose my Big Sister. It seemed as if the whole world had changed. Every time I came home from school, it was not quite like coming home again. Big Sister was also Auntie's favorite daughter. Auntie could not bear to let Big Sister's remains go out at once. She had her coffin placed in the hall of her courtyard for one hundred days, during which she chanted Buddhist scriptures every day to propitiate her soul. I had not been coming home from school regularly, as I was living in the dormitory, but now I came home every afternoon after classes and cried a few minutes beside Big Sister's coffin before going back to school.

One day, when I came home to cry, I found that the latticed doors to the hall were locked, and Auntie was sitting near the railing in front of the hall.

"Lansien," she said to me quietly, "all my loved ones have died—all but you. You are my only one left, thanks to your adopted luck. But you must take good care of yourself and not disappoint me. Although your Big Sister is gone, she will continue to watch over you. I have great hopes in you. Be good and don't do anything that may bring me grief. You know, Lansien, even I do not go too near the coffin now. After one hundred days are over and she is interred in our old home country back in Anhwei, you can visit her tomb whenever you return to Anhwei."

I promised her not to go into that hallway again. But I continued to come home every afternoon and stood for a while in that courtyard.

Since that calamity, nobody wanted to live in that courtyard until 1934, when I had the rooms renovated for temporary use, while my own house—my husband's—was being built. I was not at all afraid to live in that courtyard. I knew Big Sister loved me. When my second daughter Nova was down with diphtheria in it in 1934, some old members of my own family, who were living in the other courtyards, started to whisper a little. But Nova got well, and got married just the other day.

A great change occurred in our school. Our honorary principal and founder, Governor Chou Yüshan, was transferred to Peking for duties in the capital. Vice-principal Shen was appointed Fant'ai, or Finance Commissioner of Kiangsi. The families of students would like to have a woman principal. So the gifted Miss Lü Huiju was appointed principal. Miss Lü excelled in all the traditional liberal arts of "lute, chess, books, and painting," and had been to Japan for one year, but was not much of a thinker in matters of educational policy. Her first act was to change the school to a normal school. She emphasized form at the expense of substance. Because of differences over policy, she discontinued the services of most of our old teachers. Many of us changed schools, Kuanhung's father died that year. Three of her brothers went to Japan to study and took her along. Suchüan went to Laura Haygood School (Methodist) in Soochow. After staying on for three months and finding life not the same, I asked Grandfather whether he would approve of my going to McTyeire School of Shanghai. Grandfather said it was all right, except that he was afraid that the Chinese studies there would not be so good. I had better wait until Father came back from Tayeh and talk it over with him.

A new difficulty about my plans was that Father was losing badly in his mining business. There had been a flood in Tayeh and the pits were damaged severely. He even had to draw heavily on his savings reserved for my education. Grandfather wrote to him that, so long as Father agreed to my going to McTyeire School, he would support me himself. But Father did not reply for a long time. Winter vacation came—winter vacations were long, important vacations in China. I went to Tayeh to see Father, especially about my going to McTyeire.

Both Father and Uncle Ch'eng agreed to my going and said that they would accompany me to Shanghai themselves.

In Tayeh, my luck struck a near-miss. When I lived in Tayeh before, we youngsters used to buy the Hupeh provincial lottery tickets. One sheet of ten coupons cost six dollars and would be worth fifty thousand if you got the first prize. Father used to laugh at our patriotism because, if we bought such things regularly, it would, in the long run, amount to contributing a steady income for the provincial government. But I was not wanting in the gambling spirit. When I returned to Tayeh that winter, my cousins on my aunt's side and on my mother's side invited me to join them again in buying some lottery tickets.

"You ought to buy a whole sheet this time," said one of my cousins. "Since you want to go to McTyeire School, you should be well provided for. "

"It takes both luck and a ticket to get a prize," I replied.

"There is no reason why I should get anything this time after wasting a lot of money just on tickets and tickets. I am tired of exchanging real money for the shadow of fortune."

"Be a sport," urged another cousin. "Besides, the postman has already, brought our tickets and it isn't nice to ask him to take them back."

So, just to be accommodating, I made a gesture of throwing away sixty cents of big money and bought one coupon—instead of buying several coupons, as I had usually done before. The other nine were divided among several people, among them one of the guards at the gate, who took four coupons.

We won. It was Third Prize—ten thousand dollars. The retailer deducted two thousand dollars for expenses and celebration. The guard got thirty-two hundred dollars. He resigned his job, returned to his land, bought a farm, and lived happily ever afterwards. My coupon was good for eight hundred dollars. After sharing my good luck with relatives, friends, and servants, I took exactly three hundred and ten dollars with me to supplement my school expenses. Since I have never met a person who got as big a lottery prize as I did and since the amount spent in lotteries by all my acquaintances added up to rather more than three hundred and ten dollars, or even eight hundred dollars, my father was still right about the patriotic effect of our activities with lotteries.

After the Chinese New Year's holidays in 1908, Father and Uncle Ch'eng accompanied me to Shanghai to enter McTyeire School.

15

WRITING TO MY FIANCÉ FROM McTYEIRE SCHOOL

CONTRARY TO MY expectations, I did not find McTyeire a better school than Lüning. Rules and regulations were taken more literally. Because of the importance of keeping high standard of respectability in order to attract students from the better families, many things which my liberal grandfather smiled at were frowned upon by my teachers. Instruction was more stereotyped. Questions outside the lesson of the day were discouraged. All this whetted my appetite for doing the wrong thing because it was the wrong thing.

My schoolmates were mostly from families of Protestant Christians or families of merchants working in foreign firms. Foreign girls would not, of course, enter our school, since they went to schools established by foreigners for foreign children in order not to become literate in Chinese when they grew up. Even at McTyeire, which was for Chinese girls, Chinese was secondary to English. At Lüning I had been weak in Chinese and strong in the other subjects. When I entered McTyeire, I was placed in the top class in Chinese, second class in mathematics, and fifth class in English. I often had to ask my schoolmates to help me out in my English lessons.

If I did not quite like the school, I liked the friends I made there. I remember best, well—er—Ch'en Chaohsing, P'an— P'an—well, I give up. You see, they all talked the Shanghai dialect, and although I never used to speak it in my school days, I knew all my schoolmates by the Shanghai pronunciation of their names. It is such a wrench to pronounce their names in Mandarin. So, to start over again, in Shanghai pronunciation, I remember best Zung Tsausing, Pe

Nyokme (now Mrs. L. T. Ch'en), Sze Vongme (Mrs. Ch'iao), Wong Zoeyien (Mrs. J. C. S. Tung), Dong Nyokzoe (Mrs. T. F. Tsiang), and Ting Me'ing. Me'ing was my quarrelling friend. We quarrelled all the time, sometimes seriously, sometimes just for the fun of it. She liked to boss everybody and I hated to be bossed by anybody. So, for identical and opposite reasons, we both finally became doctors, and we had a good laugh about it when, after many years, I visited her hospital in Tientsin. Nyokzoe is the most constant personality I have ever met. Unspoiled by prominence, unruffled by crises, she is the same simple, lovable self today as when I first saw her over thirty years ago.

In the summer vacation of 1908, my personal problem came to a head. Ever since Father made my cousin promise to finish his studies before getting married, he was more guarded in speaking of possibilities of any final break. I also felt that it would be unfair to have acquiesced when Father put up his conditions and then make him eat his word. Yet my freedom was at stake. Thus, a constant fight was going on within me, which might have hurt me seriously, but for my generally happy-go lucky nature.

That summer, Cousine Lang (Auntie's niece) had a bad boil. They treated her by applying hot compresses and such things. If it would only come to a breaking point, then you would be able to clean it out and get well, they told her. One day, I was talking with Grandfather and the subject drifted from methods of treating boils to marriage systems. Inevitably, I applied what he said to my own case. It was only five months from my nineteenth birthday, or twentieth birthday by Chinese reckoning "Grandfather," I said, "when is my boil coming to a breaking point?"

Grandfather was silent for a moment. He looked at me with his eyes of wisdom that brought four thousand years of China into the twentieth century:

"My dear *child!*" he said. "If that is how you feel, we shall certainly have to do something."

He studied my face for a while and continued: "Are you really determined? Juiching is a fine boy, you know. You will not regret it?"

"No," I replied simply.

There was the question who should bring up the question to whom. There was no precedent to follow, because the thing was unprecedented. I thought at first that, since the families had made the engagement, they should be responsible for breaking it. On the other hand, since it was on the ground of freedom of the individual that I based my move, I should write to my cousin myself. Grandfather was in favor of the latter way. So I took my brush and paper and drafted my letter of proposal to my fiancé to break our engagement. I showed my very literary composition to Grandfather for correction. One passage said:

"If, by bringing unhappiness to the husband's elders, one brought discredit to one's own parents, then it were better to mend matters beforehand than leave regrets to the future."

My idea was, first of all, to win my freedom, of course. If I could do that, I would not like to hurt anybody more than I had to, nor to bring any more disharmony between relatives than there was. By putting the question partly on the plane of my unfitness to serve the parents-in-law, which was an all-serious consideration in the old family system, I was trying to save the face of everybody concerned. When Grandfather read my draft letter to this point, he said:

"Ch'uanti, you have grown up. You have proved your right to freedom. For you have not only made a good case for yourself, but also made a brave effort to maintain harmony in the family. I know that you will succeed in solving your own problem and hope you will succeed in your effort to effort to help others."

"I don't know," I said. "I am afraid to think what a row Big Uncle and Aunt Ch'eng will make as soon as they hear of this."

"You still have five months in which to think it over," Grandfather said. "When you need me, I will help you with all my authority.

Meanwhile, go your school and study just as if nothing had happened."

I folded up my drafted letter, sealed it in an unaddressed envelope, and returned with it to Shanghai at the end of the summer holidays. Cousine Lang, who was present at my talk with Grandfather, was the only other person to share the five month secret.

In November, Emperor Tetsung and the Empress Dowager died in close succession. Two-year old Henry Puyi (who later became puppet ruler in Manchuria) ascended the throne. We students demanded a one-week recess for national mourning. The principal, Miss Richardson, said that McTyeire was a missionary institution and had nothing to do with Chinese national affairs. We replied that we were Chinese people; that a missionary school was to teach us to embrace religion, not to renounce our country. We had not been particularly loyal subjects of the Ch'ing dynasty, and I had been proud of having come from a revolutionary-minded family. But now national honor was at stake, and when it took the form of a one-week vacation, the movement was irresistible. We elected our teacher of Chinese, Mr. Fan Tzumei, to negotiate with Miss Richardson. Finally we compromised on a three-day recess.[1] A memorial service was held. The students had yellow worsted in their hair, which was fourth degree mourning. The foreign faculty wore black bands. It was quite impressive.

In the same autumn, Father came to Shanghai on business. He sent Cousin Chungying to take me out to stay with Father for a few days.

---

[1] Poor girls, you didn't know how to bargain! Over at Kiangnan Provincial College, we had a two-week vacation, and I was able to return from Nanking to Changchow to eat fresh-water crabs.—Y.R.C.

When Chungying brought me to the hotel, Father noticed the yellow worsted that was still in my hair. "Why, whose mourning are you wearing, Ch'uan'er?"

"Oh, that. That was for the Emperor. Not that we care much about the dead Manchus, but it's a question of maintaining national honor in a missionary school, you know."

"Sh—! This is not home. This is a hotel. You must be careful with what you say, Ch'uan'er."

We had a riotous time going places, Father and Chungying and I. We shopped, we dined, we bought clothes, or rather Father bought them for me. He had a golden hairpin made for me.

One evening, after Father had had a successful day in his business in town, I took out my drafted letter and showed it to him. He sighed and said: "If you insist on doing it, I cannot force you not to. But aren't we being unfair to your cousin?"

"Well, in a revolution," I replied, "somebody will have to be sacrificed. He is just unfortunate, if having had to go to school can be called unfortunate. Father, I have made up my mind."

"Well, then, will you add a declaration in your letter that you will never marry again? Since he is being sacrificed for an idea, it's only fair that you should match his sacrifice with yours. I have always treated you as a son. You can teach, and be independent."

"But Father," I objected, "if this is going to be a revolution, it must be a revolution with no conditions attached. Moreover, since in all likelihood he will marry somebody else,[2] why should I be bound, and bound to nobody? If the idea is to break the tradition, I should all the more plan to marry. But that's a question that depends upon whom I meet and whom I like, and has nothing to do with the present case. Of course I won't marry anybody I meet on the street just for the purpose of breaking the tradition. The right person may

---

[2] He subsequently married the sister of Third Brother's wife.

or may not come into my life. But you don't want to prevent him from coming, would you, Father?"

"All right, Ch'uan'er, you shall have your wish," he said. "But you will appreciate my position. I cannot openly support you. Since Grandfather wishes it, I don't think Big Uncle or Aunt Ch'eng will disobey. If they make me the excuse, just say that I knew about it.

I had three more days of good time with Father in Shanghai before he left for Tayeh on finishing his business. Never had Shanghai autumn days been so bright and beautiful.

The day after my birthday, I mailed the letter to my fiancé. His reply did not come until two weeks later. He did not say yes or no, but blamed me for not understanding his difficulties. For my part, I regarded it as agreed.

When I returned to Nanking for the winter holidays, I was surprised to find Father back home from Tayeh. Was anything the matter? Then Cousine Lang explained to me what had happened. As soon as my cousin got my letter, he consulted Aunt Ch'eng and Big Uncle about it. That was why it took him so long to reply. Aunt Ch'eng was angry with Big Uncle. She railed at him for having brought to this world such a disobedient daughter.

"You are right, my sister," said Big Uncle. "I've had enough of this nonsense. Tomorrow I will take her out of school and order her to be married to your son at once. If she refuses, I will put her to death."

"But don't forget that Lansien is no longer our daughter," Auntie said, against her usual feelings about such relationships. "Since she has been adopted by Second Brother from birth, it is for Second Brother to decide."

Then Grandfather asserted his authority:

"You ought to be ashamed of yourself," he said to Big Uncle. "At your mature age, can't you think of anything but putting a child to death? Let me tell you, these things have been going on with my knowledge."

Big Uncle gasped; Auntie's face relaxed—so Cousine Lang told me.

"Say no more," Grandfather continued. "When Ch'uanti returns for the winter holidays, I will send for your Second Brother. I will then make the decision for them."

That was why I found Father home from Tayeh when I returned from school.

When the question was opened again, everybody repeated what they had said before, except that Big Uncle did not mention killing me any more. Addressing his remarks specially to Big Uncle and Aunt Ch'eng, Grandfather said: "I have no illusions about happy marriages always resulting from free choice, but you be sure that no good can come of compelling girl to marry someone against her wish. I have seen too many abuses in the old system. If a family like ours cannot make a start in reform, who else's can? You are always talking about your mother's orders. All right, I am your father. I now countermand her orders. That is final."

Big Uncle shook with suppressed anger. But having been brought up in the school of obedience, he obeyed Grandfather's order to permit my disobedience. He only added: "Then she must never marry again."

"But why should—"

"No more now," Father interrupted, and then added in a whisper, as he pulled at my dress, "That won't count."

Thus, on one half of an interrogative sentence, ended successfully my nineteen-year fight for unconditional freedom. For the first time in my life, my self was my own.

16

MY GRANDFATHER

I HAVE SAID so much about my grandfather, because he had such a decisive influence over my formative years. My early life can very well be called "Life with Grandfather. And this chapter may very well be called "Grandfather's life in my autobiography." You will see, among other things, how Buddhism and the revolution were combined in the same person and why he was such a champion of freedom in general and of my freedom in particular.

My grandfather's formal name was Wenhui. His style, or courtesy-name, was Jenshan. He was born in 1837 in Shihtai, in southern Anhwei, and was the sixth child and first son of my great-grandfather. When three days old, he was engaged to my grandmother, who was six years old. It was common practice then to have the girl several years older than the boy, so that she could take care of him, if married very young. When my grandfather was nine years old, his fiancée had the smallpox. Being less lucky than her granddaughter, she came out of the sickness terribly disfigured. Her father sent a special messenger to Peking, where my great-grandfather was an official, to break the news to our family and to relieve my great-grandfather of his obligation. When asked by his parents how he felt about it, Grandfather replied: "I don't mind. Don't they say of girls:

> Once pockmarked,
> Thrice alluring
> Without pockmarks,
> No love enduring?"[1]

---

[1] I ma² san¹ ch'iao⁴.

So, promptly at fourteen, Grandfather was married. At the unveiling of the bride on the wedding night, great-grandmother burst into tears. So handsome a boy, and so unusually bright! To think that he would have to live all his life with such a girl! When, after three days, the formal returning day for the bride, the groom's family called on the bride's family, the father-in law said:

"Jenshan, I will permit you to marry another wife in the future. It will be agreeable to me, so long as you treat my daughter well and maintain her equal standing in your home."

Grandfather thanked him without saying yes or no. Bigamy in the sense of marrying two wives (not concubines) was not normally allowed by society. The only exception was when one of two aged or deceased brothers had a son and the other had in which case the son could marry two wives to be daughters-in-law of the two houses and thus perpetuate the two branches of the family. But grandfather had no such responsibilities. His father-in-law made the very unusual concession purely out of goodness of heart.

About this time began the T'aip'ing uprising, led by Hung Hsiuch'üan, who was something of a Christian, something of a fanatic, and something of a racial revolutionist. The movement spread like wild fire. By 1853, Nanking fell to the plundering T'aip'ing hordes. Tseng Kuofan began to train his Hunan troops for his loyal defense of the dynasty. As my great-grandfather was a friend as well as classmate of Tseng Kuofan in getting the *chinshih*, or doctor's degree—they were of the class of 1837—he sent my grandfather to Tseng to help him in military affairs. In a short time, he was given assignments of considerable responsibility. When the new famous Hunan Army was on the march to reconquer Anhwei from the T'aip'ings, grandfather tried to persuade Tseng to take this opportunity for a revolution. He said to Tseng Kuofan:

"I am happy to serve under your leadership in putting a stop to killing and plunder by these fanatics and in restoring peace and law

---

Pu ma² pu yao⁴.

in the land. But why must we continue to be loyal to this decadent foreign dynasty? Now that we have a first-rate army of our own Han people, isn't it now a fine opportunity to regain our freedom?"

Tseng Kuofan smiled and said a few words of admiration for my grandfather's character. The next day, he despatched him to send his respects to my great-grandfather at Hangchow, to which the family had moved from Anhwei, and gave my grandfather a job there, the job of taking care of food supplies in the rear. Here ended his first revolutionary activities. Here also started his first and last romance.

Shortly after he arrived at Hangchow, he met a refugee girl in the neighborhood. Young people of opposite sexes did not use to meet, not only in Grandfather's time, but not much even in my time. But those were unusual circumstances. Life as refugees was not conducive to the observance of ordinary conventions. Besides, the place was Hangchow, on the shores of beautiful West Lake. My grandfather saw Ch'iaoku ("Clever Maiden") every day. He would bring a volume of poems to her, and she would chant them to him—we never just read poems in China, not the classical poems—in her melodious Soochow voice. The West Lake moon, waxing and waning in the reflections, was just like the moon over the lakes of any other country, except that it was more beautiful.

Things went so far that my grandfather had to confess to his elders his wish, and reminded them of what his father-in-law had promised. My great-grandfather consented. Even my grandmother agreed to what she felt to be honor-bound. But my great-grandmother wanted to wait until my grandmother gave birth to a child. If it was a girl, my grandfather would be permitted to marry Ch'iaoku; if a boy, then she would not permit the marriage. It would not have mattered if it had been a question of taking Ch'iaoku as concubine. But since she was of a respectable family, that would not have been a possible alternative.

When her time came, Grandmother gave birth to Big Uncle, my actual father.

Grandfather used to tell us children about those old days when we took turns in fanning him or otherwise attending to him during summer evenings in the big courtyard in Yenling Hsiang. When he reached the birth of Big Uncle, and the consequent loss of Ch'iaoku to him, I looked around a little and said:

"If you had asked me, Grandpa, I would have given up Big Uncle and myself in exchange for the other grandma!"

After the close of that episode in his life, Grandfather would wander alone in the streets of Hangchow after office hours. One day he picked up a volume of *Lengyen Ching* or *Suranga*. He had always been interested in science, philosophy, and religion, and this Buddhist work was such a great find that he kept reading, standing in the old bookshop, quite forgetting where he was.

My grandfather never took the universal civil service examinations. Until these examinations were abolished in 1905 when modern schools began to be established, every young man who could afford to devote ten to fifteen years to the learning of some two dozen standardized Confucian classics took this road to personal advancement. But Grandfather was never interested in following this road. His revolutionary sentiments must have had something to do with it. But there was an even stronger reason. Grandmother was no different from most young women of the time in wishing to become the wife of a high official. Because his own wish had been thwarted, Grandfather's aversion to become an official became a determination. Now, with this unusually good find in a subject which had always had an absorbing interest for him, he felt that he had found his life work. He collected rare editions, visited temples and talked with monks and lay Buddhists and pursued research in textual criticism and interpretation of Buddhist thought, and organized the Chinling Buddhist Press, as I told you before.

But Buddhism baked no bread—or rather boiled no rice—not for a lay Buddhist, anyway. When my great-grandfather died, the burden of family support fell on my grandfather. Tseng Kuofan had just reconquered Nanking. He summoned Grandfather there and asked him what he would like to do. As he did not want to be an official, he gave him the job of supervising the construction of the new Viceroy Yamen, which later became the office of the National Government. This was how I, a "native" of Shihtai, Anhwei, happened to be born and live in Nanking, Kiangsu. That was, also, how a tradition of construction supervisors started and continued for three generations in our family—Grandfather supervising the building of the Viceroy Yamen, Big Uncle and Father supervising forts and mines, and Sixth Brother Yüsheng supervising the building of the National Central Museum in Nanking, until World War II interrupted it in 1937.

Shortly before he died in 1872, Tseng Kuofan told his son Chitse to take special care of my grandfather.

"Yang Jenshan is going to go far," he said. "Take good care of him, but do not force him to do anything. He is at his best when he does what he likes."

In 1875, Tseng Chitse was appointed Envoy Plenipotentiary to England and France. He asked my grandfather whether he would be interested in going abroad, and offered him the position of Councillor in the newly established Chinese Legation in London. Grandfather accepted the offer. Thus began a long interlude in his Buddhist studies, during which his scientific interests had full play. Big Uncle went along as attaché, and later was sent to France and Germany to study civil engineering.

Grandfather sent little money home, leaving Grandmother to carry on the best she could with the rent from farmlands in Anhwei. He spent practically all his salary on scientific instruments, with which he intended to equip a modern school when he returned. He bought clocks and watches, materials for making terrestrial and celestial globes, transits, telescopes, cameras, and thermometers—such as we used to fool our teachers. They all thought that he was eccentric if not crazy.

Something crazy did happen in the diplomatic household. When my grandfather and his colleagues set up house in London, they found that there was a beautiful porcelain pot in every bedroom. One New Year's Eve, the younger members of the staff planned a Chinese dinner for the English stenographers, copyists, etc., there being no typists then, of course. When the girls entered the dining room and saw a big First Rank Pot, flanked by four other equally enormous dishes in the same kind of flowery tureen, they started to snicker and giggle. When their hosts urged them to sit down, they backed away and laughed louder. It was beyond the diplomatic vocabulary of those English girls to explain the cause of their mirth, but the idea finally did get across. With characteristic self-possession and humor, Grandfather said:

"Well, we must take a photograph of this memorable occasion."

And so we still have, in our Yenling Hsiang house, a picture of that table—unless it was placed in the courtyard which was burnt after the fall of Nanking in 1937.

The story was of course most hush-hush during those days, when the Chinese were self-conscious and easily offended at being considered ignorant of foreign usage. But as the nation grows surer of itself and its citizens find it rather pleasant to be called "Chinamen," the story was gradually taken more and more in the spirit in which my grandfather took it.

I have not told you the most amusing part of the story yet. What makes me chuckle most is that people have started to ascribe the story to so-and-so and to themselves. If they are too young to have been there, at least they feel proud to have known or to be related to the gentlemen of the *faux pas*. They move the story to Paris, or to Washington, and ascribe it to Wu Tingfang or Li Hungchang, and narrate it to me with circumstantial evidence from their friends. They narrate it to foreigners. For China enjoys a laugh at herself now.

Grandfather stayed abroad for five years. After returning home for a short stay, he went abroad again with Liu Chiht'ien, Minister to England, still as Councillor in the Legation. This time he took Father along instead of Big Uncle. They represented China, as I told you, at the Paris World Exhibition in 1889, the year in which I was born. After a stay of four years, during which he bought a great many more scientific instruments, he returned and devoted himself entirely to scholarship and education. With Governor Chou Yüshan, as I have told you, he established Lüning School. He made Yenling Hsiang a meeting ground of scholars. Many even came with their families to stay at Yenling Hsiang, with its endless courtyards. There were classical scholars like Ch'en Sanli, Ch'en Hsi'an, and Cheng Hsiao-hsü, students of Buddhism like Mei Kuanghsi, K'uai Jomu, and Ouyang Chien, revolutionaries like Sun Shaohou and T'an Szut'ung, and many more who came for shorter visits. Among foreigners who frequented Yenling Hsiang were Li T'imot'ai, Li Chiapo, and Fu K'aisen, or, in English, Timothy Richard, Gilbert Reid, and John C. Ferguson. Through Richard, he became acquainted with the Japanese Buddhist Nanjō Bunyō, from whom he obtained some of the most important material for the editing and reprinting of the *Tripitaka*. With Richard, he was co-translator of Asvaghosa's *The Awakening of Faith*, Shanghai, 1907.

The activities at Yenling Hsiang were not really those of underground revolutionaries under a Buddhist cloak. Among the visitors, there were even strong royalists, such as Cheng Hsiao hsü, who later turned puppet premier under Henry Puyi, because of his loyalty to the defunct dynasty. The relation between scholarship and the revolution was much more organic. The young men were inspired in finding how the universalism of Buddhism and the liberalism of Western thought were integrated in the same catholic personality. Those who thought conservatively respected the teacher too much to cause him trouble. Those who were seeking direct action found added courage for their convictions. If the authorities were fooled in thinking that a club of innocuous Buddhist scholars was the last place in which to look for revolutionaries, my grandfather did not mean to fool then.

17

OCTOBER 8 AND OCTOBER 10, 1911

HAVING SPOILED ME in habits of independence of thought and freedom of action, Grandfather suggested that I had better prepare myself for the medical profession. When you are a doctor, everybody will seek your help and you will not have to seek help of anybody else. But as Father had expected me to become a teacher, I had better consult him about my plans for further education.

Father was then living near Poya Lake, Hanyang. He had not been able to get along with the Japanese engineers at Tayeh Mines, who had become more and more arrogant towards his Chinese colleagues, as the Hanyang-Tayeh-Pinghsiang Company became more and more indebted to Japanese creditors and stockholders. He had left Tayeh and was transferred to the Iron Works at Hanyang. So in the early spring of 1911, I went to Hanyang, opposite Wuchang and Hankow.

Father approved at once my plan of studying medicine. There were no modern medical schools in China, and the choice lay between England and Japan: England, because he and Grandfather knew the country; Japan, because Second Brother, my schoolmate Lin Kuanhung, Kuanhung's brothers, and quite a few other friends were already there. I had been corresponding with Kuanhung, and it was about this time that I had been induced by her to join Dr. Sun Yatsen's T'ungmeng Hui, or the Revolutionary Party, the predecessor of Kuomintang. (Both Grandfather and Father knew about this, but we never talked about it openly at home.) Another advantage about going to Japan was that the family could support me in Japan, if necessary, while going to Europe or America would be a much bigger undertaking. For opportunities like the one I had missed for going to America without taking an examination were not to be had every day.

While I was discussing these things with Father, a telegram came from Auntie in Nanking, saying that Grandfather was seriously ill. So Father and all the children gathered a few necessities and hurried back to Nanking by the first boat going down, and later Fifth Uncle followed.

There had been a flood in Nanking. Grandfather had taken the whole family out to see the flood and exposed himself to excessive heat. When we arrived home, he had been ill for a month and was not improving. His mind was as clear and active as ever, but he was unable to eat. The attending physician found a cancerous condition of the stomach and was concerned about the heart condition.

Believing that he did not have long to live, Grandfather called together his pupils and members of the family to arrange his affairs. The Buddhist Press was assigned to a board of three men, Ch'en Hsi'an (who had taught me at Wuchang) in charge of finance and management, Ch'enIfu in charge of external relations, and Ouyang Chien in charge of editorial work. He reaffirmed his previous will, that the Yenling Hsiang property was to go to the Press, but that his family had the right to veto the sale of the property by the management. His pupils K'uai Jomu and Mei Kuanghsi proposed that a separate house should be erected by subscription for the Yangs to live in. But Father did not want any public funds to be raised for the benefit of the family. After much discussion, an arrangement was made which has lasted to the present time. The westernmost courtyard was to be made into a shrine and tomb for my grandfather, and various branches of the family were to take turns in living in that courtyard to take care of the shrine. The next row of courtyards were for the rest of the family to use. The eastern half of the premises, including the front door at 49 Yenling Hsiang, was for the use of the

Press, except that all the wood blocks for printing the books were housed in a courtyard behind the shrine courtyard.[1]

On some days, Grandfather seemed to be almost his normal self again, though he still had to lie in bed. He called his family and his pupils together and enjoined them not to be extravagant with his funeral ceremonies.

"Soon there will be great changes in the nation," he said. "Do not be bound to elaborate conventions, but make everything as simple as possible. If anything happens while I can see it, I will remain where the *Tripitaka* is. You young people should go where it is safe."

Then, turning specially to K'uai Jomu, he said:

"I have some favors to ask of you. This granddaughter, Ch'uanti, is an unusual child. Will you help her realize her ambition to study medicine abroad? This grandson, Chungying, should do well in pursuing the study of Sanskrit. Will you give him every encouragement in that direction, so that he may continue the line of Buddhist scholarship?"

K'uai Jomu promised. Years later, though I went abroad under quite different circumstances, he did help me afterwards in establishing my hospital in Peiping. About Chungying, my grandfather made one of his few mistakes in judging personalities. Chungying turned out to be a very poor student in his school days and a very good engineer today.

On the 12th of the eighth moon, while I went out in a ricksha to do some shopping on Huap'ailou, I was startled to hear a very familiar voice calling me, "Yunch'ing!"

"Why, if it isn't Kuanhung herself!" I exclaimed, as we both scrambled down from our rickshas. "I thought you were still in

---

[1] These arrangements were "documented" in the form of phonograph recordings of speeches made by Judge Mei Kuanghsi and Ouyang Chien in 1936.

Japan. Why didn't you tell me that you had come back? How are you? And where are your brothers? Have they come back too?"

I fired my questions at her without waiting for an answer.

"I can't tell you much now," she said rather quietly, in contrast to my boisterous reception. "I'll tell you all about it when we get home. Can you come to my house?"

"No," I replied, "Grandfather is very sick, and I have to go back and stay home as soon as I have done my errand."

"Oh, I am so sorry to hear that. Then I'll come to your house and pay my respects to Grandfather Yang."

Grandfather was as surprised as I was to see Kuanhung back. When there were not so many people around, she told Grandfather that her brothers had come back especially to join the revolution. They were sure, Kuanhung said, that this time there would not be such unnecessary sacrifices as there had been in the previous abortive attempts. Kuanhung also told Grandfather that she had already been in the Tokyo Women's Medical School for a year. Thereupon, Grandfather put my hand into hers and said:

"Kuanhung, here is your companion. Yunch'ing is going to study medicine, too. With the unity of mind and heart such as you two have, you will be able to do anything."

Kuanhung also spoke of her interest in Buddhist works which she and her two brothers had been reading. So Grandfather told Fifth Uncle to go to the stockroom of the Press to bring her copies of *The Awakening of Faith in the Mahayāmā* and some of his own works on Buddhism.

Two days later, Second Brother also returned from Japan. We knew why he came back, but outsiders only knew that people gathered at our house to inquire after Grandfather's illness.

On the morning of the 17th of the eighth moon, a number of Grandfather's friends and pupils were holding a discussion about various affairs, to report to him after the meeting. I was sitting at his bedside.

"Ch'uanti," Grandfather said, "you had better take a rest on my screened porch. You children must be all tired out from attending to me day and night without rest."

I went to the back porch and fell asleep. I had not slept for many minutes, but I had slept soundly enough to have forgotten where I was. I did not know whether I was in Tayeh with Father or in Wuchang with Big Uncle, whether it was day or whether it was night, when I was awakened by Cousine Lang's trembling voice, calling:

"Come! Come quick!"

When I returned to the front room, the whole family streaming in. The men's meeting had just adjourned. K'uai Jomu, holding high a sheaf of papers in his hand, led the group in to report on the discussions. He started to speak, but when he saw the peaceful countenance of my grandfather, his hand fell and his head lowered.

Having been something of a granddaughter in our house, Kuanhung was almost as grieved as ourselves and volunteered to wear heavy mourning, like a member of the family. Big Uncle arrived from Hupeh two days after and broke down with remorse for having returned too late. At times I was able to observe that we grandchildren cried even more sadly than our parents.

Funeral rites were dignified and relatively simple. Everybody seemed to work methodically and with quiet despatch. There was a strange atmosphere of tense expectancy.

Right opposite our house and looking east from Yenling Hsiang, was a small lane called Sungt'ao Hsiang, in which was the mansion of Chang Hsün, garrison commander of the Nanking district. Chang had been a nodding acquaintance of Grandfather's, and his guards and orderlies often chatted with our servants when they met on the street.

On the 19th of the month, two days after my grandfather's death, Old Ts'ai, the gateman, rushed in and said:

"The Chang's mansion is being heavily guarded today. One of the soldiers has just told me they've started a revolution at Wuchang. General Chang has closed all gates of Nanking and ordered the execution of all members of the Revolutionary Party. Any man found without a pigtail on his head will be arrested as a revolutionist. What shall we do?"

A pigtail, or queue, as you know, had been the symbol of a man's submission to the Manchu rule since 1644, and the lack of it, except for Buddhist monks, was prima facie evidence of being a rebel.

Everybody looked at Second Brother, who had just returned from Japan and was without a queue. Second Brother looked at Third Brother, Sixth Brother, and Ouyang Chinyuan—all three boys had had their queues cut off just the other day.

Thus we brave young revolutionists found ourselves face to face with our first practical problem, when the long wished for revolution finally came on the 19th day of the eighth moon of the third year of Hsüant'ung, in other words, October 10, 1911.

18

SITTING OUT THE REVOLUTION

THE FIRST SHOT of the 1911 Revolution was ordered by Li Yuanhung, who was commanding the 21st Mixed Brigade at Wuchang. The story has it that he had to be fished out from under a bed and forced at the point of a pistol to issue the order. You may call him stubborn or overcautious if you like. But in fairness, I must say that those who accused him of being timid, or even opposed to the revolution, did not know what they were talking about. For I know that, during his stay with us at Huap'ailou, Uncle Li had not at all been cautious about wishing the end of the corrupt monarchy, at least not when he was talking with Grandfather or Father. He had not minded a little girl playing in the room, who presumably could not understand or remember what was being discussed.

When finally greatness was thrust upon him, his only mistake was his failure to realize that it was later than he thought. At the touch of his hesitant brush and seal, Wuchang fell like ripe melon. Nanking echoed practically in the time for sound to travel—no, faster than that, in the time for electricity to travel over the telegraph wires. Thus the Revolution spread quickly over the land and began to touch us in the form of personal problems.

Everybody was of course anxious to know how things were going outside. I knew I would not be allowed to go out. So, making sure that no one was looking, during the general confusion at Yenling Hsiang, I, together with Kuanhung, slipped out of the house, hired two rickshas, and went in the direction of the Viceroy Yamen on Tahsing Kung. When we passed Huap'ailou, we saw a lot of soldiers nailing queueless heads by the ears to a wall, the heads of executed revolutionists, they said.

"This is it," Kuanhung said. "You'd better go home, Yunch'ing. I am going to my home, too. My family is too deeply in this. I don't want you to get involved?"

"But I am a full member myself," I said.

"Sh—, not so loud here on the street! You should be with your family and help them get out of here."

As she told her ricksha boy to turn into Ts'ang Hsiang, where her family was living, she called back to me:

"Goodbye, Yunch'ing, till we see each other again! Either very soon, or not at all!"

I returned home and reported what I had seen.

"This is serious," said Big Uncle, as he looked at the boys. "The idiots! However can they get out of this house? A fine season in which to cut off your queues!"

He continued to ask me some other questions about conditions on the streets, before something dawned upon him, with a sort of delayed action common to preoccupied minds, when he suddenly shouted at me:

"Ch'uanti! Who told you to go out? Who gave you permission to leave the house? You might have got into trouble!"

Then we resumed our worrying over the four boys.

Choruses of monks were chanting Buddhist scriptures to propitiate the soul of the departed. Grandfather had never taken such formalities too literally, but it was the thing, and the family felt better for having these things done for him. While Big Uncle was watching the monks, with their shaven heads, ambulate in and out of the courtyard, his face suddenly brightened.

"I have it," he said. "Why don't we borrow the robes and the caps from those monks and let the boys get on the train in them? You girls can go with them, and we older people will be safe enough to remain and observe our mourning at home."

The idea was so original that smiles broke out over the hitherto sad and worried faces. Here, at last, was a perfect solution of an impossible situation.

"But you can't do that," I objected. "What would people say if they saw a group of young ladies traveling with a lot of monks? It would surely arouse suspicion. And if an inspector should tell the monks to remove their caps and find that they initiation marks burned on their heads, then we're surely in for trouble."

"Ch'uanti," said Big Uncle, "you are right there," which was a very unusual thing for him to say to me. "It's true that General Chang Hsün is our neighbor, but he knows that we have dealings with the revolutionists. He can choose at any time not to know us any more and send over a searching party.

While we were worrying our heads off over how to keep them on, a servant announced:

"General Chang!"

Yes, it was Chang Hsün himself. After a few very tense seconds, we were greatly relieved to find that he came as a good neighbor to pay homage to the deceased scholar. Big Uncle, as chief mourner, returned his kowtow, as the custom required. Then he made bold to ask him:

"General Chang, may I venture to ask a favor of you? Our young women folks are getting scared. And—and we have in our T'ienyin Convent some young mo—er—nuns, who originally came from good families known to us. I should be most grateful if you would be so kind as to arrange safe conduct for these young women to take a train to Shanghai. Is the Interurban train still open to passengers under present conditions?"

"Yes, I should be glad to be of assistance. I shall detail a guard to escort them from the Viceroy-Yamen Station to Hsiakuan and see that they get on the through train at the main station there. And they may bring a few pieces of baggage if they wish."

Big Uncle thanked him profusely for this unexpected friendliness. I tried to peek behind the curtain of mourning to see what this General Chang Hsün looked like, but Mother pulled me back.

The next morning, October 13, the guard came and told us to get ready at once. Fighting would break out at any moment, he said. The next train might be the last to run on the Interurban. So Mother and we girls and the "nuns" (Big Uncle's brilliant revision of his bright idea)—there were twenty-four of us all together—started for the Viceroy-Yamen Station. There was considerable difficulty in getting rickshas and we had to either double up or lug luggage. Mother was the oldest of the party. Auntie remained home. At the last moment, she told Father to help the guard to escort us to the Hsiakuan main station.

While we were waiting for the Interurban to arrive at the Viceroy-Yamen Station, the Republican troops began to attack the Yamen. Chang Hsün's soldiers replied with fire. All was confusion at the station. Our party huddled in a group by a sort of misguided animal instinct. For we knew nothing about taking cover or falling on our stomachs. There was not enough room there for all our stomachs, anyway.

The train thundered in. Before it quite stopped, everybody began to scramble for the steps. Our husky nuns shoved four big boxes in first. They got on and started to pull the rest of the party in. I insisted on staying below to give each one a shove. The train started to move, and Father and Cousine Lang and I were still on the platform. Bullets were whistling and whamming by thick and fast. A man standing next to Father cried, "Aiyo!" and blood started to stream from his pierced ear. I don't know where I got my strength from, but with a shove, I got Cousine Lang in. I jumped on, and with a big "Heyowei!" I not only pulled my two-hundred-forty-pound father up the steps, but also accelerated him enough to start with the train. No, Father wasn't going with the train to start with, but had intended to go back home after seeing us off. He even still had his hemp mourning robe tucked inside his street robe, as he had had no time to change. But under the conditions, the only thing for him to do was to get on. He could then go home from Hsiakuan by a safer road than by way of the Viceroy Yamen, or he could even go with us to Shanghai.

The Interurban train passed the Drum Tower Station. Crowds milled among baggage and boxes piled mountain-high. As the train was already dangerously full—I had both hands on the railing and one foot on the steps—it did not stop, but left the refugees behind, to weep and stamp their feet on the platform. The same scene was repeated when the train shrieked past the San P'ailou Station on to Hsiakuan. When we reached the main station of the Shanghai-Nanking Railway, Father bade us goodbye. Mother tried to stop him. But he said he had to observe the mourning—no son was supposed to leave the house until forty-nine days after the death of his father. So he and a servant boy started for home by God knows what way.

The six-hour journey took us only nine hours, and we entered the foreign concessions of Shanghai, safe haven for both revolutionists against bad governments and plotters against good governments, but, for us, just safe haven. We engaged three carriages and went to half a dozen hotels before we finally found rooms in a bug-infested hotel in the French Concession. Nobody slept much. I kept worrying about Father, wondering whether he succeeded in getting home, with Mother saying my thoughts aloud over and over again all through the night.

Next morning, Third Brother and I went to the Arsenal in the South End to look up Cousin Lang, brother of Cousine Lang. But the Arsenal had been shut down and nobody was allowed in, nor could we get any information about Cousin Lang. So we set out on our own to look for a more permanent place to live. Every likely place was taken. Finally we got a "one-up-one-downstairs" apartment in one of those *lungt' ang*-style tenement houses. Twenty of us slept head-to-head and foot-to-foot on the floor of the upstairs room. Two servants slept with their bodies partly on the stairs and partly on the landing. The room downstairs was our dining room, kitchen, and basement. We cooked by grass fuel. Since the stove had no chimney, smoke filled the place whenever we cooked. My sisters-in-law had never been to a market before. They found it fun to go to the market, carrying baskets on their arms, but hated to stay "home." Second and Third Brothers went house-hunting, for some place where we could stretch our legs without kicking somebody else.

My job was to try to get news from Nanking. I knew that the headquarters of the Revolutionary Party was in a certain locality in the French Concession, but I knew neither the exact street nor the house number. So I rode around in what I thought were the most likely places, and thought up plausible names of relatives to inquire about. We had taken some jewelry along, especially gold things, as the most convenient form of money. There were regular daily exchange rates for gold, and we could get cash for it without much loss. But I rode so much in rickshas that a gold ring lasted me only three days.

On the fourth day, I met Kuanhung's brother Lin T'isheng, on the street, and thus found the headquarters at Hsuehp'ing Li on Route Vallon. The Lins lived only three doors from the office. I was very happy to see Kuanhung there and was introduced to her women comrades, some of whom I had already known by name. I was glad to learn that Nanking was going to fall to the Republican army imminently, but was worried when they told me that General Chang's soldiers had started looting in the city. Foreign missionaries had been negotiating with Chang Hsün for a peaceful retreat, and he was apparently making some suitable preparations for it. Kuanhung wanted me to stay with her group. But I told her that since Father had not come out with us, I had to take care of the women folk of the family.

(Possibly because of my early years of wearing a boy's attire and being called "Little Master Three," I always automatically assumed the part of a man whenever there was an emergency.)

After this I rode to Route Vallon every morning after breakfast, spent the day there, and returned to my family after five o'clock. My standing in the party was much younger than that of the Lins, who had introduced me, so I just listened to the news and discussions and talked mostly only with Kuanhung and her brothers. I was told at Route Vallon that Nanking would fall in a matter of days but that I had to keep mum about it. So when I returned to my family and my sisters-in-law complained about the misery of a refugee's life and wanted me to tell them exactly when the revolution would be over, and when we could pack up for home, I just had to tell them to be patient.

"How can you expect a dynasty of two hundred sixty-seven years to be changed into a republic in a few days? Endure hardships now and we shall enjoy freedom forever."

It was not quite in my style of talking, at least not to my family. But I heard so much of this line during those days that it came out very easy and fluent.

After twelve days, Nanking fell, and I returned home from Shanghai and found everybody safe and sound at Yenling Hsiang, under a Republican flag. I had sat out the Revolution.

19

HOW I GOT MY NAME "BUWEI"

BECAUSE OF URGENT duties, the Lin brothers went to Nanking as soon as communications were reopened. Kuanhung and I went with them, while the other members of my family at Shanghai waited for almost a month before Father said it was all right for them to return, and went to Shanghai himself to escort them home. Kuanhung and her brothers had moved into a house right next to ours. The headquarters of the Revolution had moved to the Viceroy Yamen. Kuanhung often took me to the meetings, at which plans were discussed for sending expeditionary forces to the North, for the Revolution had not yet reached Peking, where the boy emperor P'uyi was still sitting on his throne. In fact, he did not abdicate until the next February.

Among many problems of revolutionary reform, the equality of women with men was often discussed, and various measures were proposed. After a time, Kuanhung and I began to feel that we were not being very useful as members of what was supposed to be a class of leaders. We had enough enthusiasm; we thought we had the right attitude and the right aims. But we were ignorant and inexperienced. We admitted secretly, between Kuanhung and me, that we were not the equal of men. But sometimes, when we saw men in responsible positions, with powers to do things they knew nothing about, we consoled ourselves with the thought that some men, too, were not the equal of men. If we could not do anything about other men and women, we could at least resolve to get ourselves properly trained, so that we would know the right things to do and the right ways of doing them.

Kuanhung and I spent long evenings talking over these questions. She was planning to resume her medical course in Tokyo. I, because of Grandfather's influence, made her agree with me in planning to go to England with me to study medicine there. After completing our training, we would come back and work together. When we told her brothers about our plans, they thought they were very good. One of her brothers said jokingly:

"Since you girls talk so sensibly on these questions, we'll give you the equality now."

Then Kuanhung told me about another like-minded friend, who had studied medicine together with her in the Tokyo Women's Medical School, and who had also promised to work with her at the completion of her training.

"What's her name?" I asked.

"Kuan Yiwu," she said. "She was originally called Hsünyen, but I gave her the name Yiwu, it's much nicer."

Kuanhung was always presenting her friends with new names, not nicknames about some trivial sides of their personality, but real, serious names that you could actually use. The mentioning of Yiwu reminded her of her favorite pastime. So she said:

"Yunch'ing, I want to give you a name, too. I know you will become a great woman, so you must have the word *wei* [great] in it. And you will start making great strides towards greatness now. So you must have *bu* [stride] in it."

"So you are going to call me Weibu?" I laughed.

"Yes, Weibu. No, Buwei—Weibu—Buwei. Yes, Buwei is better. So from now on you will be Yang Buwei."

"I don't like it, Kuanhung. It sounds too much like a man's name. Seriously, I don't think 'Buwei' sounds like me. Imagine me called

'Yang Buwei'! Ha ha ha! No, Kuanhung, I don't want to be 'Buwei.' "

"All right, Yunch'ing," she said with resignation. "We won't talk about it any more. Since you don't want to be 'Buwei', then don't be 'Buwei.' All that matters to me is that you are you."

My decision to study medicine needed no strengthening. But an additional impetus was added unexpectedly in the form of a series of disasters. The youngest daughter of Lin Pingnan was down with high fever and a very sore throat. The men were out and busy with the revolution most of the time. Ninth Sister in-law—that's how we all called Pingnan's wife—was busy with the house they had just moved into, without the help of enough servants, and did not give the child much attention. Although her aunt Kuanhung was a medical student, she had only taken some pre-medical courses and knew nothing about diagnosing a fever. All she knew was reading a clinical thermometer and putting on an ice bag, which looked professional enough to the family. On the third day, while the girl's fever was running without let-up, Ninth Sister-in-law's second boy Tsungtse, too, came down with high fever. Then Kuanhung recalled that her textbook had said that, if a fever remained high for several days, it was a sign of some contagious disease. So they hired a carriage and sent both patients to the Presbyterian Hospital at Four Poles (Street). The next morning, before the American woman doctor could tell what the disease was, the girl died. The boy, Tsungtse, had a badly swollen eye. Another doctor was called in for consultation. He diagnosed the case as scarlet fever and gave the family to choose between sacrificing the boy's left eye and running the very probable risk of the infection reaching the brain. So they had to save the boy's life at the expense of his left eye.

Only then did the family begin to take the danger of infection seriously. Everybody stayed away except the mother. But the day after Kuanhung came to stay with me at my house, she had the fever just the same. Pingnan's eldest son and eldest daughter, at their house, also got it. So all the patients were sent to the hospital. I insisted, against warnings, to stay in the hospital to watch over Kuanhung, taking such precautions as were possible under the circumstances. After a week, the Lin patients were getting well. Another brother of Kuanhung's, Sixteenth Brother, came from Shanghai to see her. Seeing me in the room so near Kuanhung, he said: "Yunch'ing, you should be careful."

After another week, Sixteenth Brother of the Lins died at the Drum Tower Hospital. While I was trying to hide the news from Kuanhung, a servant blurted it out when he brought some things over to her. That caused a relapse. She had high fever again and became delirious.

One morning, her mind seemed to be clearing up;

"Yunch'ing," she said, "I am afraid I won't be able to join you and Yiwu any more in our plans for the future. The two of you must endeavor to carry on with the work of three."

Then, turning to her brothers, she continued:

"Don't mourn over the loss of a sister like me. What finer sister can you have than Yunch'ing? Help her in every way, as if she were me, and I should be as happy and grateful."

For days after it was no longer necessary, I continued to feel like going to the kitchen to warm over milk or measuring off medicine every few hours. The rest of the time my mind seemed to have run out of ideas. My family and the Lins were concerned about my condition. Soon afterward the Lin brothers hastened to make arrangements for transportation of the remains back to their homestead in Foochow for burial there. They wanted to help me forget.

During that epidemic three daughters of a Rev. Wang, who happened to be living on the hospital grounds, caught the fever and succumbed. The American doctor who first attended Kuanhung died of the same disease. I escaped without a sore throat. I wondered at first why I was immune. Then, after the tension and distractions of the days were over and I began to be more conscious of my own affairs, I recalled that, when I was in Tayeh, I had had a spell of high fevers, with a parched throat and a darkened tongue. I had been given quarts and quarts of sugar-cane juice to drink, until I was sick at the sight of sugar or candy. I must have had it before.

"Yunch'ing, I am afraid I won't be able to join you and Yiwu any more. You two must carry on, Yunch'ing." The words lingered in my ears.

Poor, good Kuanhung! I was so rough and insensitive, and she was so good-natured: "If you don't want to be 'Buwei,' then don't be 'Buwei.'"

But yes, why not? I *will* be "Buwei," too. It's a good name. The least I can do for her is to remember her by that. So that was how I got my name "Buwei."

Part III
THE YOUNG WOMAN

20

PRINCIPAL YANG BUWEI

FATHER SAID that "Buwei" was a lucky name. For before I even completed my education, I became the head of a school. It came about this way. While things were very unsettled during the early days of the revolution, Father and Big Uncle and Fifth Uncle, being technical men with no important political connections, were out of jobs and were staying at home. Like the peace-unemployed at the close of a world war, they were happy over the long-term future, but unhappy about problems of the immediate present. One day I was arguing hotly and endlessly with Second Brother over something, I don't remember what. We got on Big Uncle's nerves and he wanted to stop us.

"Why don't you young men and young women stop talking and get started doing things?" he said. "All you do is to run around all day, talking about revolutions today and independence tomorrow. And what have you accomplished? You haven't a thing to show. If you party members are such important persons, why can't you declare independence and at least take care of yourselves?"

It was against my principles to take advantage of a person who was down and out. But it was also against my principles to remain passive when I was provoked. Unfortunately, I chose the wrong principle this time. I answered back and made the unpardonable retort:

"How about you, Big Uncle? If you are eating at Grandfather's house doing nothing, why can't we grandchildren—"

This incensed Big Uncle so much that he took an iron tubing that happened to be in the room and started to swing it in the direction of my head. With a quick movement, Second Brother snatched it away from him, saying: "Oh, not that, Father! You might kill a person with that."

"What if I do?" said Big Uncle. "That's just what I wanted to do. The home-breaking, unfilial offspring! Using your grandfather as a shield, huh? Now we'll see who's going to shield you."

"But, Big Uncle," I answered, as I saw an opening for easy attack. "You talk as if you were glad Grandfather's dead. How can you be so unfilial as that?"

This started things. The fire spread upstairs to the older generation now. Big Uncle scolded Father for having spoiled his child beyond salvation. Mother scolded Big Uncle for treating her child still as his child. Auntie scolded Big Uncle for being so unreasonable towards her favorite child. Fifth Uncle blamed Big Uncle for starting a quarrel instead of quieting it down, as a big brother should. Finally, Father led me out of the house to stay temporarily at a distant cousin's house, so that the sight of me would not continue to anger Big Uncle.

If I were writing a story, I would have to wait a week, or at least let three days pass, before allowing the following to happen, in order to make it appear more realistic. But since I am writing an autobiography, I must tell the truth. On the very next day after the family quarrel, which all started from Big Uncle's taunt about my independence, General Po Wenwei, Military Governor of Anhwei, sent his secretary, Miss Huang Ch'i-hsiung, to see me, with an invitation to be the principal of Ch'ungshih School.

Ch'ungshih or "Real Things First" was a sort of vocational finishing school for girls. At the start of the Revolution there had been organized a Women's Expeditionary Corps—shall we say "WEC"?—which was to be sent out to fight in the North. When fighting was over, before the women soldiers were needed, the corps was disbanded, and a school on a sort of "G.I. Bill of Rights" plan was organized to finish the education of the girls. This, then, was the Ch'ungshih School.

With such a special group of students of widely varying ages and background, Po Wenwei was at a loss to find a suitable principal. He had known of me and my family through his associates, many of whom were Grandfather's pupils. When his secretary Miss Huang told him she was coming to our house to see my Big Sister-in-law, who was a relative of hers, he told her to look me up, too, and to offer me the position of principal in the newly organized school.

I consulted Father about the proposition. Father said: "It is a difficult job, but seeing that you are good at deciding things in emergencies, I don't see why you cannot manage it. Besides, with such disharmony troubling us all the time, you had better stay away a while. You know Big Uncle's grudge against you for breaking your engagement. He has to find outlets for his suppressed feelings. I will go out soon myself, too. You think it over."

For one day and two nights the question turned over and over in my thoughts, showing a new picture of things at each turn. The general sent one messenger after another, requesting me to see him. If I did not go to call on him, he would be willing to come over to call on me. As I hated to make such a show of self-importance, I finally went, with Miss Huang accompanying me.

Po Wenwei did not at all look the military man I had imagined him to be. Kindly and soft-spoken, he looked rather like a classical scholar—in fact, he had been a *hsiuts'ai* (bachelor's degree) before he entered the army, a not too common combination for men of his generation. Between reminding me of my grandfather's public-mindedness and addressing me as Yang Hsiensheng-*hsiensheng* being a term of address for all men and only professional women—he quickly made me feel how ungracious it would be to decline.

"Would the general be kind enough to make me acting principal for one year, so that a more suitable permanent head of the school can carry on after things get started? I should like to be relieved at the end of the year, so that I can go abroad to study medicine.

"Yang Hsiensheng," Po said, "your very modesty proves that you are capable of the job. But you must accept the regular position of principal; otherwise you will not have the necessary authority. As principal, you may count on my full support. Don't hesitate to do what you honestly think is right, even if you argue with my old-fashioned father—he is chairman of the board, you know. Some of the staff were army officers. If you find any of them incompetent, I give you full power to fire them. The students are of very uneven qualifications and you will have to be patient with them. But if any of them should make trouble, just report them to me and I will court-martial them."

"But, General, you are not going to execute the girls!"

This brought a hearty laughter from him, as he found me bold enough to play on his figure of speech.

"As for your plans for studying medicine abroad, Yang Hsiensheng, I shall see to it that you get an Anhwei provincial scholarship for six years. What country would you like to go to?"

I thought that England was the best country for medicine.

"All right," he said. "I shall have all arrangements made for you. With your ability and background, you are entitled to get a scholarship in any case. But I should appreciate it if you will serve at Ch'ungshih School at least until everything gets well started."

I thanked him and agreed to the conditions. As I came out of his office, I found quite a little crowd gathered around the entrance, among whom was Po's brother. I overheard the people say:

"What a young principal!"

"The general is ruining the school."

"What will you bet she is not twenty?".

"Whe-whew!"—or the Chinese equivalent of that.

If I walked awkwardly past the crowd, I did not feel so. I smiled a smile, such as I imagined a school principal would to an audience at her inauguration.

I returned home and told Father. Father was greatly pleased and enjoined me to live up to my part. The letter of appointment was sent over in the same afternoon. My salary was one hundred eighty dollars a month, plus non-accounting expenses of two hundred dollars.

I took office the next morning. The school was in the former mansion of Chang P'eilun on Fuch'eng Bridge (Street). There were over one hundred and twenty sixteen-by-twenty-four-foot rooms, grouped around courtyards with year-round flowers.

Eighty rooms were assigned to the use of the school. The remaining space was used for General Po's Nanking office and for his family's residence.

I had to apportion the use of the eighty rooms—ten for teachers' quarters and offices, ten for handicraft workshops, thirty for students' dormitory, and the rest for classrooms, business offices, and maintenance. To save space, I made all students who had homes in Nanking live at home—I did not tell them that, with my home only half a li from school, I had been a dormitory student at Lüning.

Although Ch'ungshih was planned as a vocational school, I wanted to give the girls as much general education as possible. For the rather illiterate and mature persons, I had to let them "major" in weaving, sewing (with sewing machines), knitting and crocheting, or embroidering. For the younger students, I established two primary and two secondary grades, with a view to giving them a vocational training after they had some general schooling

At this school, I took some valuable lessons in human affairs. I learned that in dealing with things, you spent much more time and energy in dealing with people than in dealing with things. After my nice little scheme of general education was put into effect, up came the chairman of the board of directors, Po's father, and wanted to change the school to an all-handicraft school. When the handicraft students had learned to weave one pattern of cloth, I told the teachers to teach them other patterns and spend some time in explaining the principles of weaving and the construction and repair of looms. But Chairman Po wanted the students to produce one or two patterns in quantity so that the school could sell the cloth.

I prohibited smoking in the school; I got into trouble in trying to enforce that. Things came to such a pass that the Kiangsu Provincial Commissioner of Education came over to investigate what the troubles were. I said to him that, as I understood it, the board of directors was to receive reports from the school and decide on long-term policies. They were not supposed to meddle with every detail in running the school in place of the staff. The commissioner had understood as much. After the investigation, the Chairman of the Board of Directors interfered no more. I got along with him so well afterwards that he even sent his youngest daughter Ch'infang, the general's sister, to study in my school. Soon Mrs. Po Wenwei, too, became an auditor. Relatives of the Pos came out from their homes in Anhwei and became regular students. I not only took care of the school, but often helped with the family affairs of the Pos.

I enjoyed my work as principal of Ch'ungshih School and regarded my accomplishments as gratifying. But I had not expected that, in addition to dealing with things and dealing with people, I had to deal with ghosts. The house was haunted.

21

CHASING GHOSTS AND SUPERVISING EXECUTIONS

THE MANSION which had been converted into Ch'ungshih School and General Po's residence and office had an enormous amount of space. It had a tradition of being haunted by ghosts and foxes, the kind of foxes which were believed to be able to appear and disappear supernaturally and play tricks on human beings. When you feel oppressed and cannot breathe or move in your bed, it is a spiritual fox that is sitting on your chest. We don't have nightmares in the lower Yangtze provinces, we have nightfoxes, so to speak. When, however, a general's headquarters and a modern, unsuperstitious school moved into the place, we were sure that we had enough of the "positive principle" to drive all ghosts and evil spirits away.

But tradition was long and stories continued to be told. So, after the new school settled down into routine, things began to happen again. Every night something would rap in one room; something else would shuffle in another. Then some students began to hear voices coming from dark, unoccupied classrooms. There was even singing, laughing, and crying from empty places. Students, many of whom were older than myself, would come to me and ask to be transferred to better lighted and more populated courtyards.

Since I knew from frightful experience that ghosts were nothing but dried lotus leaves tied to my pigtail, I was able to act the fearless leader. Every evening I would hold one of those kerosene "safety" lamps together with a box of matches on windy nights and make a round of the courtyards. I talked to the students in bright, daytime tones, and reminded them that they had been soldiers of the

Women's Expeditionary Corps and therefore should not be afraid of anything. My rounds included not only the part belonging to the school, but also the Pos' residence and office. Those who believed in ghosts said that I was blessed with enough of the "positive principle" to repel the evil spirits. Those who did not believe in them were glad to see me pass by with a lamp, anyway. But there were two incidents which I have never been able to explain to this day.

My courtyard, like most of the others, had a width of five rooms in a row, with a hall or reception room in the middle and two bedrooms on each side. My bedroom was next to the right of the reception room; two women of the staff, dean of studies and dean of students, were on the opposite side of the reception room, within hearing distance, for loud voice, from my room. One night, after the clock had struck twelve and I had gone to bed, I heard the noise of chairs being dragged about in the reception room, followed by the sound of laughter. So I called loudly: "Are you still up so late? What are you laughing about? What have you done that's so funny?"

There was silence. I thought they had not heard me. So I just turned on my other shoulder, with my better ear up.

Another burst of laughter and giggles. I rolled out of bed, lit my kerosene lamp, pulled out the bolt and flung my door wide open. The chairs were all out of arrangement. The corners of the tablecloth were still swinging—there was no wind. But there was not a soul there—not one that was attached to a body. Both the front and back doors of the room were closed. My first reaction was to suspect that the ladies in the opposite room had been making those noises to frighten me, but I found their door still shut.

"Did you hear that, too, Principal?" they said in trembling voices.

"Come out, girls," I said. "There is nothing to be afraid of. Everything's all right."

They unbolted their door and showed a pair of pallid, scared faces. I tried to reassure them by grasping their hands. Their hands were damp and cold. If they had planned to frighten me, they certainly did not look the part. Soon the people in the rooms on the opposite side of the courtyard lit their lamps and spoke. They, too, had heard the noises, but had not dared to move until they heard me get up. I sat a few minutes in the opposite room and told everybody not to say anything about it the next morning, in order not to frighten the students. But the story was out just the same. All I could do was to make up some naturalistic explanation, such as the wind, the cracking of wood due to expansion and contraction, etc. My calm manners and modern-sounding words stopped their talk, but did not satisfy myself and probably did not quiet their fears.

In many middle schools in China, that is, high schools, there is a period of study hours in the evening when the students do their "homework." The study hours in our school were from eight to ten. One of the classrooms used for this purpose consisted of a row of five rooms, with all the partitions removed. On the opposite side of this classroom was a similarly converted room for housing thirty looms. The students reported more than once that they had heard noises from the room of looms while they were doing their homework on the other side of the courtyard. As I thought it might be cats and mice that had got into the looms, I made a point of inspecting all the looms and locking up the door myself at the close of each day. One night, about a month after the midnight incident, it happened to be my turn to supervise the study hours. Shortly before ten o'clock, when the class began to sound a little restless, with papers rustling and a few books closing, one of the looms in the room opposite us seemed to have started to weave. The sound lasted for about half a minute and stopped. The class was in an uproar.

Who is tampering with the looms this time of the night? I thought.

Taking hold of a large lamp, I called a few of the more courageous students to follow me across the courtyard. I unlocked the door, entered with the students, and immediately shut the door again, in order not to let anybody or anything go out unnoticed. I looked inside, and saw that, on one of the looms, the vertical pull-cords for controlling the designs of textiles were still swinging back and forth. On the half-woven cloth lay the cob of an eaten corn, still warm to the touch. The eight of us searched everywhere among the thirty looms, but found nothing. I said aloud: "If there is any ghost or monster here, please dare to appear!"

Nothing appeared. Not a cat or mouse or dog, not to speak of a human being. There was no hole in any of the walls or windows. There was no wind. All was quiet in the big, long room, with eight women among thirty looms and the warm cob of an eaten corn. Since that incident, which I still cannot explain, there were no more noises. Teachers and students were able to sleep in peace, until one day something really serious happened.

As commander of the Fourth Army, Po Wenwei had a branch headquarters outside the West Gate near the main barracks. One morning, six or seven telephone calls came from the West Gate office for General Po. It was February, 1913, just before the old-style new year, when everybody needed money. All bills, you know, must be settled the day before the 5th of the fifth moon, before the Mid-Autumn Day (the 15th of the eighth moon), and, most important of all, on the old style New Year's Eve. There were complaints over insufficiency and inequality of pay. The first telephone call asked whether the general would come out to settle the differences between the soldiers and the paymaster. But the general was away in Anking. Then they reported that the soldiers were in an ugly mood. Would somebody come out at once to maintain discipline? No, followed another telephone call, don't come out. Mutiny had broken out. The telephone calls became more incoherent and less intelligible. Finally couriers arrived, saying that the mutinous troops were on their way into the city, threatening to burn down the general's residence.

Po's family all came over to the school for protection. I was not sure that the school was any safer than the rest of the place, since it was within the same gates and the soldiers would not be able to tell the difference. I had better go and see what the guards were doing for a defense. I found that Po's younger brother had ordered the iron gates closed, had sandbags piled behind them, and ordered the guards to stay behind the sand bags, with all their guns pointing outside in one direction.

I had never studied military science. All my knowledge of war was from reading the philosopher Hsün Tzu, the *Story of the Three Kingdoms*, and such ancient stuff. But somehow the disposition of the guards behind the gates did not look right to me. There were only about 130 men all told there, and they had better make the best use of themselves. I suggested that they should barricade themselves on two sides inside the gates and direct their fire in many directions over a wide arc, that they should not fire when fired upon, but only as the attackers came near and tried to force the gate. I suppose that is what you call "cross-fire" nowadays, but both the captain of the guards and I thought the idea rather original. So the captain rearranged the defense, while Mr. Po and I continued to argue over the relative merits of the two formations.

As I was sure that 130-odd soldiers, no matters how efficiently deployed, could not hold out indefinitely against a mutinous horde, I tried to get reinforcements from Ch'en Shihch'i of the Eighth Division, which was stationed in the city. Telephoning through the municipal exchanges was slow in any case, and was even slower then, as everybody that had a telephone was trying to telephone for news. So I got hold of General Po's military telephone and called up General Ch'eng Tech'üan.

"This is General Po's residence," I said. "Send over some troops at once. We are being surrounded by mutinous soldiers."

But before the mutineers entered very far into the city, they were all caught and disarmed. Twenty-eight leaders of the mutiny were court-martialed, to be executed by beheading on the same afternoon.

General Ch'en Shihch'i came over to see how things were in our place. When Mr. and Mrs. Po Senior, Po Wenwei's parents, told

Ch'en how I had directed the defense preparations, he said, to my amazement, "Principal Yang, you will join us in supervising the executions."

I did not know what to say or what to think. Then it occurred to me that, since sooner or later I would have to get used to corpses and death if I went in for medicine, I might as well start my training now. So I went along.

This was a different sort of thing from voices and moving looms. There was something poetic about those events in the night. But this execution business in broad daylight was literal and brutal.

Yuenren, pour me a glass of—er—sherry, before I go writing!

Well, after it was all over and we returned to the headquarters, word came that five families in the neighborhood had been robbed during the confusion. Would somebody go call on them to bring them reassurance and inquire after their health? They wanted me to go.

I said: "Of course, Po T'ait'ai is the logical person to make such calls. What am I in the government to do such things?"

But Mrs. Po was very diffident about it. She insisted on my going with her at least.

"I tell you what, Yang Hsiensheng," she said, "I will tell them that you are my teacher and our family's chief of staff."

I laughed and agreed to go along. Before we had taken many steps outside the gates, as we were passing near the execution ground, with a splash, I stepped into a puddle. My dress was bespotted all over. When I realized what color it was, I was a thoroughly scared woman. I had stood the previous scenes with composure. But this caught me unprepared. I don't remember what perfunctory inanities I mumbled during those calls, as I was feeling sick all the time. I found later that I could not eat; I threw up everything I tried to swallow.

On the third day after the mutiny, Po Wenwei returned from Anhwei. He thanked me for taking care of his family and complimented me on my handling of the situation.

"It was only a case of 'the quick wit that comes in an emergency,'" I said. "Anyone who would keep a cool head could have done as much. But I hope, General, that in the future you will see to it that your subordinates will always give fair and just treatment to their men. I think it was a pity that those men had to be punished."

Po bowed ceremoniously and agreed.

I suddenly wanted to go home. Though Yenling Hsiang was only a mile from Ch'ungshih School, I usually went home only about once a week, just to say hello to everybody and then returned to the school. This time, I felt run down and wished to rest in Yenling Hsiang for a while. But the Pos wanted to take care of me. They would get me the best doctors. The students would also be afraid at night if I did not stay in the school. So I remained. Every day the Po ladies would bring me special foods to restore my appetite. They sent Ch'infang, Po's youngest daughter, to sleep in the room next to me. From that time on, our acquaintance grew into a lasting friendship. She practically nursed me back to health. I was able to work after two weeks and my appetite returned to normal after two months.

You know, I am generally such a helpful person that I have often missed the opportunity of making friends by accepting the help of others. The way my friendship with Ch'infang started was quite a revelation to me. My husband says that he is happy to have married a very helpful wife, but that he likes me best when I am helpless.

22

RETURN OF THE NATIVE TO ANHWEI

YOU MAY HAVE wondered why I often say at one moment that so-and-so went to Anking, and the next moment, referring to the same event, that he went to Anhwei. The explanation is that Anking is the capital of Anhwei province. Situated rather centrally on the northern bank of the Yangtze, where "north" is more or less west, it is Anhwei par excellence. As I have explained before, a Chinese is a "native" of a province where his near ancestors (in some cases even remote ancestors) were born. As my grandfather and father (and Big Uncle) were born in Shihtai, southern Anhwei, I am automatically an Anhwei woman. I just happened to be visiting Nanking when I was born. Moreover, just as an American woman keeps her American citizenship when she marries a foreigner, so I keep my provincialism, though I am married to Yuenren Chao of Changchow, Kiangsu.[1] During my numerous trips up and down the Yangtze between Nanking and Wuchang or Tayeh, I crossed the whole width of Anhwei on water every time, and it was a standing joke in my family to call me a "house-boat native."

Now came my chance to set foot on the soil of Anhwei. It was about April, 1993, when Po Wenwei invited me to visit Anking, so that I could get a little rest from practically twenty-four-hour duty for weeks on end. As I was particularly interested in arranging with the Anhwei Commissioner of Education for my scholarship for studying abroad, I accepted the invitation. Arriving at Anking, I was

---

[1]But you remember, my dear, I was actually born in Tientsin, Hopeh. –Y.R.C.

borne in a blue-covered sedan chair to the mansion of the military governor. The first thing I said, after exchange of greetings and politenesses, was to ask him when I could resign and go abroad. Since everything in the school was in running order, could I leave before the end of my year? Po tried to persuade me to stay. When I persisted, he said he would talk it over with me next month on his trip to Nanking

I was put up at the Women's Normal School. Two very pleasant ladies, Miss Kao and Miss Yao, kept me company in my sightseeing.

The second day Po Wenwei gave me a big dinner party. There were Police Commissioner Ch'i, Commissioner of Education Wu, Principal Wang of the Normal School, Principal Kao of the Women's Normal School (who later became the wife of Commissioner Ch'i), a Mr. Chang and his Japanese wife, who spoke very fluent Chinese with a southern-Mandarin accent. It was a sort of mixed stag party, so to speak. I was the guest of honor in the capacity of "Yang Hsiensheng" rather than "Miss Yang," and Mrs. Chang, was included, probably out of courtesy to a foreigner—though as a wife in her own country she would have been a sort of slave.

Conversation at a Chinese dinner is practically always general. Everything one says is addressed to, or at least for the benefit of, everybody else. If more than one person talks at the same time, so much the merrier. To the Chinese mind, there is something unsociable in the Western custom of having half a dozen separate private conversations around a table, especially when you are left alone between the backs of two guests and the other guest who is being left alone at the other end of the diagonal is too far from you to be of mutual assistance.

But at this dinner, the thing that was uppermost in my mind was when I could get my scholarship, hardly a fitting subject for general conversation. I did succeed, however, in having a few words with Commissioner of Education Wu. It seemed that my scholarship had already been assigned and funds were ready for it, but that he could not proceed with the arrangements for my passport until my resignation from Ch'ungshih School was accepted; otherwise he would be doing the discourtesy of hurrying my departure.

After being thus partially satisfied with the arrangement, I rejoined the general conversation. As the other guests were all immediate subordinates of the host, they talked little, and I found myself doing most of the talking. I usually do, that is, at Chinese-speaking parties.

The dinner began at noon and ended at three o'clock. Then Principal Wang of the Normal School took me to see my father at his school. He apologized for not having known that Mr. Yang Tzuch'ao was my father. I said naïvely: "What if you don't know about it? What if you do? He does his job, and I do mine. What difference does it make?"

He looked at me, and I felt that I should not have talked that way;

"Daddy!" I greeted my father simply. For that is the proper form of saying good morning or how do you do to an older member of the family.

"Well, I was just thinking of you, Ch'uan'er. I heard about your coming even before you arrived."

After we all had a cup of tea, I said: "Please do not stand on ceremonies, Principal Wang, and do not bother to prepare supper for us. Father and I will go out together tonight; we have a few things to talk over. When Wang insisted on inviting us in order to express his hospitality, I became impatient and said to him: "Doesn't the proverb say, 'Better obedience than deference'?"

At this Father gave me a big stare. For I was using a phrase which properly could only be used by Mr. Wang if he agreed to my declining the invitation. Taken aback at my arrogant phraseology, he bowed himself out.

When he was out of hearing, Father said: "You ignorant child! If you want to use fine phrases, you should at least know enough to tell which is the fine end and which is the blunt end."

On the following day, I telephoned to Po and asked him to get me a ticket to Nanking, and asked him whether I could buy some local products to take to his family in Nanking. He said good, good. So Father and I went to the markets and stores and bought a big package of Anking shrimps, several catties of beancurd cheese, forty cans of soy-sauce pickles, two packages of dried beancurd, a pair of dried salted shad, and twenty pieces of "autumn stone" (saltpeter), which was wanted by some members of the Po family to cure spitting blood. Because of the general lack of inter-regional transportation, every traveler was expected to bring local products to his friends and relatives.

I ate a meal with Father in a riverside restaurant and watched the busy water traffic for a while. We went to the dock to find out about sailings of down boats, for in matters of travel, it was always good to check your information from independent sources. Then, as he started to go back to his school and I to the governor's office to take leave, I said: "Daddy, I am going."

That is the correct form, the only correct form, of saying goodbye to an older member of your family.

When I saw Po Wenwei, he said, with a smile: "Well, did Senior Mr. Yang tell you to go back?"

"My father said that I should not neglect my school duties too long. Besides, if I want to get your approval to let me go abroad early, I had better work hard and earn it."

Po laughed and said: "You have more than earned your scholarship already, Yang Hsiensheng. The only problem is to find a suitable successor. I hear that your students, too, refuse to let you go. When I am in Nanking next month, I shall talk it over with the Kiangsu Commissioner of Education, as well as explain the situation to your students. Personally, I am heartily in favor of your plan to get some solid training abroad, so that you can serve your country even more effectively when you come back."

Then, suddenly lowering his voice, he continued: "You know, Yang Hsiensheng, the Revolution is not such a simple thing. There may yet be serious trouble in the nation. We old revolutionists are only good at breaking down. It is for your generation to build up. So prepare yourselves well."

After supper with Po and some guests, I was escorted by some guards to the wharf and embarked on the down-river boat which called briefly at Anking.

I went to bed, wondering what General Po had meant when he said that there might yet be serious trouble in the nation. Outside my stateroom, the deliberate giant walking-beam engine of the old S. S. "Kiangk'uan" kept saying throughout the night:

> "Sss—EE—rious
> Troub—ble,
> Sss—EE—rious
> Troub—ble,
> Sss—EE—rious
> Troub—ble,
> ....
> ...."

23

THE SECOND REVOLUTION

AS PROMISED, Po Wenwei came to Nanking one month after I had returned and told the students at a general assembly that I was going to leave the school. Five hundred thirty students rose, demanding that Po keep me there.

"There, you see," Po said, as he turned both palms outwards toward the crowd, "it is not I who am keeping you here. What can you do under such circumstances?"

After the day's classes were over, more than twenty representatives of the students came to my office. Between sobs and tears, they tried to convince me that I could serve as effectively in education now as in medicine later. Why give up the present certainty for a future possibility? I tried to convince them that I knew nothing about education, that vocational education should not be left in the hands of amateurs like myself, that there was great need of modern medicine, and that I could be of much greater use if I got some training as a doctor. Group after group came to me to make the same appeal. Neither side convinced the other. For the plain fact was that I was set on going abroad and the students were set on making me stay. Meanwhile I kept an eye out for a possible successor.

My deceased friend Lin Kuanhung had an aunt, who was married to Vice-principal Shen of Lüning School (the school I attended before going to McTyeire). I had met her in society and heard of her name as a revolutionist and a literary woman. She was polite but somewhat pompous in manner. As she was a granddaughter of the famous Lin Tse-hsü, and as her father was also a man of literary and official attainments, I thought there might be good material for a principal in this woman. So I engaged her as an additional dean of studies, with the idea of turning over the school to her when I should leave.

To my disappointment, she came not as an educator but as an official's wife. She brought five servants with her. She demanded a kitchen and dining room for herself. I explained to her that we had always eaten with the students, one teacher or staff member with seven students at each table. But she wanted everything separate. When I tried to assure her that it was fun to feel like one of the students, she said: "Miss Yang, you are taking equality too literally. You don't even distinguish between superiors and subordinates."

"But aren't you a leader of the Revolution yourself, Mrs. Shen?" I said. "Why are you still so self-conscious about belonging to the official class?"

"You should call me Aunt Shen," she said, "since you were my niece's friend. There is no revolution in matters of seniority yet."

"All right, Aunt Shen. Since I don't even obey my parents, I can't promise to take orders from an aunt."

She got along all right, though, so far as I was concerned. But the Board of Directors and the staff and students did not look forward to such a principal, and Po Wenwei told me that I had better find another successor. Thus I made my position even worse than before I recommended Mrs. Shen. But my problem was solved for me, or rather left unsolved, when a great national problem came to a crisis. The "serious trouble," anticipated by Po Wenwei, and echoed by that steamship engine, became a reality.

You remember that the Ch'ungshih School was formed of the Women's Expeditionary Corps because they were no longer needed to fight. The reason that they were not was that Tuan Ch'ijui, Yuan Shihk'ai, and other military elements in the north refused to defend the empire and forced the boy emperor to abdicate. Apparently, the

Revolution of 1911 was completed and the Republic was established at very little cost in blood.

For the sake of unity, Dr. Sun Yatsen yielded the presidency of the Republic in favor of Yuan Shihk'ai. But Yuan was not only not a republican at heart, but actually a plotter against real revolution on democratic principles. When he had the revolutionary leader Sung Chiaojen assassinated, the patriots concluded that it was a case of either Yuan Shihk'ai or the Republic. Thus began the so-called Second Revolution of 1913. Among those actively planning the campaign were Po Wenwei, Li Liehchün, and Ch'en Ch'imei (uncle of Ch'en Kuofu and Ch'en Lifu). In Nanking, we began to hear the name Chang Hsün again, this time not as a neighborly general, but as a leader of antirevolutionary forces marching on Nanking. He had escaped and been hiding in Tientsin, but now came as a supporter of Yuan Shihk'ai to take Nanking. After twelve days' fighting, Po Wenwei returned to Nanking from the front and sent for me for a talk.

"Yang Hsiensheng," he said, "the way things look now, I am afraid we are going to fail. You will have to disband the school and bring those of the students and the staff to Shanghai who have no homes in Nanking. I am sorry you have made your name unsafe by joining our Party. Anhwei is also in danger now. Better persuade your father to come to Shanghai, too. I have provided accommodation for the school and your family."

The next day I announced the bad news to the school. A few days ago, I had not been able to disband myself; this time I disbanded five hundred and thirty students without a single voice raised in protest. Taking Mother, Sixth Brother Yüsheng, and the seventy students who had no homes to return to in Nanking, I made my second trek as a refugee to Shanghai. After getting the students settled, Mother and Sixth Brother and I went to stay with the Lin Pingnans, brother and sister-in-law of Kuanhung's.

On the fifth day, the armies of the Second Revolution were decisively defeated by Yuan Shihk'ai's "government" troops. Po Wenwei escaped to Shanghai. He sent for me by his sister Ch'infang.

"Yang Hsiensheng," he said to me, "I have to leave the country in ten minutes. Here are some funds I want to hand over to you. The three thousand dollars in cash here is for disbanding the students. Here is five hundred for your mother and brother to use in Shanghai, while waiting for your father. This letter of credit for thirty-six hundred is for you, for studying in Japan. Under the regime that will come into power, the authorities will of course cancel your scholarship, if not actually order your arrest. I have to go away with my comrades to make plans for our future efforts. But I have one request to make to Yang Hsiensheng. My father and two younger brothers are unused to conditions in this disturbed world. Would it be too much a burden to entrust you with taking them to Nagasaki? I have already arranged passage with Mr. Nagakawa of the Yokohama Specie Bank, who will notify you as soon as there is a boat. Goodbye, Yang Hsiensheng. We shall meet again in Japan."

This was a terrible responsibility. But, both by temperament and by circumstance, I could not but accept. I entrusted Mother and Sixth Brother to Mrs. Lin Pingnan, with money for half a year's expenses in Shanghai. I wrote a long letter to Father in Anhwei, telling him that I had to leave for studying in Japan, for I could not safely say much in a letter about the Pos or the political situation. I left a copy with Mother, in case the original should get lost.

Because Lin Pingnan had been active in the Second Revolution, I advised him to go with us, too. After another five days, the Yokohama Specie Bank sent word that the entire first and second class accommodations on the "Yabata Maru" had been assigned to our party. But in filling the order, we had to travel as one family. So I filled in "Yang" for everybody.

This was not my first sea voyage, but it was my first voyage abroad and the first voyage I remember well. For three days and three nights, I could not eat a thing. I lost interest in food and, with it, interest in everything else. I was worried about having had no news of Father. (No wonder he blamed me for years for leaving my family behind, to travel abroad with another family. What sort of daughter was I, not to say what sort of woman?) I blamed my unhappy state of mind for my misery, not knowing that I was to be a miserable sailor, years later, even on my honeymoon to America.

When the ship docked at Nagasaki and I set foot on solid ground, I felt a perfectly well person again, happy and hungry. A party of Japanese in kimonos and clogs welcomed us. They all spoke perfect Chinese. One of them looked very familiar. I was sure I had seen him somewhere before. It was Po Wenwei!

24

GOING TO TOKYO IN A RICKSHA

NAGASAKI IN 1913 was of course a different kind of place from Nagasaki after the plutonium bomb in late 1945. As I entered this picturesque coastal city, I could not quite believe that I was in a foreign country, soon to enter a medical school there. My first impression of Japan was not unpleasant. I did learn to be offended when children in the street called us "Shinajin," just as "Chinaman" was until recent years taken as a term of contempt, but the offense was more theoretical than felt. Until I came into personal contact with the Japanese of my own class, I found the people very nice and polite.

One illusion I could not explain was that of the unreality of the whole thing. Everything seemed to be part of a peep show, staged for my benefit. There were big steamships in the port, with a lot of people busying about, but I could not realize that these were the kind of people who owned the ships. The small, low houses, and the streets, gay with paper lanterns and hanging signs on cloth, looked all very temporary. I imagined that there would be real houses and real streets somewhere beyond.

I asked myself: "Is this the kind of country where I am going to stay for several years? Is this the kind of place where there are colleges to enter? Maybe Tokyo will be more like a real city. Why don't we go on? Why do we have to stop at Nagasaki?"

As was usual with Chinese travelers in Japan, we did not, nor could we afford to, go into one of the few Western-style hotels, but went into little toy-like huts—rooming houses, if you like. I hesitated, and almost blushed, when I was told to take off my shoes and leave them at the door. But I did as everybody else did. There were no tables or chairs in those eight-by-ten-foot rooms. We just sat on the *tatami*, or strips of mats, spread over the entire floor. The size and price of a room were usually reckoned according to the number of strips of *tatami* in it. In one of the wooden walls or partitions, there was a sliding door, revealing a spacious cupboard, in which were stored bedding and things. You took them out at night and spread them on the er—well, I thought of it as the floor at first, but after I slept on it a few times, I began to feel that I was going to bed every time I came in from the street and took off my shoes. I never quite learned to live the Japanese way.

One evening, while I was wondering about the new manner of living, I heard strange noises of hammering and chiseling in the next room, where the Pos were staying. When I asked them what they were doing this time of the night and was told to come and look, I found a lot of broken bits of gold chains and bracelets spread all over the tatami. The Pos had used up nearly all their money. They were waiting, uncertainly, for some remittance from supporters of the Revolution from the South Seas, but meanwhile had to change whatever they could into cash for maintenance. The jewelry they had would perhaps last two or three months for the party of political refugees. That was why everybody had to stop at Nagasaki. It made me feel so bad to see the patriots reduced to such circumstances that I said impulsively: "I don't need those thirty-six hundred dollars. I still have a thousand dollars' worth of jewelry myself, which will last me quite a while." (One could then live on about thirty *yen* a month in Japan.)

I ran to my room, returned with my letter of credit, and said: "I'll just take five hundred dollars out of this. The rest is everybody's. It was everybody's money in the first place."

"But Yang Hsiensheng," Po Wenwei protested, "it was already wrong to force you to study in Japan instead of England. I must not do you further injustice."

After pushing the letter of credit back and forth several times over the smooth *tatami*, he finally agreed to my proposal. I would take five hundred dollars out of it for my own use; his children and his sister Ch'infang, who were going on to Tokyo with me, were to take another five hundred, and the balance was to go to the rest of the party.

After making suitable arrangements for his family and associates, Po Wenwei left for the South Seas to plan his future work there.

My trip to Tokyo was in a small party of five, consisting of Lin Pingnan, Miss Po Ch'infang, Po Wenwei's two children, and myself. None of us spoke any Japanese. I sometimes tried a little English, but usually the English words I happened to know were not the same ones that the Japanese I spoke to happened to know, and when we did know the same ones, we did not know that we did, as we did not pronounce them alike. So I soon stopped trying. Instead, we found that we could go a long way by writing Chinese characters. There was plenty of opportunity for misunderstanding of characters, too, but if I chose a few characters remotely synonymous to what I wanted to say, there was a chance of my being understood. Thus if I wrote the usual Chinese characters for "railroad station," it would not mean anything to the Japanese, or possibly "the fire engine has stopped." But if I wrote the Chinese characters for "a horse stage for automobiles," then the rickshaman would promptly take me to the railroad station. After all the centuries of misuse of Chinese characters in Japan, it was a wonder that I still got along there better in characters than in English.

When it was about time for the train to arrive at Tokyo, I saw a big sign in characters which I read as "Tokyo Station." So we got off the train and went into a hotel. Next morning we asked the maid to order some rickshas to go to Miss Su Shuchen's address in the

Ushigome district of Tokyo. After a long time, the maid came back shaking her head and hands, talking in what was obviously a very negative tone. Two Chinese passed by and stopped to ask us if they could be of assistance. I said we were trying to order some rickshas for going to Ushigome.

"Ushigome?" They wondered. "Why don't you take a train? Nobody takes a ricksha to Ushigome from here."

"Well, we don't know the city, you see."

"But you can take a train to Tokyo and then engage rickshas from there."

"Take a train to Tok—but isn't this Tokyo? Isn't that the Tokyo Station?"

When our compatriots explained to the people in the hotel, that we had taken Yokohama for Tokyo, everybody broke into laughter, the first and one of the few frank and hearty laughters I have ever heard from the Japanese.

25

GETTING A SCHOLARSHIP

I ARRIVED in Tokyo between laughter and tears. For, when our party finally found Su Shuchen's house in Ushigome and her mother asked us why we were one day late, I started to giggle and was unable to speak. But when Mrs. Su saw Pingnan, she thought at once of Kuanhung's death and started to cry. The rest of our party and other members of the Su family looked on puzzled and embarrassed. This sobered me up immediately, so that I was able to explain coherently what we had done.

Miss Su had found a house for us nearby. For thirty-five *yen* a month, we had two small rooms, a hall, and a small kitchen, in which was a gas stove on the floor and a faucet over a wooden sink, also on the floor. We had to work kneeling or sitting with folded legs. When the vegetable vender and the fish vender came to our door, our housekeeping began.

Our minds, however, were not on food. We had to learn the Japanese language first. To give ourselves more time, we hired a maid for five *yen* a month, plus food. We got a Japanese tutor to give us four hours of intensive language instruction every afternoon. As I saw my money being used day after day, I studied the language harder and harder. For I had heard that any Chinese student who gained entrance to one of the recognized institutions of higher learning in Japan would be eligible for a scholarship from China. Starting with the beginner's syllabary of *a, i, u, e, o, ka, ki, ku, ke, ko,* etc., in

October, 1913, I finished by next April by passing my entrance examinations, done in Japanese, into the Tokyo Women's Medical School.

Now, the catch was that, while I could read Japanese visually, I had not yet learned to speak the Japanese language. I had learned enough then to make purchases and ask people what city I was in, but could not read Japanese aloud. You see, in the Japanese system of writing, all the important ideas are written in characters, with roughly the same meanings as in Chinese, while words for grammatical relations (like "to," "on," "by," "and,"—and "not"!) are in Japanese characters, called *kana*. There are only fifty-one *kana* characters (in two graphical styles), but thousands of characters. The characters are pronounced by the Japanese in Japanese of course. It is as if you see "etc." and pronounce it *"und so weiter"* or if the figures "97" and pronounce *"quatre-vingts-dix-sept."* What I did and many Chinese students in Japan did was to read the characters in Japanese books in the Chinese pronunciation. All we needed was to learn the relatively few *kana* characters and some Japanese grammar, and we could "read" Japanese. In this way, I could neither be understood when reading aloud to a Japanese listener, nor could I understand a Japanese when he read in his way. But this was where I cashed in on the catch: I passed my written examinations.

It was some time after I entered the medical school before I could follow the lectures and learned to say the terms in Japanese. Thus, when I was given the list of 206 bones of the human skeleton in three forms, in Chinese characters, in German, and in Latin, it was not three times 206 units, but four times 206 units, that I had to memorize. For, in addition to the terms in characters (which I naturally pronounced in Chinese), I had to memorize a whole set of 206 Japanese pronunciations. And so it went for the rest of my course of study.

As pressure of school work increased, and as all the rest of the Po family later came to Tokyo, I moved out to live alone in a Japanese boarding house, where I could have more quiet. For 25 *yen* a month,

I got a room with six strips of *tatami* and three meals a day. The food was terrible, but my constant hurry to get back to my studies served as sauce. Occasionally, the Pos sent over some Chinese dishes to supplement my fare, and I sometimes bought myself some eggs. But I had to be frugal with my limited means. I had worked hard to gain entrance to the medical school, with an eye on a possible government scholarship. After I got my entrance, however, I became timid and did not dare to apply, for fear of being spotted as having been connected with the Second Revolution.

Half a year after I entered the medical school, a new person entered my life. This was Kuanhung's schoolmate Yiwu, whom Kuanhung had told me about shortly before her death. Yiwu was an old-timer in Japan. She had studied in a Japanese middle school when her father was in Japan and had learned not only to speak Japanese like a native, but also knew all the manners and mannerisms, such as bowing deep and sucking in air to punctuate her polite remarks. She had been back home in Tientsin for two years and now returned to Japan with a Hopeh provincial scholarship for studying medicine. Having heard a great lot about me from Kuanhung, she looked me up as soon as she arrived. We were friends at first sight. I am friends at first sight with everybody, anyway. She wanted to live with me together. Two could live more cheaply than one, you know. As I was tired of eating Japanese food, I joined her to keep house again.

I knew nothing about cooking. Yiwu knew less. We had a maid, but since the reason I left the boarding house was to get away from Japanese cooking, I did not want to see another Japanese cooking. As Ch'infang, who could cook a little, was no longer with me this time, I had to cook by trial and error. The only thing that guided me was my knowledge of how a dish should have tasted after it was done. How truly was necessity the mother of invention! For I had to invent a lot of strange dishes before I discovered one that was not so strange.

My friendship with Yiwu did not start too happily and it ended with—well, of that in due course. Yiwu liked good clothes. So did I. But I hated to wear Japanese clothes. (Later, when we started to treat patients, no Japanese patient would accept a Chinese woman doctor in Chinese dress.) So we wore Occidental-style clothes. (I did not return to Chinese attire until my first sojourn in America.)

Yiwu promised to help me get a scholarship, but on condition that I should not take up the regular medical course at the 1925, after same time with her, but wait until she was one year ahead of me. It would not look well for an old-timer like herself to be in the same class with a greenhorn like me. But I refused to agree.

After two months, the Chinese Supervisor of Students notified me that I was awarded a six-year scholarship from Anhwei province. (So it was only vanity that had given me the persecution complex of being afraid to be spotted as a revolutionist against Yuan Shihk'ai's government.) The scholarship carried a monthly allowance of thirty-six *yen*, plus tuition fees. I even got back pay for the last three months I had been in school.

Now that I was freed from financial worries, Yiwu suggested that we should live well. With my jewelry and seven hundred dollars Chinese money and three months' back pay, we could have things and go places. We would dine at a *seiyō ryōri* one day and go to the most expensive movies the next. Since my three squirrel robes were not in proper style, we had them converted into two fashionable coats at a foreign-style furrier. Each of us had a three-piece grey serge suit made to order, as well as two summer dresses. Since we hated to sleep and sit on the floor, we modernized our rooms with two real beds, two full-height desks, two enclosed bookcases, and four chairs. It wouldn't do to have dirty secondhand copies of anatomy textbooks lying around in such an elegant room. So we traded in some of our textbooks for brand-new copies. Fellow Chinese students who dropped in remarked that revolutionists must have money.

But as reward for her efforts on my behalf, Yiwu wanted me to keep the promise which I did not make. At the end of the year, she would not let me take the final examinations. She would fall sick, so that I would have to attend to her and miss my classes. When she called me ungrateful, I would offer to renounce my scholarship, anything rather than fall one year behind, unless I actually flunked the courses myself. Once, her voluntary sickness caused her to flunk an examination, which I passed. When my name got into the habit of being always one or two names above hers in the published order of marks, she could stand it no longer and left me.

But this was only the first episode in my life with Yiwu.

26

STUDYING MEDICINE

AT LAST I settled down to the study of medicine. As usual, I was quick in finishing my homework. I acquired a taste for serial movies, which were the fashion in those days, or they were the ones the Japanese liked to import from America. There was a series called, in Japanese, "The Strange Hand" (the original name in English was probably *The Claw*), starring young Lionel Barrymore. They changed chapters every Wednesday at 2 p.m., just the hour for my inorganic chemistry. I was so anxious to know how the story developed that I cut several classes in succession. When the examination came, I had to stay up two nights to get a barely passing mark. They told me that I should have slept, to let my knowledge soak in while resting. But the trouble with me was that there was not enough chemistry in me to soak.

I never bluffed at examinations. The Japanese girls, who were using their own language, liked to write long papers. But as it was all I could do to remember to insert the right *kana* characters and do such grammatical acrobatics as putting the object before the verb, in addition to remembering the subject itself, I always wrote as briefly as possible. Once, a teacher passed around my paper in the class as a model of conciseness. He was not aware that I did not know enough to be diffuse.

Japanese lectures, in the style of many other things they borrowed from the Germans, were regular *Vorlesungen*. In fact, it was the fashion to have titles in German, *Vorlesungen über* this and *Vorlesungen über* that, on the backs of books of which the inside was in Japanese. The professor read his notes aloud, page by page, in class, and all the students scribbled at top speed without once looking up. It was important to get everything down, as many students could not afford to buy books, and the library facilities were not such as would enable the students to do regular assigned readings.

Chinese students, on the other hand, rarely wrote out their notes in full, because, in the first place, they did not know the language well enough to write fast enough, and, in the second place, they did not believe in the system.

For my part, I tried to find out what books my professors had published and bought those which were nearest to the course being taught. I would look them over and bring them to class, and, in almost nine cases out of ten, I could find the place where the professor was reading himself. All I had to do was to mark the place and note down such changes as he had made since he wrote it. My Japanese schoolmates thought it such a pity to deface the nice new books. "You will lose so much value on them when you turn them in to the secondhand bookstores," they told me.

I felt initiated when I took up my dissection tools and started to cut up dead Japanese bodies. Four students were assigned to a body in "alphabetic" (i.e., *kana*) order, except that all Chinese students were placed in an order we did not quite understand. My group consisted of three Chinese and one Japanese. This latter objected strongly to being placed in my group, which I attributed only to race prejudice. While this girl was usually forward in things, she never moved ahead, but just looked on, while the three of us did the dirty work. When we found a particular nerve or artery we had been looking for, she would come over and hold a pair of forceps and touch it very gingerly and then quickly return to her manual. Each time she did this, she would go away and wash her hands. What a fastidious girl for studying medicine, we thought. Then we found that similar things happened in the other groups where there were Chinese students.

There was a Korean student by the name of Kyo, written with the same character as the name of a Chinese student Hsü. So they "recognized relatives" and made friends with each other. Although Koreans were Japanese subjects, Miss Kyo was also placed out of alphabetic order in a Chinese group. She smelled something wrong in the air, literally. She discovered that the body given her group was that of a patient who had died of tuberculosis of the skin, and none of the bodies used were properly sterilized. She made a big row to Dr. Washiyama, the woman president of the medical school. Her husband, Dr. Yoshioka Jitarō, was also present. From Miss Kyo's report of their talk, the Chinese students learned that most of the bodies assigned to them carried contagious diseases, and, moreover, that it was against the law to use disease-carrying bodies in a class for normal anatomy. The administration reprimanded the laboratory people in charge, and the matter was closed.

Irritations, big and small, were part of the regular fare of Chinese students in Japan: you would find insufficient quantities of chemicals; you would be given defective histological specimens. Sometimes you would meet with promoters of Sino Japanese friendship, but they usually wound up with reminding you of the war of 1894, when Japan annihilated the Chinese navy. One expression of friendship took the form of advising us nice Chinese girls to marry Japanese men—this from the men, of course. And yet the Japanese wondered why Chinese who had studied abroad in Europe and America always spoke well of the country they had lived in, while the majority of those who studied in Japan learned to love the country less than before they went there.

I must say, in fairness to Japanese opinion, that there were all sorts of Chinese in Japan. Because of the cheapness of steamship fares and living expenses there, there were unlimited numbers of Chinese students *not* studying in Japan. Now, I do not believe that large-scale transporting of people from one country to another, out of their cultural environment, necessarily contributes to international understanding, certainly not as a short-term result. Witness the wholesale importation of Chinese laborers into America during the last century. Witness the thousands of homesick G.I.'s in China during World War II. They may have contributed toward exchange of cultures in the wider, anthropological sense, and I believe that, in both cases, the long-term effect has been to the good. But they have been far less effective as cultural ambassadors than, say, a hundredth of their number of real students could be and have been.

As more and more young, people went to Japan to get "glazed," as we describe it, with the name of a returned student from abroad, the Japanese began to organize special, easy courses, even special schools, for Chinese diploma-seekers. They ceased to welcome serious students and made excuses for not admitting Chinese students to the best courses. So the whole thing worked into a vicious circle. We were getting what we were asking for. As time went on, Japan-returned students acquired a name in China of being only second-rate-trained. Hence the general desire of Japan-returned students to get a second coating of glaze by going to Europe or America. I went a step further. I married an American-returned student and went to America with him. But of that more later.

27

THE TWENTY-ONE DEMANDS AND SINO-JAPANESE FRIENDSHIP

CHINA'S RELATIONS with Japan came to a head when on May 7, 1915, while Europe and America were fully occupied with the World War, China received from her "ally" the infamous "Twenty-one Demands." If they had been accepted, China would have become a vassal state of Japan, with Japanese supervisors of police infesting all the provinces. Even those of the demands which were accepted were humiliating and damaging enough, until corrected at the Washington Conference of 1921.

When the news of the demands came out, a large proportion of the seven thousand Chinese students in Japan quit their studies and planned to return. Many of those who remained organized "blood and iron" groups, preparing themselves for doing espionage in case of war. I was under great pressure to join the patriotic activities. But knowing how weak and unprepared the country was, I was sure that it would not come to war, but some compromise would be reached, at China's expense, of course. I advised my fellow students to continue studying until we really had to return or get interned. "Why not take this opportunity to experiment on and kill some Japs instead of practicing on our own patients?" I reasoned.

"You and your exams," they would reply. "What's the use of a profession if you haven't got a free country to practice it in?" For I was then taking the final examinations of my pre medical. Of eleven Chinese in my class, only three remained. As we passed the picket line into the examination halls, the pickets would abuse us and say: "Pack up and go home, girls! Want to stay and marry the Japs?"

Of the three girls who took the examinations, there were, besides myself, Yiwu and Feng Ch'iya. I am glad I got to know Feng Ch'iya, for it was at a party in her honor that I later met her nephew Chao Yuenren.

Having finished my pre-medical course, I returned to China, for a summer vacation. I stayed most of the time with Father, who was then Assistant Manager of the Shenchia Chi Paper Manufacturing Company in Hupeh. He spoiled me as he had never spoiled me before. He gave me all the good things to eat I had missed abroad. He had more than forty new Chinese dresses made for me, also six dresses to take to Yiwu. He asked me what branch of medicine I was going to specialize in and where I would like to have my hospital set up. He would make preparations, so that it would be ready for me when I returned again. He arranged parties for me and introduced me to everybody as "my daughter Dr. Yang Buwei."

"You know," he told his guests, as he drank to their health, "I would rather have one daughter than ten sons. Now look at Yüsheng. I don't know what's going to become of you, Yüsheng, if you keep on being such a truant. You know what, Ch'uan'er, I want you to take Yüsheng with you to enter a middle school in Japan next autumn and make a man of him—like yourself."

When Father came to Shanghai to see me and Sixth Brother Yüsheng off, waving to us from the dock, I had no idea that that was to be the last I saw of him. He never saw me as a real doctor.

I returned to Japan when World War I had been going on for over a year and the white man's prestige had sunk very low. Apparently trying to offset some of the increased ill will from the Twenty-one Demands, the Japanese tried a campaign for friendship between the yellow races. The government sent a special official, Okubo Shintarō, to arrange with the Chinese Supervisor of Students to implement the new policy. They picked out Yiwu and me as the best representatives from China, probably because we wore smart-looking

European attire—I like to believe that we looked all right in any attire.

Our newly formed connections may have helped us in getting a chance to practice at the Imperial University and the next door Mizui Hospital in our third year—medical students did not usually begin practicing until their fourth year. There were two or three thousand patients at the Mizui Clinic, and each student had ten or twenty patients a day, under the supervision of specially assigned instructors. One of my supervisors was a Dr. Go, whose grandfather had emigrated to Japan from China. Not every Japanese of Chinese origin felt Chinese in himself. But this one was very good to us. When there was an especially interesting heart case, he would send for Yiwu and me and let us examine the patient for half an hour, or as long as we liked.

My interest was in internal medicine—even before I practiced doing operations. I loved especially contagious diseases. They were so exciting. Once, a girl standing next to me in the laboratory spilled a test tube full of live bacteria. As she screamed, "Cholera, cholera!" everybody ran toward the door in panic. I snatched a bottle of carbolic acid and splashed it all over the place. On another occasion, when the Spanish influenza had gone around the world and reached Japan and many of the students were trying to study the virus, I thought I was taking all the precautions. But one night I developed a high fever and ached all over. After I got well, I concluded that it was not necessary to have a disease in order to understand or be able to treat it. I did not understand it any better after having had it than before.

My interest in internal medicine did not decrease, but something happened which changed the direction of my profession. An order from the Chinese government came to us through the Supervisor of Students to the effect that all women holders of government scholarships in medicine should specialize in gynecology and obstetrics. This rather disturbed me. I did not like to be so limited. Besides, most children seemed to like to come into the world at night and I hated to have to get up at night. However, it made no difference to me yet, as every student had to learn something of everything until the end of the fourth year. Meanwhile I had a chance to interest myself in the other branches of the profession.

During the fourth year, the class was sent to visit and sometimes practice in the Public Health Department, military hospitals, psychopathic hospitals, etc. Partly because Yiwu and I were women, and partly because of personal connections, we were able to see rather more than most other Chinese students were. At one army hospital, we were allowed to see many preparations for war. (The Japanese did not do any actual fighting in World War I except taking Tsingtao.) One thing that impressed me was the long-term preparation for army rations. There were dumps and dumps, piled mountain-high, of dried, half boiled rice balls. They told me that every year, whether it be a good year or a year of famine, a stated amount of rice had to be set aside for the rice reserve. If and when war should come, the troops could carry this concentrated ration and have it ready for use by soaking it in hot water for fifteen minutes.

"We of the yellow races should join hands to expel the white man from Asia," they always told us. "Our army will annihilate Russia's army. Our navy will annihilate America's navy (which later they partly did). If you Chinese know enough to follow us as your leaders, we will be prosperous and great together."

Such friendly talks were contradicted not only by action on the political plane, but also by the behavior of individuals toward the Chinese. With all the kindnesses shown us in small matters, there was always an overbearing superiority that you felt in every contact with them. Of course I told the story of the rice dumps and the all-annihilating Japanese army and navy, first to my people at home, and later to Americans when I went to America. But the Japanese were right about us girls in one thing. It was quite all right to show us what we liked to see because they knew that nobody would take us seriously. Just so much Chinese propaganda.

28

GRADUATION AND RETURN

ALTHOUGH I LOVED contagious diseases (and had some of them), and acquired a taste for bacteriology, I finally had to buckle down, as ordered, to the study of gynecology and obstetrics. I went to fewer Lionel Barrymore movies. I stopped going to Sino-Japanese friendship parties. There were no Sundays or half-Saturdays off and there were no vacations. I had to take the rare opportunity of joining the Kitasato Seminar and other seminars and meeting the leaders of the profession.

I must say that the Japanese scientists were scientists and had a world point of view—when they were talking science. Men like Kitashima and Hata (co-inventor of "606" with Erlich) did command my admiration and influenced me more than just by way of imparting knowledge. They shifted my center of the medical world from England to Germany. When the Supervisor of Students informed Yiwu and me that we had an opportunity to be transferred to America if we wanted, we declined, preferring to wait until we had a chance to be transferred to Germany.[1]

One professor, Dr. Matsui, took enough interest in me to insist on giving me a higher mark than I wanted. It was at a general examination for graduation, when I was supposed to make a prescription for a patient with myopia, astigmatism, and everything else. My ophthalmology was little better than my inorganic chemistry, and when

---

[1] I don't blame you, my dear. For some of my best American professors of that time were "returned students" who had studied at German universities.—Y.R.C.

I was sure that I had done enough to get a passing mark, I handed in my paper and started unceremoniously to go away.

"Yō San, Yō San," (the Japanese equivalent of "Yang Hsiensheng"), he called after me, "you can do still better than that. I know you can."

I walked along the gallery-like passage, with the professor chasing after me and round and round, holding a case of assorted lenses in his hand. That was the last I had to do with lenses and things. Today I have to ask my husband what is the definition of a diopter.

The last two or three years in Japan rushed by like a rapid river. Except for a week's trip to the summer resort of Kamakura, and another trip, with Yiwu and Dr. Yen Chihchung (son of the educator Yen Fansheng), to the winter resort of Hokone, all those busy years seem to have been one continuous session.

Even the flurry of excitement over Yuan Shihk'ai's abortive monarchial movement and the World War Armistice is now very much foreshortened in my memory of that period. For, at the end of those years, one thing stood out in strong relief.

In May, 1919, shortly after I joined a seminar on heart disease, I received a letter from Father from Haining, Chekiang, where he was mayor. He expected me to be home by August or September. Because I had told him before that I should like to open a hospital at Peiping, he planned to go there first to buy one of those old *wangfu* or mansions, so that I could have it converted into a hospital when I came back.

But "Heaven does not follow man's wishes." They told me that two days after he arrived at Peiping, he took sick. On the third day, he could not speak. On the tenth day, he passed away. The doctor could not diagnose what he died of.

I did not know a thing until the news reached Mother and Mother wrote to me from Nanking. My first impulse was of course to rush home at once. Then, when I felt that I could not imagine my country without my father in it, I thought I had better stay abroad for another year. But Mother sent me one telegram after another. Yiwu also urged me to return to start a hospital with her. So I decided to return.

Yiwu and I were quite friends again. You know, for friendship, there is nothing like living apart and crying together. We had been living separately during the past three years and so had fewer occasions to quarrel. My father had always encouraged us to stick together and to plan to work together. He had always something for her whenever he sent food or clothes to me. When he died, my tears felt less bitter and more warm for my friend's tears, which kept mine company. So when we started on our journey back to China, after a stay of six years in a foreign country, there was in me a subdued glow of confidence and feeling of adventure, which would have given way to worry and brooding if I had had to travel alone. Besides, I still had the illusion of a big, old mansion waiting for me in Peiping.

Our train crossed the Strait of Shimonoseki at night. In Seoul, capital of Korea, we spent one night at a Japanese hotel. The rickshamen would not take us to a Korean hotel, seeing that we were in Occidental dress. After another day's journey, we arrived at Mukden at midnight. All changed trains. We got into the train for Peiping and found ourselves the only passengers in a whole car. Suddenly martial music broke out on the platform. What? A military band to welcome the returned students back to China?

Twenty soldiers rushed into our car and two military policemen stood guard at both ends. Were these men sent in to be our bodyguards or to arrest us? No, they just sat down quietly, and, to our relief, quite ignored us. I pulled up one of the drawn shades to look at the platform. There was a tall, big general, with a heavy mustache and heroic features, talking with a rather short, thin gentleman, with a small mustache, in a flowing gown.

"Who's that?" I asked one of the officers.

He sized us up a little, and then replied: "That's Commander-in-Chief Chang, seeing Governor Lung off to Kwangsi."

"I see, so that's Chang Tsolin and Lung Chikuang. I thought Lung Chikuang was a tall, big fellow."

"None of that," the officer whispered. "You mustn't call them directly by names. You'd get into trouble if you weren't foreigners."

Yiwu and I winked to each other and decided to be foreigners. We carried on a conversation, half in Japanese, half in what we thought was English, with a sprinkling of long medical terms in Latin and German.

"How long have you been in China, ladies?" the officer asked. "You speak very good Chinese. Where do you people live?"

"We were born in Tientsin," I replied, putting on the best Tientsin accent I knew or made up. "We have traveled quite a lot and so acquired a rather mixed accent."

Yiwu spoke in Japanese and tried to stop me from further nonsense.

"So you can still talk Japanese," the officer said.

"Yes," I said, "we have been traveling in Japan lately."

Realizing that we were getting more and more involved, I did not dare to talk any further.

Months afterwards, I had a great argument with a man about the appearance of Chang Tsolin.

"Chang Tsolin is a short, thin man," he said. "I am a northeasterner and I ought to know."

"No," I said, "Chang Tsolin is a tall, big fellow. I ought to know, because I saw him and you did not."

I saw him all right, but the him I saw was the other fellow and the other fellow I saw was he.

The two important persons must have had an all-night conference, for the train did not start until next morning. There was no sleeper or diner service for ordinary passengers and by morning we were getting very cold and hungry. As venders began to gather and spread their tempting foods along the train, we called an attendant and handed him a silver dollar to buy us some breakfast. He came back with two armfuls of things and had two boys help him bring in some more. I thought some of the things were for the other people in the train, but no, they were all ours. I counted two small spiced roasted chickens, eight pairs of pot-stewed large prawns, twenty spiced hard-boiled eggs, ten large sesame-sprinkled hot-biscuits, and ten puffed fritters. We were overwhelmed with such a lot of rich foods, we didn't know where to put them between us, let alone inside us. When the attendant saw our embarrassment, he said:

"T'it'ai," (for he could not imagine that two unmarried young ladies would travel unescorted the way we did), "I thought you were buying these things for friends inside the Pass.[2] When you eat a meal around here, it costs you only a few coppers."

That reminded me. So I bought two large roasted chickens for fifty cents more to make a presentable little something for Yiwu's family at Tientsin, where we were going to stop over.

I found a hospitable welcome at Yiwu's home. Her family was however not as demonstrative about her return as I had expected, that is, even allowing for Chinese reserve. When I started to leave for Peiping the next morning, I had taken for granted that Yiwu was going to spend a few days at home, but, to my surprise, she went with me, as if she had spent a night at a hotel.

Peiping, at once the most cosmopolitan and the most Chinese of Chinese cities, was an impressive place to enter even from other Chinese places, not to say after a six-year stay in Japan. The effect increased on me as our train skirted along the inside of the outer wall for mile after mile, with the magnificent Temple of Heaven looking

---

[2]That is, in the provinces inside Shanhaikuan.

at us first from our east, then from our north, then from our west, and then from our south, as we finally arrived at the Eastern Station of the Peiping Mukden Railway.

Stepping into rickshas, we went straight to the Shihtai (Anhwei) Guild Building, where Big Uncle was staying. I had not been on speaking terms with Big Uncle for eight years. But when he saw me this time, he broke down into great wailing, as was proper for greeting between relatives when there was death in the family. He pitied me for having to bear the whole burden of a family right after my homecoming. Having been abroad for so long, I could not bring myself to cry aloud at a specified moment. But the meeting affected me so much that it practically marked a complete reconciliation between us. In fact, I had a hard time convincing my husband about my early unkind accounts of Big Uncle, whom he met later as one of the nicest old gentlemen he had ever known.

29

THE FILIAL DAUGHTER

WHEN BIG UNCLE expressed concern for me, I re assured him with the saying: "Heaven never puts man on a dead-end road." As I now had a profession, it was naturally up to me to support Mother, Sixth Brother, and his young bride.

I did not realize how badly off Father had been and the truth came to me only gradually. But just to be prudent, Yiwu and I went to a small hotel, the Peking Hotel on Hsi Hoyar—not the Grand Hôtel de Pékin. As was my habit, whenever things went wrong, I tried not to think of the past, but to plan for the future. I wished I could start practicing at once. I called up Dr. Yen Chihchung, of whom Yiwu and I had seen a good deal in Japan, and asked him about regulations for starting a hospital. He was then Chief of Section on Hygiene in the Ministry of Interior.

Police Inspector Yang, a distant cousin of mine, who had been attending to my father's affairs at the time of his death. From him, I learned that Father had died without leaving a thing. When I asked him whether Father had discussed money with him, he asked me whether Father had written to me about it. I said that he had not mentioned figures, but promised to buy a house and medical equipment for me, and that when I sent him a budget for twelve thousand dollars, he did not tell me that he could not do it. (Later, when I went to Nanking, I learned from First Cousin Ch'eng, my father's treasurer, that Father had drawn from his account at the Chekiang Industrial Bank fifteen thousand dollars, of which he had carried nine thousand dollars in cash in his vest pocket on his way to the north, the rest being given to Mother and used to buy jewelry for me. Only a negligible part of this was subsequently accounted for.) When I told the inspector of what I knew of the situation then, he offered to find a public building for us and to advance funds for repairs and fixtures, which we could later pay back gradually from income. Yiwu and I thanked him profusely. But Big Uncle and Third Brother were opposed to accepting this generous help from our mutual distant relative. Since, however, they were unable to suggest any other we had to accept the offer.

Dr. Yen also came to see us at the hotel and promised to help us in our public relations. We also looked up Lin T'isheng, one of the Lin brothers we had known, who not only helped to arrange contacts for us, but advanced more than three thousand dollars for our initial expenses.

After four busy days in Peiping, I started for Nanking to see Mother, Auntie, and the rest of my Yenling Hsiang family.

Mother was in heavy mourning dress of coarse hemp. I told her of my plans to open a hospital. She was pleased that I was "as good as an eldest son" and took out a hemp dress for me to wear. I was already in an all-black foreign-style dress. But that did not look at all proper in Chinese eyes. Auntie also advised me to change to hemp. Since I already had undertaken the burden of supporting the family, what difference did it make to wear coarse clothes for a few days? It would make a good impression. So I agreed. They were greatly surprised that, after having been abroad for six years, I ceased to agitate for revolutions and came back knowing propriety. After all, it was good to let children go out and study. This pleased me greatly, as I felt that I had won my revolution in advocating education for women. So I behaved more and more nicely. When the chorus of monks came chanting to propitiate the soul of the departed, I did the kowtowing, as an eldest son would. When mourners came, I returned their kowtow to thank them, no longer insisting that the Republic had abolished the kowtow.

On the sixth "Seventh," that is, the forty-second day of mourning, it was the custom for a married daughter's family to present feasts as sacrifices to the deceased, after which the food was used to entertain the guest mourners. Although I was not married, I offered to cook a regulation feast of twenty-four vegeterian dishes for the occasion. Everybody laughed at the idea. Aunt Ch'eng, who was still bitter over my breaking my engagement with her son, and who knew that I had always hated household work, said sarcastically: "That's right, Ch'uanti. Your cooking will be only fit for dead people to eat. Your father won't mind it. Since he loved you so, he would call it delicious, no matter what you cooked. But a chief mourner can't go out of the house, you know. You had better write out a list of the things you need and send the cook out for them."

This was a hard one for me. I did not know all the names of various kinds of foods. Even today, I prefer to go to the American market myself and point to things, asking for some of this and some of that. On that occasion, I would have given myself away if I had written down the name of some of this and gotten some of that instead. So, borrowing some street clothes from Cousine Lang and young Cousine Chinghua,[1] I slipped out of the house with them and bought some forty kinds of fresh and preserved foods and brought them into the kitchen. I told them only to help me wash and cut, but not to tell me how to do the cooking.

Complete vegetarian dinners in China often contain imitation meat dishes which are not only supposed to look like animal food, but also taste like it. The trick consists largely in the skilful use of soybean products and gluten of wheat flour and good vegetable oil. I had never cooked those dishes before and had only my memory of having eaten them to guide me. I had to use quite a little imagination and invention. Most of my dishes did not look or taste like the ones I meant them to be, but they tasted just as good. If my peastarch

---

[1] I just received a letter from her from Nanking the other day after having had no word from her since Pearl Harbor.

roast duck was not plausible duck, it might pass as vegetarian ham.² "After busying myself in the kitchen for half the night and all the next morning, I produced not twenty-four dishes but thirty-three dishes, most of which I did not know what to call.

It was customary for the family to do ceremonial crying as the dishes were offered on the sacrificial table. But everybody was so interested in my performance that they forgot to cry. Service over, Mother divided the food onto four tables for the family to eat. Aunt Ch'eng was completely won over. Auntie, on her part, was happy because I made good her implicit trust in me.

I planned to return north first, to get things settled a bit. But Mother wanted to go with me at once. Big Uncle wanted Auntie to join him, and Third Brother wanted Third Sister-in law to join him. So we went north together in a big family party .

---

²But some of the vegetarian ham you have made for me tastes like mock turtle.—Y.R.C.

30

MY HOSPITAL IN PEIPING

ON JUNGHSIAR HUTUNG, inside and a little to the west of Ch'ienmen, was Senjen Hospital, a name I had I thought up as Yiwu and I discussed our plans on the train from Mukden to Peiping. Since Kuanhung and Yiwu and I each had a character for "tree" in our surnames, the three of us together would have formed the word *sen*, "forest," written as three "tree"-characters combined. Since Kuanhung's death left only the two of us to carry out our original plans, I added the word *jen*, "benevolent," consisting of the character for "two" and the character for "person." So Senjen Hospital it was called. The application for license called for the names of a director and vice-director, if any, and the two of us filled in our names. We had a staff of two nurses, one ricksha boy, one cook, one maid, and one errand boy. I tried to get number 606 for our telephone, although our practice did not call for the use of the medicine under that name, but the nearest I got was "South 706."

The grounds consisted of two rows of four courtyards each, the main row, counting from the entrance, being office and waiting room, dispensary, our living quarters, and kitchen and service, and the side row being used as ward for in-patients. The dispensary was an important part of the hospital. For, while prescriptions by the old-style herb doctors can be read and filled by any herb drugstore, Western-style drugstores in China mostly sell only patent medicines and drugs in quantity and do not, as a rule, fill prescriptions. We had to lay in a large stock of all the important drugs and have our nurses fill the prescriptions. We were, however, so scared of their misreading the decimal points that we had to supervise most of their work.

We were both fortunate and unfortunate in being among the earliest, if not the earliest, non-missionary women doctors to set up practice on our own. We attracted not only patients within our sphere, but all kinds of cases, especially children's. Because of my interest, I had previously given more attention to internal medicine than I needed to. Now I was glad that I had. Sometimes people would pay a dollar's registration fee just to "see the doctor." I think they meant it literally. Others were more frank and got introductions to pay calls on us. It would not do to say that you were busy were busy or that your hours were such and such. We just had to see everybody. If some who came were not patients, they might bring in patients, so we were advised.

In China, where everything is on a friendly basis, your patients could not feel that they had repaid you enough by giving you money. I even blushed when I received my first pay. Many patients would rather do things for you by spending several times the regular fee, but you wouldn't get a cent in cash. They would send you presents, give you big horizontal tablets of praise, and make you the guest of honor at three-hour banquets.

One dark winter morning, at about five o'clock, the doorbell rang, followed by urgent knocking on the door. The doorman came in nervously and said that an automobile with four soldiers was at the door. Would I come out at once? As I got dressed, I told one of the nurses to go out by the side door to bring a policeman from a neighboring police station. When the visitors saw me come out with a bodyguard, they all laughed.

"No, Doctor," they said, "we have not come here with a warrant. We have been sent here by Regiment Commander Wu of the Nanyuan[1] Barracks, who has heard the fame of Dr. Yang. Mrs. Wu is seriously ill. So we have come with an automobile, specially

---

[1] A southern suburb of Peiping, now the city's main airport.

borrowed from the Division Commander, to bring Dr. Yang to Nanyuan."

I asked what Mrs. Wu was ill with. They could not say. But since our hospital had to take every case that came, I had to go, though I had no way of proving that these men were not kidnapers. I went inside, washed my face hurriedly, and left word with Yiwu that, in case she did not see me again by noon, she had better tell the police and find out whether there was a Regiment Commander Wu in the Nanyuan Barracks.

Though I was accompanied by two nurses, one policeman, and four soldiers in the large automobile, I found it a very lonely ride to go through the wild outer city of Peiping and out of Yungting Gate into the dark, silent country. The car seemed to be going in the right direction all the time, and I was relieved to be received by Commander Wu and shown to Mrs. Wu's bedside. I examined her and found nothing wrong with her. She had been pregnant for something like five months, but that could not be called anything wrong. The only complaint seemed to be some pains from gas in the stomach.

By that time I had learned enough about the practice of practicing to do something to please the patient as well as something to do her real good. It would have been sufficient to give her some rules about right eating and living, but I had to give her in addition some pills— "tablets," when we mention them to patients—to be taken at stated hours. Otherwise, what were doctors for? It was the fashion among devotees of Western medicine to insist on being given a hypodermic for any and every ailment. Mrs. Wu insisted on having one. But all I had in my kit was morphine, which was rather too strong medicine for an ordinary stomachache.

A week afterward, I was invited to a banquet in town by the Wus. Two weeks later, a two-by-four-foot tablet with four big characters CHO SHOU CH'ENG CH'UN ("At the touch of the hand comes spring") was carried to the hospital, followed by two loads of presents of foods and silks, for which I tipped the bearers twenty dollars. So the more flourishing my practice became, the more I had to spend in time and money.

In China, as elsewhere, a doctor does not doctor himself or members of his own family. But things beyond my control brought calamities to my home and almost to my medical reputation. There was a common belief, in which my mother shared, that death in the family within three years of the coming of a bride was attributable to the bad luck she had brought into the house, and this made the relation between mother-in-law and daughter-in-law very difficult. Both of them were making life more and more miserable for themselves and for everybody else. As for my position, you know how hard it is for one member of a family to try to give orders to another member, doctor fashion. Add to this the fact that the family belonged to a different medical tradition of several thousand years.[2] I was in the impossible situation of being wanted but not listened to. For this reason, I had long engaged a missionary maternity hospital for my sister-in-law.

When her time came, she was down with pneumonia. I advised her to enter the hospital at once, but both she and Mother balked at the last moment at going into a foreign hospital. They could disregard instructions at will if I took the case. But Auntie warned me not to have anything to do with it. She reasoned that I could do no good without cooperation and all I could do was to ruin my reputation with the case. In order to lessen responsibility and increase authority, I persuaded the family to call in two other doctors, who of course thought alike in such a simple, though serious, case.

I must say that the will to live is no mean factor in a patient's power to pull through a crisis. It is no doubt something that is finally translatable into physico-chemical terms, but in terms of common sense, "the will to live" is about as understandable an idea as any.

---

[2]Grandfather's modernity had very little influence on his daughters-in-law, probably because propriety always required a rather remote formal relationship between a father-in-law and a daughter-in-law.

Now the shock of my father's death and of the loss of an expected fortune had altered the whole life picture for the bride, and of course for my mother. There was probably more than mere medical conservatism in the sabotage against medical care. You can keep a person from committing suicide, but you can't make a person want to live if he doesn't want to.

Mother, on her part, had been given to seek escape in wine. While excessive drinking had no such inelegant connotations as in other countries, but quite the contrary, it was nevertheless just as bad for one's health. The death of the daughter-in-law and child was another shock to Mother. I warned her repeatedly of her heart condition. Perhaps I should not have done so. One night, after I had had a very full day of calls until eleven o'clock at night, I went to see how Mother was. Sixth Brother was sitting with me at her bedside. Something one of us said made her laugh. After that, she was silent.

Circumstances had made brother and sister out of cousins: Sixth Brother, son of Fifth Uncle, and myself, daughter of Big Uncle. We had been rivals for favoritism—father spoils daughter, mother spoils son, of course—until the death of both our adopted parents brought us closer together. Although Brother had been married and widowed, he was so much younger than I that I suddenly seemed to be the only one to prop up for him. My usual reaction was of course to think of what next. I would have to work harder than ever. At the same time, I had better get my brother started at once on further education and training. But according to Chinese custom, children had to remain behind mourning curtains for at least forty-nine days, preferably one hundred days, before going out of the house. The political revolution had abolished the kowtow, but there was no explicit ruling about such matters. High officials could be given a "leave of grief" with pay, but what about doctors pay, if that, on a day-to-day basis?

So I started a little revolution of my own in a matter on which the Revolution with a capital R was silent. We would follow all the conventional forms of funeral rites, wearing hemp dresses and hemp sandals and all that, but at other times we would go about our business as usual. I would wear a black foreign-style dress and Brother would wear a gray robe. He approved the idea, but did not dare to tell other members of the large family about it. I said all right, just leave it to me.

On the third day of mourning, when some eighty relatives and friends were present, I made a grand speech, announcing my intention to modify the usual conventions. Besides declaring that Brother and I would go about our business as usual, my most drastic proposal was to move the coffin out in only three weeks. I promised to undertake to have a proper tomb built for my parents in due time. I quoted such passages from the classics in my favor as I could think of—you could of course prove anything if you knew your classics well enough. I got a good hand from my audience, who said that after all Miss Three was a straightforward person of straightforward words, like T'anch'un in *Dream of the Red Chamber*. A few years afterwards, I made good my bravado. I wish more of my elder relatives were living to see Father's and Mother's tomb, built according to the most propitious "winds and waters"—so propitious that Brother became a successful engineer, got married again, and has now a big family.

31

PLANS AND INTERRUPTIONS

HAVE YOU EVER noticed that life consists mostly of interruptions, with occasional spells of rush work in between? After I had my way in abolishing long mourning at home, I made big plans for future work—until the next interruption. I found my hospital growing too small. It did not have enough rooms. None of them was really suitable for an operating room. A number of girls applied for training for nurses. I wanted to take them, but had no facilities for giving them such training. So, when Third Brother returned from a trip to Tientsin in early 1920 and told me that Li Yuanhung wanted to see me, I took this opportunity to go to Tientsin.

At that time, Li had retired from public life. Perhaps he could help me in my plans. Third Brother went with me. Mrs. Li came out first. She wore a Chinese-style short black jacket and trousers, and looked just as she had fifteen years before in Wuchang, except that she was a little stouter. You could not tell from her simple manners that she had been the first lady of the land. As we were exchanging small talk, suddenly somebody behind covered my eyes with both hands.

"Who is it?" I asked.

Everybody laughed.

"Are you still as naughty as before, Ch'uanti?" a voice behind me spoke in an unmistakable Huangp'i, Hupeh accent.

Li asked me about my work and my plans. I told him that I wanted to avoid having too close connections with the government, but suggested that if a board of trustees could be formed to raise funds to develop our hospital as a private organization, that would suit me best. I wished to have an X-ray unit, a bacteriological laboratory, a good operating room, and equipment for a training school for nurses. Li asked me how much funds I needed. I replied that eighty to a hundred thousand dollars would do it. He said: "All right, you draw up your plans in detail and get some additional prominent people to be trustees I should be glad to serve as a member. But don't you give up halfway, you know!"

"Thank you, Uncle Li," I replied, "and don't you decline this presidency they are offering you! 'The Revolution isn't completed yet,' you know!"

"As quick as ever," he laughed. For at that time, Ts'ao K'un had been elected President through wholesale bribery and there was great unrest in the country. Li was asked to be President again and he declined.

I had to hurry back to Peiping, as Yiwu had been limiting her practice to children's cases and I was handling all the maternity cases and had to be more or less on twenty-four-hour duty. There was at least one good thing about riding in a train. I had a few hours' rest from telephones.

I returned full of plans. Suddenly everything came to a stop. Not a patient came to the door. Civil war had broken out between the Anfu and the Chihli groups of militarists. The city gates were closed for six days, and few people dared to go out of the house. No vegetables came into the city. But the stocks of ducks, eggplants, and watermelons were plentiful. Ducks sold for forty cents each, because there was no feed and the Peiping ducks were reared in such a way that they would die if not kept constantly overfed. So Yiwu and I, and occasionally some doctors who dropped in, spent our time eating ducks, eggplants, and watermelons.

I soon got bored with staying indoors. The Ministry of Interior had issued Red Cross flags and armbands to hospitals. I welcomed these things both for protection and for adventure. Putting on an armband, I went out on the street in ricksha. There were many wounded soldiers being brought into the city. I was just on the point of offering to take some into my hospital, when I met Dr. Yen, who stopped me from doing it. I thought that his manners were a little blunt. But later when he and Dr. P. Z. King[1] showed me and Yiwu around in the military hospital under them, I concluded that I could not have managed what I started to undertake, not in the same hospital with the other kinds of patients.

As business picked up slowly again, Yiwu and I began to resume making plans for expanding our hospital. Yen and King often dropped in and gave us advice. To get people to consent to be trustees, Yen was to approach his own father Yen Fansheng, the leading educator from Tientsin, Yiwu was to approach Ch'i Hsiehyuan, her father's acquaintance, and I was to approach Hsiung Hsilin, K'uai Jomu, Lin Pingnan, Po Wenwei, and Ts'ai Yuanp'ei. With the exception of Ch'i, who still had to be approached, everyone consented. Then, on September 18, 1920, came another interruption.

My classmate Feng Ch'iya had a distant nephew and niece: P'ang Tunmin and his first-cousin wife Feng Chihwen, both of whom had also been our contemporaries as students of medicine. The P'angs had already set up practice in Peiping. On the arrival of Ch'iya, they gave her a welcome party at their home, to which they also invited Yen Chihchung, P. Z. King, Dr. Yü, Yiwu, and myself. We were a cozy little group, with common interests and common memories. We talked shop and joked in allusions which nobody outside our circle could understand. Then we were interrupted by the entrance of a young man, dressed in shabby foreign clothes, who changed the whole atmosphere of the party. In fact, he changed everything.

---

[1] Another contemporary of ours who had studied in Japan. He is now Minister of Health.

Part IV
AND THE YOUNG MAN

32

CHAO YUENREN SAUNTERS IN

"THIS IS MY cousin Chao Yuenren," Mrs. P'ang introduced the uninvited guest, "who has recently come back from America. He is teaching mathematics at Tsing Hua College[1] and happens to be in town today. So I asked him to join us."

Since there is no "How do you do?" in Chinese, we just nodded acknowledgment pleasantly and said nothing. When Dr. Pang started pouring wine into the guests' cups, Yiwu declined by turning her cup upside down. I was going to follow suit, when I noticed that Chao Yuenren was doing the same thing, and I stopped. Yen smiled subtly. As usual, I talked much and loud. Once in a while, Chao Yuenren would make some dry remarks. We all laughed politely, as they must have been American jokes.

After the dinner, he herded all of us to one corner of the small room, set up his camera at the other corner, pressed the shutter release, dashed across the room and sat on the floor before us, and, after trying to keep us still for five minutes, dashed back to the camera and pressed the shutter again. After he left, we had one topic of conversation for the rest of the evening.

---

[1] A preparatory school in Tsinghua Yuan, a northwestern suburb of Peiping, for training students to be sent to America under the returned American-indemnity fund. (See pp. 75-76.) Since 1925, it has been a national university.

The next morning, while I was checking some prescriptions the nurses were filling, Mrs. P'ang came, saying, as she walked in: "Yunch'ing! Yiwu! I have brought a stranger to call on you ladies."

"All right, Chihwen, please make yourselves at home in the inside parlor. Yiwu is there. I'll be with you as soon as I am through."

"You said you've brought a stranger," I said, as I joined them later. "But I met Mr. Chao last night." (For nobody is stranger to me for a second time.)

So we entertained our callers with grapes, chocolates, French, pastry, and tea. It was a good way to dispose of the loads of gifts from our patients. After I looked over a few out-patients, Ch'iya dropped in and asked me if I had anything good for lunch, for she and I had often cooked together while in Japan. With very little persuasion by the four lady doctors, Chao Yuenren was willing to stay for lunch, too. Since, in the Chinese system of eating, an extra guest means just setting an extra bowl and an extra pair of chopsticks, sitting down to an uninvited drop-in meal is as casual and natural a thing as accepting a cigarette handed to you. Our conversation drifted to photography. As Ch'iya was only visiting Peiping for a few days, to return soon to Wusih, she started an impromptu afternoon party to visit the Central Park and called up Pang Tunmin and another cousin. So we went to the Park with a battery of three cameras. Chao Yuenren, who is the sort of man who will keep any bad photograph so long as it contains more than you can draw from memory, beat all the rest in quantity by taking more than twenty pictures, each one with some person or persons in it.

Although Chao Yuenren called very often, for a person living several miles out of town, I talked very little with him, but let Yiwu and Mrs. P'ang, who came almost every day, entertain him. I had my hands full with my morning's out-patients and afternoon's visits, and urgent calls seemed always to come at night. Peiping is famous for roasted chestnuts, not the kind that cracks and gets burned and still raw inside, but the fragrant, meaty kind, roasted evenly in sand. One evening, I happened to be able to join the group and we had a goodly supply of hot roasted chestnuts. Mr. Chao proceeded methodically to shell and skin all the chestnuts and offered them to the three ladies. I liked roasted chestnuts, but my stomach did not. So I kept them in my hands, and, while Mr. Chao was not looking, gave them to one of the nurses.

The next morning, Chao Yuenren came again. Noticing that I was knitting, he said: "You are just like an American, Dr. Yang, always doing something. You never seem to need a rest."

"No, I can't rest," I said. "If my hands and feet are not moving, I always think up things to do, except in sleep. And then I may be even busier, when I dream."

He smiled. Yiwu smiled and started to say something, but as she often did, she said half a sentence and then quit.

"I can knit, too," Chao Yuenren said. "Once I knitted a whole glove."

Everybody laughed. I said: "Doesn't the proverb say, 'A man who sews and mends in poverty begins and ends'?"

As he took leave, he said at the doorway: "I hope you won't mind, ladies, if I can't come again so often from now on."

"Of course not," I replied. "I know Mr. Chao must be very busy with teaching. But any time you happen to be in town, we should always be glad to have you drop in."

On the evening of the next day, there was a noise of some body tripping over and breaking something in the dimly lit courtyard.

"May I come in?" said Chao Yuenren, as he tried vainly to put my best pot of chrysanthemums together again. "I said I wasn't coming, but here I am again."

Yiwu and I laughed and reached for some bandage and iodine, but found that the only injury done was to my flower pot.

By this time, I was pretty sure how things were going, though I did not know exactly which way things were going. But I had my ideas about it. Although the way Yiwu was cooperating as Vice-Director of Senjen Hospital was not entirely unexpected, since I had known her for six years, I did have some illusions at first that she might change a little when she got really started. But I was wrong. She attended only to children's cases, and of these she assigned to the nurses the job of vaccination. As in her student days, she was sick, or anyway stayed in bed, about once every two or three days. While she liked foreign, modern ways in food and dress, her idea of a nice lady was entirely of an older tradition. She must be frail and weak, unable to keep her balance in a breeze. She must pine and sigh, and if perchance she smiles, the smile is all the more charming under a knitted brow. Such was the traditional idea of an elegant lady, as one read in Yang Kueifei of *Song of Everlasting Regret*, or in Lin Taiyü of *Dream of the Red Chamber*.

It was a far cry from the idea of a Lin Taiyü eating French pastry to that of a colleague in a two-doctor hospital. As the year wore on, I wondered more and more what was to become of Yiwu. Since I had lived with her so long, concern about her welfare troubled me as much as about my work. Finally I had a brilliant idea—to see if I would make a successful go-between.

33

A "BYSTANDER'S" POINT OF VIEW

WHEN CHAO YUENREN called again, I made myself busier than ever, so that I could have less time to help Yiwu entertain him, especially on days when Mrs. P'ang did not come to the hospital. If anything nice came of it, it would be a meritorious deed which, according to Chinese tradition, would add years to my longevity. Though I could not tell which way things were going, they could at least be allowed to take the natural course, given the right conditions.

September 27 was the first anniversary of the opening of our hospital. A year back, during the confusion of starting an organization by a couple of inexperienced hands, we had not had much of an opening ceremony. Now our place looked fairly presentable both inside and out. We had already collected quite a few horizontal tablets, and the goodwill they represented. I had just completed my first year of practice by delivering the second child of the same mother. So we started a rather elaborate celebration this time. Besides showing visitors through the grounds and entertaining them with tea and refreshments, there was also a program. Mrs. Hsiung Hsilin was the principal speaker. Chao Yuenren was also asked to do something. He stood on a chair and made a speech imitating a foreigner's Chinese and sang a foreign song.

On Mid-autumn Day, Chao Yuenren gave a dinner to the four lady doctors, his aunt Ch'iya, his cousin Mrs. P'ang, Yiwu, and myself. The table was set at the compound in Tsing Hua College, known as the "Yamen." There was a tradition, I learned subsequently, that the room in the Yamen compound next to the college telephone exchange was the most lucky room on the campus. No bachelor teacher could live in it without getting married within a year's time. That was Chao Yuenren's room. No wonder the four lady guests attracted so much attention.

I was never quite clear what Chao Yuenren's special line of study was. One day he came and told us that from now on, he would probably be able to see us more often (as if he had not been seeing us very often).

"Bertrand Russell is going to lecture at the National University of Peking," he said, and I have been asked to be his interpreter."

"Who is Bertrand Russell?" I asked. "What is he going to lecture on?"

"Oh, he is a British philosopher. I specialized in philosophy when I was at Harvard, you see?"

"Why should a sensible man ever want to study such an empty subject as philosophy?" I wondered to myself. But all I said was just "Oh."

Sensing my disapproval, he added: "But he is going to lecture on mathematical philosophy, and that's just what I studied. That's why they want me to be his interpreter. If he lectures several times a week, I shall have to move into the city."

"Then you will have to move into the hospital." I said it just as a nonsensical joke. But Yiwu gave me a stare. However, he did not quite hear my remark.

The next day, Chao Yuenren came in a suit with properly creased trousers.

"What a well-dressed gentleman!" I exclaimed.

"I am leaving for Shanghai to meet Bertrand Russell," he said. "That's why I have borrowed a good suit."

"By the way, Yiwu," I said, "you were going down south to see Governor Ch'i about that business of sponsorship. Why not go together? I should like to take a trip, too, if I weren't so tied down with the hospital here."

I always speak before I think. Since I hated to travel alone, nothing was so natural as to suggest a trip together if people who knew each other were going in the same direction. When Chao Yuenren said that he was going to take a roundabout way via Hankow and down the river in a boat, a trip I visualized with pleasant memories, I said: "Yiwu, you have never been on a boat on the Yangtze River, it will be a wonderful trip."

Yiwu gave me another stare, and I stopped.

We got a picture postcard a couple of times, addressed to both names.

"What a stingy man!" Yiwu remarked each time. "He would not even buy two cards and two stamps."

"Isn't he a stingy man!" I echoed each time.

After a tour through Shanghai, Nanking, Hankow, and Changsha, Chao Yuenren returned to Peiping in company with Bertrand Russell and Dora Black. They stayed in the Continental Hotel on Morrison Street. From there, Chao Yuenren either called or telephoned almost every day. He always talked with me longer over the telephone, because, no doubt, I was naturally more talkative.

One evening, Russell gave a lecture on the analysis of matter at the High Normal School. More than a dozen of our medical acquaintances went there together. There was a big audience gathered in the indoor gymnasium. We came back discussing the lecturer and the interpreter. Some said that the lecturer spoke more clearly than John Dewey, but that the interpreter was not as good as Hu Shih (who was then interpreting Dewey's lectures at the University).

"You must make allowances for the difficulty of the subject," I said. "Many of the terms evidently have never been translated into Chinese before. He has to make them up. Besides, how can you properly explain a subject like the analysis of matter to an audience of two thousand?"

For a time, Chao Yuenren seemed to be getting on well with Yiwu. Anyway, I managed to be busy all the time. One day she suddenly decided to take that trip down south to interview Governor Ch'i. Chao Yuenren and I saw her off. Coming out of the East Station, we were met by our respective rickshas. I was going to return to my hospital. But Mr. Chao said: "Let's dismiss the rickshas and walk back to the hospital, shall we?"

As I knew it was just an American custom to escort a lady home, I agreed and walked the mile with him from the station to the hospital. Perfunctorily, I invited him to come in, and he did.

Then I asked a stupid question: "Are you still coming to the hospital?"

It was just another of those things which slipped out aloud because I was saying it to myself. When he smiled, I was so embarrassed that I hurriedly excused myself to attend to the patients. He asked me if I had time to go to Russell's lecture in the evening. I said I would try to, unless I was called away, and if he liked rinsed lamb, would he come for dinner before going to the lecture?

After the lecture, he escorted me back again and wondered if he could stay for a few minutes. So I wheeled out my sewing machine and sewed away as we talked. It happened that there were few telephone calls that evening, and the nurses answered all of them. I had never realized that I was such an interesting conversationalist. When he rose to take leave, it was past midnight.

"If I may change the quotation a little," he said, " 'I have learned more in one night's talk with you than in my ten years' study in America.' "

How this man can flatter, I thought to myself. Probably he felt obliged to come as usual out of politeness. Maybe he would come less often gradually.

After this he came almost every day. One evening, we forgot the time. When I arrived with him at the University, Bertrand Russell had been standing helplessly on the platform for more than ten minutes. For his Chinese vocabulary apparently included neither "analysis of matter" nor "analysis of mind." As Mr. Chao stepped on the platform, Russell was heard saying *sotto voce*: "Bad man, bad man!" All eyes turned toward me. The unheated lecture room became hotter and hotter, and, as soon as the lecturer finished his last paragraph, I slipped away without waiting for the translation.

Yiwu stayed with my folks at Yenling Hsiang in Nanking. In her letters she asked what visitors came to the hospital. I told her that Mr. Chao often came, sometimes staying quite long. She wrote that there was no prospect of finishing her errand in the immediate future. Then I wrote that she had better not wait but come back right away. I reasoned that, although Chao Yuenren was very good to me, it might be because America-returned students were used to having female company. He might be even better to her when she came back. For several evenings, we went to the East Station to meet the through train from Nanking. But on the evening when Yiwu did arrive, we missed her, because she went out by the rear exit by the Water Gate.

Yiwu was sick after her return. She liked to have visitors around, and Chao Yuenren was among them.

One evening, Chao Yuenren called me up.

"May I see you tomorrow morning?" he said.

"Yes, of course, I shall be in tomorrow morning."

"No," he said. "I want to see you alone. Can we meet at the western rocks in the Central Park? Will seven o'clock be too early for you?"

"I always get up at six," I said, "unless the telephone makes me get up at five."

When I arrived at the western rocks, he was already there.

"You are so high up there, Mr. Chao," was my form of saying "Good morning!"

When he came down to earth, he said: "I don't know what to do, Dr. Yang. I appreciate what you have been doing for your friend. But I fear that you may do her more harm than good. I like to be nice, but I ought not to allow myself to be misunderstood. Perhaps I should have made myself scarce, as I once said I would. But, why should—" and he stopped.

I had suspected that my brilliant idea was not succeeding wonderfully. Now I knew that it had definitely failed. The way things were going, there was danger that both my seven-year-old friendship and my one-year-old business would be wrecked.

As Mr. Chao and I strolled silently in the park and finally stopped under the pailou with the inscription "In Memoriam Iuris Vindicati," I said: "Yes, Mr. Chao. You had better stop coming to see us. I am sure that will be best for you and best for me."

I turned around and slowly walked away.

"Yunch'ing!" he called, just loud enough to be heard ten paces away:

I turned around.

"Yunch'ing," he repeated, still standing under the pailou, "will it have to be thus?—us, I mean?"

"Us? What do you mean, us?" would have been my usual quick reply. But I was not quite myself that morning—or was I more myself than ever before? While this had never been one of my brilliant or stupid ideas, it did not come as a surprise. The surprise was that it all seemed so natural.

"Yunch'ing," Yuenren continued, as he walked toward me. "I cannot."

We strolled in the park, back to the foot of the western rocks, past the colonnade of "Comes Rain Now" tea houses, through the pinegroves, under the Pavilion of Mottoes, through the Temple of Land and Grain, to the front of the park—until increasing numbers of the day's visitors woke me up and reminded me that the park did not quite belong to "us," and that I was keeping many patients waiting in a hospital.

What do you think of the Chinese proverb which says: "Those who are in it are blind; those who stand by are clear"?

34

THE REPATRIATION OF AN EXPATRIATE

I WANT TO BORROW a chapter from Chao Yuenren's autobiography. But he has not written any. So I shall have to write one for him.

Chao Yuenren was the only child, and a thoroughly spoiled child too, of an old family of Changchow, Kiangsu. He was born in Tientsin in 1892 and "returned" to Changchow when he was nine. He had the usual classical education at home under a severe teacher, a lenient father, and a musical and mathematical mother. When he was eleven, both his parents died and he became a complete truant. He spent the better part of his time flying kites and fire-balloons, boiling kerosene over the kitchen stove, taking clocks and watches apart, and putting some of them together again—scientific experiments, he called them. After one year of primary school in Changchow, he went to the preparatory department of Kiangnan Provincial College in Nanking. There he met his teacher, David J. Carver of Hermitage, Tennessee, and decided to go to America. He found in Philip Van Ness Myers' *General History* a chapter on the world state and immediately signed up as citizen. Maybe, he thought, the seat of the world government would be in America, too. In 1910, after I had refused an offer of a scholarship, without examination, to study in America, he took the competitive examination under the same auspices, and qualified as number two in a list of seventy successful candidates.

He began as an electrical engineer on board S.S. "China," became a physicist by the time he got on the transcontinental train, a mathematician when he graduated from Cornell University in 1914, and a student of that "empty subject" philosophy when he finished his doctorate at Harvard in 1918. Harvard sent him traveling around as "Sheldon Fellow," and, while thus freelancing at the University of California, he was offered a position to teach philosophy at the National University of Peking. Tao Mengho, who was then traveling in America, brought the offer to him in person. But Chao Yuenren thought that he had enough philosophy to last him for a while. So he went back to Cornell as instructor in physics. There he got interested in acoustics and watched his senior colleagues wading in miles of wire and calling that "wireless telephony." Then a cablegram came from Tsing Hua College, asking him to teach mathematics there. So he mimeographed a circular letter to bid goodbye to all his friends in America and returned to China, after having lived ten years in America.

Chao Yuenren made love to girls, or boasts to have. But he did not go very far with them, because he was engaged. Shortly after his parents' death, his older relatives arranged a match for him with a girl he had never seen nor could see. For his case was different from that of my fiancé, who was my first cousin. His fiancé was only a distant relative and should not of course be seen until unveiling night. What the engagement did to him, however, was only to strengthen his resolve to go abroad and stay abroad. He wrote from America to his folks to have the engagement broken. But they would not take him seriously. It was not done, not among the Chaos, any more than among the Yangs. So he remained abroad and made half-hearted (?) love to engaged girls.

But Chao Yuenren had few qualifications for being a lady's man. He passed ladies and gentlemen of his acquaintance on the street with equal absent-mindedness. That was how he acquired the title of "prof"—to rhyme with "cough"—a title he has held since his sophomore year at college. His suit was rarely pressed and his shoes were rarely shined. Once, when he was a student at Harvard, a street urchin walking behind him called out: "Hey! That guy needs a haircut!"

And it usually took more than one such reminder to send him to a barber shop.

When Chao Yuenren returned to China in 1920, he did not return sincerely. He got a leave of absence from Cornell to have a look at things, possibly to get his freedom, and would return to his job in America in a year's time. He had been thoroughly Americanized and wanted to live in America. He carried out his plan in making that return trip when the year was over. But something else happened that made him stay in China forever, or at least made him want to return to China every time he remained too long in America. I like to think that I contributed something to that something which repatriated the expatriate. But there had to be something already there that I could work on. He had to be a patriot to start with.

What is patriotism? Patriotism is your mother tongue. The reason why I am so thoroughly Chinese is because I speak nothing but the Chinese language. I have tried to speak Japanese and English and German, but whatever language I speak comes out Chinese in spirit. Anyone who wants to learn Chinese grammar can profit by studying the kind of English I speak. The reason why Chao Yuenren is so thoroughly Chinese is because he speaks the whole Chinese language. His mother spoke Mandarin; his first teacher taught him to read in the Changchow, Kiangsu dialect; when he interpreted for Russell in Hunan, the Hunanese asked him when he "had come back to the province"; when he visited Kwangtung province, they asked him where his home was in the Provincial City, i.e., Canton. He feels at home on every spot of the good earth because he is accepted everywhere as a part of it. This happy state of affairs, however, did not come about until he slowly grew into it. He had the right natural aptitudes, combined with his childhood experiences in varying dialect environments. But ten years away from the country was a serious interruption in the growth of the Chinese speaking patriot. He came back with an English-speaking and American-feeling mind.

I did not talk Chao Yuenren out of philosophy. A little philosophy is a harmless thing. But I think I talked him into Chinese linguistics. Not that I suggested to him a change of profession—I could not have done that. While I knew enough philosophy to disapprove of it, I did not even know that there was such a thing as phonetics, let alone linguistics. What I did was better than I knew or he knew. Remember that remark he made that time about one night's talk with me being better than ten years' study in America? We talked in Mandarin; we talked in the Hupeh dialect; we talked in the Yangchow dialect; we talked in the Shanghai dialect.[1] His accent was like that of a native; my accent was like that of a native of Nanking. But I spoke enough of each to revive his feeling for those dialects. He was happy to be with China. He had been urged by V. K. Ting, Hu Shih, and Chiang Monlin to turn his avocation to serious purposes. Linguistic Survey of China. Unification of the National Language. There was the job for him. Yes, come to think of it, these things had always turned over and over in his mind. Hadn't he guessed at the right time-pitch graphs of Chinese tones even as a child? Hadn't he taken time off for a course or two in phonetics at Cornell? It wouldn't be a change of profession; it was just a return to his old love. Why not come clean with a confession of it?

Thus, Chao Yuenren found his work and found his country. Because he found me.

I needed this rationalization badly, because I was leaving my own affairs in a terrible mess. What am I going to do with my hospital? What am I going to do with to do with my medicine? Those were my second thoughts when I left the Central Park that December morning.

---

[1] Curiously enough, I did not speak a word of the Shanghai dialect during all that time I was at McTyeire School. This was the first time my knowledge of the dialect came out of me aloud.

35

PLANS FOR LIVING

WHEN MY DAUGHTER Rulan sighed the other day over the perennial dilemma of marriage versus career, I scolded her roundly, because she only repeated old phrases, and old phrases could lead to nothing new. Moreover, she had no cause to worry. For, very soon afterwards, she got married, and both she and her husband Pian Hsuehhuang have been asked to teach at the same university in China. There is every prospect that they will live and work happily ever afterwards.

This is of course not what a mathematician would call a general solution. There are too many variables involved. Mine must have been a singular case, with indeterminate solutions.[1] As for young women in general, my advice to them is usually something like this. Get as much education and training as you can find opportunities for. Try to find work in your line for a while before getting married. Marriage and family will make serious inroads or interruptions in your work, and that cuts down on the chance of a woman's getting to the highest degree of eminence in the professions, but that is not the same thing as saying that no married woman can attain eminence or that a married woman has to give up all her work for all time. No woman need be ashamed to have acquired a major interest in the development of the family. But in proportion to the largeness of interest and outlook she has acquired in her formative years, she will be able to make the growth of the family a help, instead of a hindrance, to her own growth. By the time the children are off her

---

[1] I suspect that something has happened between text and translation here.—B.Y.C.

hands, she will find herself, not a back number in the larger society, but a prouder member of it.

Self-justification again. For now I get my largeness of interest and breadth of view when I take a look at my children standing in a row. Four daughters is a small family as Chinese families go, especially when there is no son, but it is a large family for us moderns. In the field of science, you do get out of date in the space of twenty-five revolutionary years. When I plunged into marriage, I knew what I was in for and what I was getting out of. I had to get out of practice, at least in my special line. I was both glad and sorry that I had been forced to specialize in gynecology and obstetrics: glad, because I hated the subject and did not find it so hard to give it up; sorry, because if I had had an opportunity to continue my interest in pathology or bacteriology, I might have been able to keep up some practice or research. Even dentistry or ophthalmology (another pet aversion of mine) could have been scheduled for less primitive hours of the day. When one or two of my daughters said that they wanted to go into medicine, I said:

"No, dears, you look almost as pretty as I did at your ages. The country needs more women doctors, to be sure, but leave it to the less marriageable ones."

Thus, thanks to my advice, Nova is still able to work in a chemical research laboratory after becoming Mrs. Huang P'eiyung.

Though I was trying to be reconciled to the desertion of my profession, I did not expect that it would come so suddenly. I had hoped to be able to run the hospital for a while longer and put it in better shape. But my colleague insisted that it should be wound up at once. We turned it over to Dr. Chu Chünkuo, whom I called Sister Hsiang, another classmate of ours in the Tokyo Women's Medical. The name of the hospital was changed to Chijen ("succeeding the two persons"). Yiwu left Peiping and me.² I moved to a courtyard apartment on Chienkar Hutung, in the same house with two British missionary ladies. Sister Hsiang still often called me in for consultation, but there were no more fifteen nights' consecutive midnight telephone calls. The only late telephone calls were from Yuenren, who sometimes called past eleven and talked until after midnight.

Yuenren could not yet marry me, since he was still engaged to that Miss Ch'en, whom he had never seen. I teased him by advising him to have a look at her before deciding, and I still tease him about his literally questionable taste. Since he had met my ex-fiancé Ch'eng in Peiping, and neither of us ever saw his fiancé, he did not know what he was missing, while I did know what I was missing. But he did not find this situation funny. For nothing was funny to Chao Yuenren that did not contain any Spoonerism or add anything to his budget of paradoxes.

Since both Yuenren and I had had bad luck with our engagements, we thought we had better not get engaged to each other. We found it such a wonderful thing to understand each other without words. When months afterwards he did say something more explicit, I did not even use the word "yes." There is no word for "yes" in the Chinese language, anyway.

What is it that brings man and woman together? In the first place, the man and woman, of course. Secondly, a common mother tongue in varying accents, as I have told you before, proved to be strong binder in our case. It is of course important that both should laugh at the same things. At first, we did not think that we did. I think people are funny; Yuenren finds fun in things and words. But when I made him more people-conscious and he made me more thing-conscious, we knew when a joke was coming and would both find fun in watching and classifying our audience. We rarely laugh at the wrong time, because we like and dislike the same people and things.

---

²She was subsequently married, and I met her only once, in 1934, after her marriage.

Over this glowing background, a throng of memories passed during the year 1921, which are easy enough to describe, but hard to express the feel of. I shall tell the events as they happened, but shall have to keep the feel to myself—to ourselves.

I had made grand plans with Kuanhung and I had made grand plans with Yiwu, but it was a different thing to make plans with Yuenren. We did not exactly plan, and we did not exactly drift, we grew in a generally agreed direction. As Yuenren often says, life is like mahjong. You start with a given hand, good, bad, or indifferent. At every turn, you see something new or receive something new. You act entirely on your own responsibility, though you are always strongly influenced by both your inheritance and your previous actions. Once in a while, somebody calls "p'ung!" and you are thrown back for one, two, or three plays. At other times, you are able to call "p'ung!" and get a break for yourself. The expert player is supposed to play hard hand. He would rather hurt himself than give others a chance to complete a *hu*, or "game." Yuenren's style is to play and let play. He likes to complete a big game himself if he can, but wants to see a big game completed, anyway, even if somebody else wins it at his expense.

Except that we were planning to be married soon, we had only rather vague ideas as to what our plans were going to be. Yuenren was going to change his profession, as I told you. He was going to be a linguist or philologist. I still cannot tell what the difference is. Anyway, it was not going to be philosophy, But after writing to his teacher William E. Hocking, he found that the only thing available for baking bread was philosophy—Harvard offered him an instructorship in philosophy. As I still had the illusion of continuing my medicine along theoretical lines, I thought it would be a good thing for me to go near the Harvard Medical School, even though I could not enter it.[3] So we decided to go to Cambridge, Massachusetts, after getting married.

---

[3] The first woman admitted into the Harvard Medical School was a Chinese woman doctor, who entered there in 1943.

"Let me introduce a new man to you," Yuenren said to me one day. "Now that I am going to America with a bride, I must tell my friends in America by writing them another circular letter. You will find a brand new man after you have seen the way I write my circular letters."

"I don't want to meet a new man," I said.

"What's your favorite color, Yunch'ing?" he asked, ignoring my remark.

"You know perfectly well I like green. What's yours?"

"You know perfectly well I hate green, he replied untruthfully. Thus began the series of Y. R. Chao's *Green Letters* which his friends look forward to receiving once every few years. As Norbert Wiener once said to Yuenren, "Every time your *Green Letter* arrives, it's a red-letter day for me."

The *Green Letters* are a sort of autobiography by installments—autoliargraphical notes, as he calls them. He starts with something like, "February 29, if it weren't 1925," and goes on to an account of his travels at the rate of 3,000 miles or a mile a page. With the inspiration of W. A. Hurwitz and R. W. King, he makes up proverbs, such as, "If you have nothing to say, don't say it well," or makes perversions of real proverbs like "Shrink before you squeak," or "Woo as you would be won by." After breaking out into some nonsense verse, he will have a few fantastic ideas about how the Chinese writing should be reformed or how music should be written in such a way that it will play back if you run the sheet through a machine like a player piano. Then he gets angry at British actors, because if they knew the Chinese tones their style of acting would not be so cramped. Sometimes, he concludes with a notice of change of address.

The *First Green Letter*, which was his second circular letter, was dated "February, March, or April, 1921." He came every day to my place at Chienkar Hutung and worked at it. We celebrated its completion by visiting the Temple of Heaven.

Then he started on his translation of *Alice's Adventures in Wonderland*. He took great pains in translating point for point. He assured me that it was an important book and that many philosophical works, including his own dissertation, quoted from it. This translation was Yuenren's maiden book. When it came out, I was happy to see a printed book with the name "Chao Yuenren" on its title page, especially as it was "dedicated to one who puts my heart into this book and into everything I do." I had no idea, nor had Yuenren, how such a book would be received. It did not become a best-seller, but it has gone through something like seventeen printings in twenty-five years, and its first edition has been sought by some American collectors. A parody by Shen Ts'ungwen, called *Alice's Adventures in China* (in Chinese), two volumes, appeared in 1928, Shanghai.

I believe in work by work and play by play. Yuenren says that that's an American superstition. He believes in work by play and play by work. He plays at his work and worries about his work while at play. This has been a common source of quarrel between us. When I wondered what the translation of *Alice in Wonderland* had to do with his plans, he said that it was the first book to write the Chinese language exactly as it was spoken. In 1921, Hu Shih's Literary Revolution was already four years, old, but Hu Shih continued to write in an intermediate style, in which literary expressions were used in a colloquial frame work. This book, which Hu Shih christened with the translation title of *Aliszu Manyu Ch'iching Chi*, was to be an exact phonographic reproduction of spoken Chinese. It was, Yuenren claimed, a philological document.

Came spring, 1921. I never approved of long engagements. That was why I broke my twenty-year engagement. Yuenren did not believe in long engagements either. So he went south[4] to break his fifteen-year engagement. He found an enlightened old gentleman Chao Chuchün, a mutual friend of both families, who was willing to

---

[4]People from Kiangsu and Chekiang always call their region "the south."

serve as a go-between in reverse. After some negotiations, it was settled for a settlement.

On the same trip, Yuenren visited his aunt by marriage, Mrs. Chao Inien, or "Amniang," in his old home in Changchow. She was pleased with the new developments and felt reassured that this foreign-educated girl could write such nice love letters in Chinese. I had forgotten that, according to the old custom, anybody in a family could open almost anybody else's letters, and I had written to Yuenren quite freely and addressed the letter, without a thought, to his aunt's care. She just opened it, as a natural thing.

After greeting me in a continuously American manner on his return, Yuenren showed me a gold-and-red leather box.

"This is your box, Yunch'ing," he said, as he handed it over to me. "My aunt Amniang and Cousine Hsin (Amniang's stepdaughter) said it belonged to my mother. Here is your key."

"Oh," I said, "just lay it there under the table. We'll look at it together some time."

We had to make up for so much lost talk that we forgot. about the box for several days. One evening, while Yuenren was with me, Sister Hsiang called and noticed the box under the table.

"What is in that beautiful box there?" she asked.

That reminded me. I took my key, opened the box, and found a gorgeous cover for a bride's coiffure, made up entirely of pearls. There were also two jade bracelets, a few small gold ingots, and other jewelry.

"Has the box been lying around just like that all this time?" Sister Hsiang asked. "Lucky thing it didn't get stolen!"

"I had no idea what was in it," I said.

"This is of course the gift from the Chao family for your engagement," she said.

"We were already engaged," Yuenren and I replied in unison. "We don't need any more engagements."

Yuenren made another of his speeches against tradition. If the jewelry had been turned into cash, what a better time he would have had in school! He would not have had to write from Nanking to his aunt Amniang or Cousine Hsin every time he needed a book the size of a Webster's *Collegiate Dictionary*. He might even have got stuck if he hadn't had the luck of getting a scholarship. But Sister Hsiang, who was a sort of big sister to us, explained to Yuenren that his mother's things were none of his business. They rightfully belonged to the daughter-in-law, and Amniang and Cousine Hsin had acted faithfully in having safeguarded the property until it found its owner.

"All right," said I, the owner, or owner-soon, "we will try to turn this into cash, and contribute it to our traveling budget."

Ordinarily, it would be a mark of unfilialness even for a daughter-in-law to change her jewelry into change. She is supposed to keep it for her daughter-in-law, and so on from generation to generation. But rational-minded Yuenren was not a filial son and promptly seconded my motion. I only kept a few of the rounder pearls for a bracelet and some jewels for a pair of earrings for memory's sake. Our decision proved to be of considerable help in riding over our later difficulties.

36

"NEW-STYLE WEDDING OF NEW-STYLE PEOPLE"

NOW THAT YUENREN and I had both broken our engagements, we were ready to get married. But who should marry us? How should we be married? Who was to give me away? Or should we have a wedding? Yuenren had been staying in the same house with Bertrand Russell and Dora Black. Like them, he wanted to put every tradition and institution under critical doubt. He hated the current tendencies toward what he called "meaningless manners and foolish flummery." I knew what correct manners were, but did not care to observe them; he did not even bother to know them. So we agreed to take the law in our own hands and planned to be married without a wedding.

While we were going over our plans for the announcements, photographs, and other details of our no wedding, came Yuenren's Cornell schoolmate H. C. Zen, himself newly wedded to Sophia Ch'en, both of them new-thinking people. He approved in principle of our plans for no wedding, but advised us to observe the minimum legal requirements. All we needed to do to satisfy the law was to have at least two witnesses and a paper, in any form, with a fifty-cent stamp-tax stamp on it. That was all that would be necessary. He had no doubt of our taking serious things seriously. But in order not to lead irresponsible young people into being more irresponsible, he advised us to be more self-conscious about being leaders of the new generation.

While our idea was to combine simplicity with originality, we got into some rather elaborate simplifications. There were to be no studio-posed photographs. So we made several trips to the Central Park with a kodak and a self-timer, and finally chose, among a number of snapshots, one taken under the Pavilion of Mottoes.[1] Yuenren drafted and redrafted an announcement in the style of his *Green Letters*, in a half-formal, half-scientific language. It informed our friends and relatives that, on receipt of the announcement, our wedding would already have taken place at 3 p.m., Mean Solar 120° E Standard Time, June 1, 1921, Occidental Chronology. Absolutely no gifts would be accepted except in the form of letters, literary or musical compositions, or contributions to the Science Society of China. Like Yuenren's *Green Letters*, our wedding announcement ended with a notice of change of address.

Our wedding did consist largely of a change of address. I moved house from 14 Chienkar Hutung and Yuenren moved house from 2 Suianpo Hutung, both to 49 Hsiao Yapao Hutung. We spent our wedding day in moving furniture around, dusting books, and getting pots and pans in order. At the announced wedding hour, we were actually in the post office, mailing our announcements and photographs.

As to the formal "no ceremony," I shall let one of our witnesses tell the story in his own words. This is what Hu Shih has to say about that day:

"Chao Yuenren often came to my house and had long discussions about phonology and romanization, as we used to do during our school days at Cornell. Then I noticed that his calls became less frequent and our discussions less thorough. At the same time, I also

---

[1] The visible parts of the inscriptions in the photograph chosen (see photograph section) are as follows:
"These are the words of [Wang] Yangming:
'Knowledge is the beginning of action;
Action is the completion of knowledge.'
"These are the words of the (ancient) *Red Book*:
'Those who put reverence above indolence prosper;
Those who put indolence above reverence perish.'"

noticed that he had been going around with my fellow provincial Miss Yang Buwei Yunch'ing. One day Yuenren telephoned to me and asked if I would be free the next evening to have supper with him and Miss Yang, and one other friend, Miss Chu Chünkuo,[2] at 49 Hsiao Yapao Hutung. Since there was no restaurant or club in that part of the city, I began to suspect what was coming. Just to be prepared, I got out a copy of the *Dream of the Red Chamber*, an edition containing my commentaries, and had it gift-wrapped. But in case I guessed wrong, I had it wrapped in plain paper outside.

"It was a cozy little supper for four in a cozy little house. There were four tasty dishes, prepared by Miss Yang herself, served in the style of an informal meal. After tea, Yuenren took out a paper in his handwriting and said that he and Yunch'ing would be honored if Dr. Chu and I would sign as witnesses. Thus Chao Yuenren and Yang Buwei were married. I was the first to present the couple with a gift."

The next day, the *Ch'en Pao* came out with a headline, "New-Style Wedding of New-Style People." When Yuenren asked Russell whether he thought we were too conservative, he replied: "This is radical enough." When the announcement reached Professor George Van Biesbroek of Yerkes Observatory, Williamsbay, Wisconsin, he posted it on the Observatory bulletin board to show his colleagues what had happened on June 21, 1921 at 3 p.m., Mean Solar 120 ° E Standard Time. Young people began to adopt weddings àla Chao Yuenren. Actually, their weddings have in all cases—not excepting those of our own daughters—turned out to be much more elaborate than ours. For no wedding ceremony could be as simple as our no wedding ceremony. One Chinese couple in America had a wedding which almost approached ours in simplicity. But on their return to Shanghai, the girl's family had them go through a full-scale wedding again, with a flowery sedan chair and all.

---

[2]That is, my classmate Sister Hsiang.—B.Y.C.

Our radicalism offended some people we did not mean to. Yuen-ren's aunt Niung sent a flower basket. It was returned, since it was not a "literary or musical composition." We have regretted it ever since. Big Uncle, who had always disapproved of my marrying after breaking my engagement, was greatly embarrassed because, just after he had told his friends that he did not know when and where his daughter-niece was going to be married, everybody received the announcement, some even earlier than he did.

We new-style people had abolished the kowtow to the ancestors. We had abolished noisy drinking and feasting. We had also abolished the mystery and suspense of the unveiling. Was that a gain? Sometimes, I wonder what it would feel like an old-style bride, suddenly and completely given to a man she had never seen in her life. I certainly wouldn't like to take any chances with a stranger. But if I had been previously assured by the gods that he was still to be he and I I, would I have exchanged a year's time together for the excitement of love at first night? No, probably. What can be more exciting than the sudden awakening to mutuality, after months of acquaintance from "a bystander's point of view"? There is no graduation in the school of love. There are many commencement festivities.

37

HONEYMOON POSTPONED

SINCE WE HAD no wedding, we had no honeymoon. We told our friends that we were going away for a month, but actually stayed in the house in shirt sleeves and aprons, arranging furniture and preparing for our honeymoon in America. We had thought of favorite resorts like Tsingtao and West Lake, but decided to "see America first."

Few knew where we were. But one day, we were awakened from our noonday nap by persistent ringing of the doorbell. I looked out of the window and saw Hu Shih and another gentleman talking with our ricksha boy, who was doing a bad job of not knowing where we were. Seeing that he could not continue like that much longer, I called out: "Hello, we'll be right down!"

"Sorry to disturb you, friends," Hu Shih said. "If you spare a few moments from under that moon, here is something new under the sun."

We were introduced to Mr. Sun Chuang, manager of the Peiping branch of the Commercial Press. He had been instructed by his main office in Shanghai to ask Yuenren to prepare a textbook for the newly standardized National Language, and then to speak for a set of phonograph records, to be made by the Columbia Phonograph Company at New York. Yuenren accepted the offer at once. The standard of pronunciation,[1] it was officially fixed them, was a compromise of

---

[1] Revised, in 1932, in favor of a system of pronunciation which is practically the same as that of Peiping.—Y.R.C.

Peiping pronunciation and a few southern characteristics, like the broad *o* for *ê* and the use of the so-called 5th Tone. Yuenren seemed to be the only person who could speak this artificial language. It sounded like his imitation of my kind of Mandarin, tinged with a strong Nanking accent. A previous attempt at record making by another company had not been successful, because the speaker, who was a native of Peiping, had made a mess of the artificial modifications. So they decided to find a virtuoso like Yuenren to speak a language that did not exist.

This new job made us doubly busy, because, after it was known that we were "back" in town, everybody began to come to see us. We had to start making up for the missing wedding banquet in installments. It was certainly fun to have a number of small parties of six or ten, but, so far as Yuenren's idea of saving trouble was concerned, I often wonder whether it would not take less time and energy after all, if a new couple entertained all their friends and relatives at one big wedding party and had it over with.

Yuenren knew next to nothing about entertaining. His idea of meeting people at a meal was to eat when it was eating time. I had eaten beautiful foreign-style meals with him when he was staying in the same house with Bertrand Russell. I learned later that it was due to the alertness of the cook who had learned that Mr. Chao was likely to have guests at any time at short or no notice.

We had a small roof garden over our house, on which we had "mad tea parties" and club meetings. Once, Yuenren invited the Peiping members of the Science Society of China to a meeting. I was going out to the hospital to see about some unfinished business there and asked him whether I had better buy some refreshments on my way home. He said never mind, he would see about them himself. I came back just in time for the meeting. Yuenren read a paper "On the Physical Nature of Chinese Tones."

After everybody had had their second or third cup of tea, V. K. Ting asked: "Yuenren, where are your refreshments? We are hungry."

"Oh," said Yuenren. He went down and was soon back on the roof with two little boxes of Zu Zu cookies, which he served around from the paper boxes, without a plate or tray.

"Is that all?" asked V. K.

"This is my favorite brand," Yuenren replied, as relevantly as the March Hare said: "This is the best butter."

He had been preparing his paper all the time I was away and forgot all about the refreshments. What both exasperated and reassured me was the fact that he was not even embarrassed about it. We still had much to learn from each other about how to have company.

We had to make a number of changes in our plans. Both Yuenren and I had enjoyed traveling on the Yangtze River but had never done it together. So we planned to go down to Hankow by train and then down the river by boat to Shanghai where we were going to sail for America on the S.S. "Monteagle." But civil war broke out in Hupeh and Hankow was cut off. So we had to go by the Tientsin-Pukow Railway. That was cut off by a flood. So we had to take a coastwise ship from Tientsin to Shanghai.

We left Peiping with a big sendoff party at the East Station. Big Uncle was among those who saw us off "Don't forget to bring back an American gold watch for me," he said to Yuenren and me. "This watch I bought in England forty years ago is a little too old. See if you can prove that they make better things in your America than in my England!"

That was the last I saw of Big Uncle, and I am glad that we parted reconciled.

I was violently seasick on board the S.S. "Tungchow." Arriving at Shanghai too late to catch our boat, we had to forfeit one fourth of the fare for our late cancellation. That cut very deeply into our already very tight budget. The only thing available for that time was a Japanese boat, "Siberia Maru," and we had to take what we could get.

Ordinarily, I became a well person the moment I stepped on firm land, no matter how seasick or trainsick I had been. But this time, I found that the room in Burlington Hotel in Shanghai still smelled like a steamship. Yuenren said it was my imagination. I carried my seasickness from one ship to another when I got on board "Siberia Maru" even before it cast off. Hu Shih, Lin Pingnan, Kao Mengtan of the Commercial Press, and others came on board to see us off. I ordered some soft drinks for everybody.

Noticing the way I played with drinking and not drinking the lemon soda, Hu Shih said: "Dr. Yang, I may be speaking out of turn. But I don't think you are seasick. Could it be that you are *hsi*-sick?"[2]

I had been pretty quick in diagnosing other women's cases, but I had never done any diagnosis from an introspective point of view. If this was it, it would mean another change in my plans. I should have to go to America purely as a housewife and come in contact with medical practice from the wrong end of the stethoscope. I had preached to young women in China against leaving their children to nurses and servants, who knew nothing about hygiene or education. I had not imagined that I would be called upon to practice what I preached, and so soon.

Thus, after changing from one plan to another, Yuenren and I sailed out on our delayed honeymoon trip over the Pacific Ocean towards America.

---

[2] To have hsi, "gladness," means to be with child.

38

IN AMERICA

THE FIRST DAY I stepped on American soil with Yuenren, I was welcomed by a bee. It flew into the taxi while we were driving up one of those steep turns to the Pali cliff of Honolulu. It was a good thing that it liked my face better than that of the driver, otherwise we should have come down much faster than expected.

Everything looked gay in Honolulu, especially those incredible fishes of the Aquarium. The people looked as if they were. having a holiday, though it was just an ordinary day. Yuenren told me that this was not a typical American place, and that some people on the continent often forgot that it was a United States territory.

Now that the voyage was more than half over, and I had, about passed my period of "*hsi*-sickness," I took more than passing interest in the store windows and went into a hat store. A high soprano of a salesgirl waited on me. Unconsciously, I pitched my voice in the same key as hers. After picking out a wide-rimmed hat, fit for a pourer at tea, I said, as I looked at myself in the mirror, "I think I'll take this one." Then, turning to Yuenren, I said in Chinese, "How do you like this one, Yuenren?"

Yuenren exploded into laughter, which puzzled both me and the salesgirl. He had been trying to restrain his laughter while I was talking in that charming high voice in English. Then, when I suddenly dropped to my natural voice, a whole octave below, when I switched over to Chinese, it was the last straw for him. But I was too pitch-unconscious to realize what I had done.

San Francisco was much more like what I thought America was like. I was almost surprised to find it so familiar. When we entered a restaurant and a headwaiter beckoned us to a table, I could swear that we had been there before. But where? I had never been to a restaurant in America. Then it dawned on me that it was the kind of scene I had seen many times in the movies.

Having seen scores of American movies may have taken some of the strangeness and freshness out of my first sight of America. But the actual give and take of living in America was of course a different matter. One engineer friend of Yuenren's, Mr. Louis Ross, invited us to eat at a cafeteria. My idea of a foreign style meal was still that of the *ta-ts'ai*, or "big dinner," served in China to Chinese patrons, with one course after another without end. The long menus on the steamship had not been very informative, either, as to what everyday meals were like in America. As I passed the winding counters with their colorful and tempting preparations, I filled my tray in no time and had to borrow space from Yuenren's tray. I took a couple of appetizers, a soup, a fish, a steak, an egg salad, a dessert, a large piece of watermelon, a soft drink, and a glass of iced tea. The various kinds of bread were too tempting not to try some of. Yuenren and Mr. Ross followed me and smiled, but placed very little on their trays. Yuenren did not even take a main dish. As he had anticipated, I could not finish eating even one-half of what I took, and, after pooling our resources at the table, we still had quite a lot of leftovers. It was not that I had overestimated my appetite. I had simply tried to reconstruct a regular *ta-ts'ai* from cafeteria. It had not occurred to me that, in the busy American life of quick lunches, variety had to be compensated by quantity.

I got an idea from this experience, or rather after a repetition of such experiences, before I finally learned. Instead of adding to the number of dishes almost indefinitely as the number of guests increase, as is the practice with Chinese dinners, why not stop with a reasonable number of dishes, say six, for the guests to share, and then merely increase the quantity with increase in the number of guests?

So this was the first idea I learned from America which I carried back on my subsequent return to China.

Though I did not order several main dishes at a meal on the transcontinental train, our funds were getting lower and lower as we traveled eastward. From Chicago, Yuenren telegraphed to his former Conant Hall roommate C. H. Hu, who was then an interne at the Harvard Medical School, to meet us at South Station, Boston, with thirty dollars, please. That gave Dr. Hu, enough of a hint. So he got a student room for us near Central Square, Cambridge, instead of reserving a hotel room.

A rooming house in Cambridge was an appropriate place for us in more respects than one. In the first place, it was within our means of that time—if that. Secondly, it gave me a totally different idea of American cities and American houses. There was not the foreign glamor, with its imperialistic associations, with which I had usually imagined foreign cities. Cambridge seemed less foreign to me than even lower Nanking Road or the Bund of Shanghai. The very drabness of the place seemed to make it countryless, at least to me, whose idea of America had been chiefly from the early-day movies. Moreover, there has always been a rather large Chinese student colony in Cambridge, which has made my children remark that, when in Cambridge, they always forget whether they are in America or in China.

Since I spoke very little English, Yuenren would not trust me with myself on the street, lest I should get lost. One day he had gone out looking for a house nearer Harvard. After a while, I bored and walked out of the house. One turn to the left, another turn to the right, and I was on a big street. There I introduced myself to my favorite resort in America, the Five and Ten Cent Store. I had read about it in books like *Guide to Studying in America*, but the real thing was even more wonderful to me. I browsed at one counter after another, until I had all I could hold for a little over two dollars. I retraced my steps and met Yuenren just coming out of the house.

"What a big scare you gave me!" he complained. "Where have you been?"

I showed him the packages.

"How did you buy so many things without knowing their names in English?" he wondered.

"I didn't have to know their names," I said. "I just pointed at the things and told them to give me some of this and give me some of that—"

"Some of *these* and some of *those*," he corrected me.

"No, that's too hard for me. But I got what I wanted, didn't I?"

After this little scrap, Yuenren told me that he had found a flat at 7 Francis Avenue, which Professor William McDougall was willing to sublet to us. Yuenren called it the "House of More Than Seven Gables," since our flat was on the third floor, on which every room had one or more corners cut off. Since we had no money to buy furniture, we spread our beddings on the floor, Japanese fashion. It lessened the chance of bumping our heads against the low corners. Seeing that no furniture was being moved in for several days, the McDougalls lent us a very welcome mattress. I had kept house on the floor before, when I first went to Japan. But I could not imagine a household without a proper kitchen. We had to use a small electric stove, which was rather unsuited to Chinese cooking. For our first meal, I boiled rice, Changchow fashion, that is, very soft. I unpacked the Kalgan dried mushrooms I had brought and made clear-soup mushroom pork with soy sauce. When Yuenren came back from outside and got a whiff of the flavors over the stairs, he said: "Mm—this smells like home!"

So, in this humble sort of atmosphere, we started our homemaking in my first, and Yuenren's second, sojourn in America.

39

THE SMALL FAMILY

A WHILE AGO, I was enlarging on the importance of taking a larger view of life when a married woman has to go through a period of restriction or interruption of activities in the larger world. But this advice is more easily given than followed. In an old-fashioned large family, such as I was raised in at Yenling Hsiang, though the chief activities were centered around the welfare of the clan, I did find quite a world of people and affairs to move about in, especially as we children, and even some of the younger wives, did not have any responsibilities for the management and economy of the household. Now that I had traveled ten thousand miles to a New World, I found myself thinking more and more like the narrow-minded housewife that I had hitherto looked down upon. Pots and pans were among the first things I picked out from the counters of the "Five and Ten." And, of course, there was always the problem of the wherewithal to fill my pots and pans.

Didn't I say that there was some philosophy at Harvard that could bake bread? Yes, but Yuenren had thought that he had better devote as much time as possible to the study of linguistics and to the preparation of his National Language Records, and, from San Francisco, he had telegraphed to Harvard that he could not teach full time. For the first few months, we had to pawn some foxes and a sable coat to supplement our self-imposed salary-cut in order to get along. I also laid out some capital for a rented sewing machine to make some handbags and tea sets parts out of parts of Mandarin coats and things I had brought.

One evening, while I was all alone and felt a sort of—well, you know[1]—I kept working on the sewing machine so as to make some noise to keep me company. Next morning, Mrs. McDougall asked me what all that noise was. When she came upstairs and saw the beautiful things lying around in my scantily furnished apartment, she suggested arranging a tea party for me. She was also attracted by my squirrel coat and wished to have it exhibited, if I was willing to have it included too, which I was. Even Dr. C. H. Hu lent a hand at sewing when he called. The William E. Hockings helped by introducing the things I made to the Harvard "Coop."

Yuenren had been contributing to the noises of the apartment by rehearsing loudly the text of his language records. For those were still the days of acoustic recording, for which one had to talk very loudly to make any impression on the wax disc. When he was ready, he went to New York for a preliminary recording. He returned two days sooner than planned, because he suddenly remembered that he had left only a five-dollar bill with me and was afraid that it wouldn't last any longer—he always remembers things suddenly. When he got back, I showed him a good-looking check, besides some cash, from sales. We bought some more furniture to make our rooms look less empty. We also planned to see something of America before I would have to stay put.

For the first time, I took a patient's point of view in an obstetrics case, when I visited a doctor in Cambridge. I got permission from him to visit New York. But I did not tell him that my program included a climb up the Statue of Liberty and a ride on top of a Fifth Avenue bus from Washington Square to Riverside Drive. It was pretty late in my year to still climb up the 168 steps inside the statue, but I came down none the worse for it. The ride on the open top of the bus on a January day, however, gave me a bad cold and Yuenren a worse one.

---

[1] Yes, I know. Cf. my footnote, p. 45.—Y.R.C.

Going from Cambridge to New York is somehow so like going from Nanking to Shanghai, that I often make the mistake of saying "Shanghai" when I mean "New York." Likewise, I have learned to paraphrase a popular comment about Shanghai and say that New York is a nice place to visit occasionally, but that I wouldn't like to live there all the time. It probably all depends upon how and where you live in New York and whom you see and what you do there. As I knew it better and better after different visits, I decided that New York was like a versatile person whom you learn to know only by meeting him on a variety of occasions, on business, at a social, at play, or even in a quarrel. There is no one New York. The New York I visited this time was to me an American playground—even though I did not go to Coney Island. It did not seem at all strange to me because, even more than San Francisco, it reminded me of typical scenes in the movies I had seen before.

I liked New York well enough to want to visit it again with Yuenren on another of his recording trips to the Columbia Phonograph Company there. But this time, my doctor put a veto on it.

"You are a doctor, and you ought to know," he said with finality.

I did find life heavier and heavier, and we moved to a small regular flat at 3 Sacramento Place, where I had only one flight to climb. Above and below us lived two Negro families, with ourselves representing the yellow color in the middle. Dr. C. H. Hu called the combination a "caramel of a house." Some American friends said that we should not live with colored people. I did not understand what they meant until I learned that yellow and red were not colors, but that black was.[2]

---

[2] Chiang Monlin told me the story that when he visited the South, he purposely sat in the sections in buses and cars marked "colored" to see what would happen. The conductor would not listen to him when he insisted that he was colored.

Three Sacramento Place is a place to remember because it is one of the places which ring familiar in my ears without effort of memory. A large kitchen, a bed room, a dining room, a study sitting room, and a back porch (which was at its best when looked out from), and a long stay gave me a first and lasting idea of home in the American sense of the small-family home. But above all, it was only when the size of my family became doubled, and finally trebled, that I appreciated the full sense of the term "small family." However, one "thing" at a time—I was not going to have twins.

Yuenren went to New York for the final recording of his language lessons. I worked some more on my sewing machine, though I did not have to work so hard any more, as Yuenren was back on full-time teaching in the second semester, and some payments began to come from the publisher on the book and records. But you know you always like to finish a piece of work when it seems to be nearly done, especially when you are alone. Yuenren arrived late at night and tried to share with me his experiences in the city and in the studio. I felt tired and unusual. Did I eat anything wrong? It must have been a strange variety of indigestion. Did I work too much on the sewing machine? My foot was not sore, but my back was.

""Back sore." That sounded familiar. As I said, "This is it," I had a fleeting sense of elation over the fact that henceforth my view of the profession would always be broader than that which any man doctor could have. However, I still had to tell Yuenren to call up the man doctor. The doctor came and sent me to the Cambridge Hospital.

I feel very much tempted to dwell on a comparison of medical practice in America and in China (new style), such as the readiness to use anesthesia and instrumental aid in America, and the conservatism of dietetic routine, each country in its own way. For I did take an intermittent interest in the first American hospital of which I had a real closeup view. But the birth of my first daughter, and my first child, was such a big event that I cannot wait to go on with memories of seeing her grow.

40

IRIS AND NOVA

MY FIRST DAUGHTER'S name is Rulan, but she is called Iris. *Ru* means in Chinese "like, as," and *lan* means "Orchid," which is part of my name "Lansien," the name Auntie "used to call me by. Since an iris is something which looks like an orchid, "Rulan" could very well be translated into English as "Iris." But somehow it happens that most Chinese call her "Iris" and most Americans call her "Rulan." A foreign flower, from either point of view, is always more exotic.

Yuenren sent announcements of Iris's birth to all friends. One of them was sent to Bertrand Russell, who had then returned to England. One of the lectures Yuenren had interpreted for him in Peiping was entitled "Causes of the Present Chaos in China." When he received Yuenren's letter saying that the 400,000,001st member of the Chinese population had arrived in our family, he replied: "Congratulations! Now I see that you are among the 'Causes of the Present Chaos in China'!"

"But no," said William McDougall, of another school of British thought, when I showed him Russell's note. "Since Rulan was born in Cambridge, Massachusetts, she is an American citizen and will become the first woman president of the United States."

Whether in China or in America, we did introduce more chaos in our home. When I returned to the house from the hospital, I found it full of a number of things, so full that I could hardly open the door. There was a cabinet-model phonograph, which Yuenren had bought while I was in the hospital, to give Iris an early start in music appreciation. There were more dishes than the sink could hold. A pile of broken dishes was found on the floor near the back door. The delivery man had knocked them over trying to open the door. Yuenren had tried to wash dishes like an American husband, but with doubtful results. Sometimes he would rather come home with new dishes from the Five and Ten than wash the dishes we already had. When I was in the hospital, he did that as a regular thing. After we had collected some three hundred pieces in this way, we needed to wash dishes only once a week or even longer. If Dr. C. H. Hu dropped in, he would don an apron and give us a holiday. Those were days long before the diaper service came into vogue. We thought of trying the same technique as we did with the dishes, but did not find it advisable to go very far with it.

When Yuenren minded the baby or took part in other household chores, there were certain matters of principle on which he would not compromise. A piece of music was not to be interrupted under any circumstances. If the baby needed a change when he had just started something on the piano, say Beethoven's Fifth, then priority had to be given to the cultivation of the child's musical taste. All other things could wait. Before Iris was a year old, she knew the Fifth so well that whenever anybody whistled or played:

she would answer, with wide staring eyes:

"Da da da da!"

Iris is now going to teach music at a Chinese university.

Another thing Yuenren insisted on was that no error in my English pronunciation or grammar should go uncorrected, no matter what I was doing at the moment. I found that heavy housekeeping with a baby was a full-time job. It not only left no time for learning grammar from books, but also left no time for learning grammar from social contacts, except with the delivery man. We did go to the movies, but they were silent.

On our later trips to America, Yuenren sometimes asked me if I had wished I had let the house go more dusty and the dishes less shiny and used the time thus saved in knowing my English better and my America better—

"My husband better, you mean," I retorted. Yuenren made no remark to that.

Now, my reply was that, had the standard of household hygiene been any lower than it already was, we might not have lived long enough to enjoy any more trips to America. Better live in a healthy place with broken English than in a place full of germs and correct English.

Like some of the other adjustments Yuenren and I have had to make, my language adventures resulted in something which is neither one thing nor the other. I made little headway with my grammar and ended with remembering only the rule that "the plural of a noun ending in *y* is formed by changing the *y* into *i-e-s*," which I had learned many years before I met Yuenren. But I am a fairly good pronouncer and finally learned to speak in public or even to broadcast from Yuenren's text. The result is sometimes surprising to Americans, because, just after a brief conversation has led my interlocuter to admire my perfect command of English, I am likely to come out with an inverted relative clause that he cannot even understand.

One thing that Yuenren still has to learn about me is that I do not believe in "knowledge for its own sake." I believe in doing things, and if I find that I have to know certain things for doing a thing, I can pick up the necessary knowledge while doing it. So, instead of learning English, I started translating a book, though I could not read much of it.

Shortly before I returned to China from Japan, Margaret Sanger had made a lecture tour in China, and aroused a great deal of interest in problems of womanhood. One of her books which seemed small enough to go through without too great difficulty was *What Every Girl Should Know*. So, this time, I took an English-Chinese dictionary and started to translate the book into Chinese.

You can get an idea of my style from the way I translated the term "ova," of which a woman is supposed to have two thousand in her system. The dictionary meaning given was the literary word *luan*. Since I was writing my translations in the modern colloquial, I wrote down, without giving the matter a thought, that every woman had in her two thousand *chi-tser*. I forgot in my hurry that although *chi-tser* is the usual term for "eggs" as a kind of food, it means literally "hen's eggs." It has since been a standing joke in our family to ask whether it was hen's eggs or duck's eggs whenever a question of translation arises.

After the manuscript was duly edited by Yuenren, it was published by the Commercial Press in 1924. It had a fairly good sale. A copy of it had found its way to Rome when, several years later, a friend of ours sent it to her daughter there as a wedding gift.

I had a brief period of relative leisure for translating that book and going to the movies. Our Sacramento Place neighbors helped by minding the baby. Nine-year-old Margaret came first and was surprised to find that the Chinese baby cried in English, since she cried in exactly the same way as an American baby did. Then came ten-year-old Marie, who would like to take care of a crying baby.

My period of relative leisure, however, was quite intermittent and brief. Not long after Iris's first birthday, there was a new arrival, and the size of the small family became doubled from what it started with.

Nova was the biggest girl among her contemporaries in the Symmes Arlington Hospital. She was about the most homely infant I had ever seen during all my professional life, with one big eye nearly an inch higher than the other big eye. Everything seemed out of proportion. But being her mother, I had to love her. As Yuenren took over the care of Rulan, I took care of Nova. When Dr. C.H. Hu called, he played all the time with Rulan and would not even look at Nova. While Iris started at eight months to say "da da da da da da da da" all day and invented the vowel sound "ö," which exists neither in Chinese nor in English, Nova was silent and glum even after she was two years old. But there is a compensation in everything. Years later, when our family was trebled, Dr. Hu had to admit apologetically that Nova was about the prettiest girl of the quartet. Incidentally, she became the most talkative member of the family—not even excepting myself.

41

THE EUROPEAN PLAN

THREE YEARS WAS the longest time I had stayed at the same address since I left Yenling Hsiang for Japan. The heavy housekeeping of a two-baby household was getting to be a great burden. As I was sure that I could not resume any medical activity under the circumstances, I became more and more restless. But I also understood by then that a married woman's plans were whatever her husband's plans were, at least so far as the locality of work was concerned. Yuenren was fortunate to have his instructorship in philosophy changed to one in Chinese, which had the advantages of both being nearer to his new interest and of requiring very little preparation. As American universities usually let their staff members audit any course that the teacher in charge permits, he made full use of this privilege by practically taking a second graduate course at Harvard. He audited courses in linguistics almost full time, even taking in half a dozen courses in music on the side. He would like to spend some time in Europe to round out his studies. But the question was, How? I was thinking of leaving him in Europe and taking the children back to China first, so that I could have servants to take the load off my housework. But Yuenren would not consider it. So our European plan had to remain only a plan.

Finally, luck came our way. Having got tired of being the only person who could speak the artificial National Language, Yuenren persuaded the Commercial Press to invest in his prediction that the government would ultimately come to recognize the natural system of pronunciation of Peiping as the national standard. He convinced them that it would be good business to have a second series of language records made in anticipation of the change. Thus originated his *Phonograph Course in the Chinese National Language (for Foreigners)*, Shanghai, 1925.

A second source of financial help came from an invitation to Yuenren by the Southeastern University (later National Central University) to teach there, and, almost simultaneously, one from Tsing Hua University, to teach there. Both places offered him a subsidy for traveling in Europe before returning to China. We debated night after night which place to go to: Nanking or Peiping. Nanking was the city of my Yenling Hsiang home and only three hours from Yuenren's Changchow home. Peiping was the place of our little prehistory and our first new home. Again, it was the husband's job that was the deciding factor. The offer from the Southeastern University was for reorganizing the Department of Western Languages and Literature. The offer from Tsing Hua was a research professorship in an Institute of Chinese Studies, soon, to be organized when Tsing Hua was to be changed from a preparatory school into a university. As Yuenren had been planning to introduce modern methods into Chinese studies, he accepted the offer from Tsing Hua.

Yuenren's former teacher, Professor James H. Woods, was sorry to see us go. He had arranged lectures on Chinese music for Yuenren to give in order to arouse public interest in China. He got the Chinese courses started for Yuenren and even took them himself. He was instrumental in getting the Charles Hall Foundation for Harvard, from which the Harvard-Yenching Institute grew into a leading center of Far Eastern studies in America. But Yuenren did not take part in the work of that institute until many years later. When it was getting started, Professor Woods said to Yuenren: "Chao, now you can write your *Dictionary of Modern Chinese*, as you have always wanted to."

But Yuenren wanted to return and survey the Chinese dialects instead. So he recommended K. T. Mei, another Harvard man, to succeed him in teaching Chinese.

Though I looked forward to the excitement of visiting another continent and returning to Peiping, I lingered enough to wonder to

Yuenren, "Is this going to be really goodbye to Cambridge and America?" I often wonder what I would have felt in such situations if I had known that I was going to make my home at Cambridge again for six years. Perhaps life is more fun as it is, than if memory worked backwards.

Before leaving the United States in the spring of 1924, I made one more gesture of keeping up my medicine by interviewing Margaret Sanger and visiting birth control institutions in New York. I had noticed that in China, as in the West, birth control was practiced by the wrong end of society. Those who had access to and made use of knowledge of contraception were mainly those who can and should bear the burden of bringing up large families. While I do not believe in any significant difference in inheritance between classes, the better-to-do certainly have better chances of educating their children. How could I reach the masses, for whom more children would mean only more slave labor? I carried this line of questioning with me for some time, until I tried some answers after I returned to Peiping.

In New York, we put up in grand style at the Hotel Commodore, with clam bouillon for breakfast, served in a silver tureen. America stands for equality and material comforts. So we booked passage in a nice little one-class boat, S.S. "Orbita," which was both small and wide and steady and slow. As I could not begin to get my sea legs in less than a week, I had a chance to get some of my trip's worth on a nine-day boat.

Leaving New York Harbor was even more of an experience than entering the Golden Gate. After the crowd of people waving handkerchiefs on the dock were no longer distinguishable, the scene seemed to be repeated once more by the friendly tall buildings waving smoke and mist along the skyline, with the Statue of Liberty standing far out at the end of the dock, also waving goodbye to us in her dignified way. When you get to know a place, you see much more than what actually meets your eye. You don't really visualize more, but you feel a great lot more behind there.

42

HURRIED TOURS

ALTHOUGH I HAD been won over to many American ways of life, I looked forward with some excitement to the first sight of England, which had been my first idea of a typical Western country. I was not prepared, so far as external appearances were concerned, for the anticlimax of seeing Southampton and London so soon after leaving New York. Another surprise was the familiarity of the scene at the dock and the railway stations. Certainly I had never been in England before, and I had not seen any British movies that I could remember. When I entered the train and got a whiff of that characteristic smell, then I began to remember. It was simply the prototype of the Shanghai-Nanking Railway, which had been built by the British with British equipment, painted with British paint.

Our plans were to "do" Europe in the summer and settle down to study in the fall. Our urgent problem was to find a suitable place where we could leave the children, as traveling about would be a burden both on them and on ourselves. We made the mistake of using a social introduction for purposes of getting practical help. When we called on a certain Dr. Head, to whom we had an introduction, he told us that "the thing to do" was to wait for his invitation and come to tea. We heard that living was cheaper in France and that there was an Association Amicale Franco-chinoise, which could help us. So we crossed the channel to Paris.

Although I did not speak a word of French, I felt somehow quite at home in Paris. The people seemed to take foreigners, not as foreigners, but for granted. The system of eating, a subject which had been interesting me more and more, was like that of China in that they had a number of dishes even for a 3.50-franc dinner. I liked also the spaciousness of the places, such as the Place de la Concorde. As Yuenren said, in his *Third Green Letter*, "You are struck by the fact that there are places everywhere." You get the feeling that Paris is a much larger city than it actually is. We encountered no language difficulty except that Yuenren spoke too good French. Like the case of my English, his pronunciation was so much better than his command of words that the Frenchmen took him to be an old-timer and made no allowances for the fact that he had never spoken French except in an American classroom.

M. Eugène Bradier of the Association Amicale introduced us to a Mme Bouillol, a lovely old soul who lived in the country at St. Aubin, near Nogent-sur-Seine. She was willing and interested in caring for our children at her home for something like 1,400 francs a month, which was the equivalent of about seventy dollars. I felt guilty about leaving Iris and Nova with a stranger in a strange country just for our own freedom for sightseeing. When we went to St. Aubin to see what it was like, we found that it was a healthy little place for young children to be in. It was a crude rural house, but they had good food there and the children took well to "Maman de St. Aubin."

Iris had started to speak English and Nova did not speak much of anything. On our succeeding visits to St. Aubin, which we made whenever our trips passed Paris, they spoke more and more French. When we finally took them back to Paris shortly, before returning home the next year, they were a couple of French country children. They ate big life-saver bread, mixed red wine with their water, and spoke French with us.

We planned to see Germany next, and then return to England in the fall. As we could not get any sleeper for Berlin, we had to sit up in a compartment for six with nine people in it. The Germans I saw seemed to be quite folk-like people, at least those who sat up nights in trains. They talked very freely and I talked with them through Yuenren's interpreting. Yuenren is what they call "a linguist who can keep silent in seven languages." He does not speak to strangers unless spoken to. I am a linguist who talks with speakers of seven languages in one language of my own. One lady said she used to live in France and could speak French like a Frenchwoman. When Yuenren tried to talk French with her, she said that, since 1918, she refused to speak French *"aus Prinzip."*

Except for Yuenren's trips to Hamburg to see Heinitz, the phonetician, and to Gothenburg, Sweden, to have a visit with the sinologist Bernhard Karlgren, our summer turned out to be a visit to a piece of China. In the first place, I saw a good deal of my Tokyo schoolmate Feng Ch'iya, who was continuing her medical studies in Berlin. Moreover, we made our acquaintances with men like Fu Szenien, Ch'en Yinko, Yü Tawei, and Lo Chialun, and Hsü Chihmo, some of whom later became very close associates of Yuenren in academic work. I got to know them so well that I even dared to write to them by using such a salutation as:

"To the four Hsiensheng ◯, 0, 0, and ⛛:—"

And each of them would recognize the faces of the other three men at once. For I have the habit of playing rough and ready as a gentleman and the privilege of being treated by gentlemen as a lady. I know when to stop, but I go as far as is fitting and I proper.

My impression of arrogant Prussia, with its angry stone lions and colossal frowns of heroes, was softened down to human dimensions when I saw beautiful Nürnberg and friendly München. From my school geography, I had been thinking of Germany simply as Germany. But now I began to think of Bavaria as Bavaria. There seemed to be no greater change in crossing the border to Zürich than in going from Prussia to the south, especially as we visited only the German-speaking parts of Switzerland.

After we spent a day in sightseeing up the Jungfraujoch and arrived at Berne in the midst of distant ranges, Yuenren said: "This is where I am going to stay. I'll get a job as minister to Switzerland."

But we stayed only long enough to see a performance of Mozart's *Magic Flute* and buy a Swiss wristwatch. Years later, on a trip to the Yellow Mountains in southern Anhwei, we stopped at a hotel in Tunchi. From a balcony overlooking the Hsin-an River, spread a panorama of mountains just like the mountains around Berne.

"Do you still want to be minister to Switzerland, Yuenren?" I asked.

"That's an insult to the Director of the Linguistic Survey," he said. "I am staying here to survey the dialects of your native province."

And so he did.

43

LEISURELY TOURS

HAVING NEARLY EXHAUSTED our funds, while payment on the second set of language records was not yet forthcoming, Yuen-ren and I had to omit Vienna and Rome and hurry back to London to catch his autumn term. Passing through France, we went to St. Aubin to take a look at Iris and Nova. They were costing "Maman de St. Aubin" quite a lot for their keep. Iris showed us the damaged edges of a table cover and told us, *"Iriche la coupé aouec chijeaux"*—she had cut it with scissors. But Mme Bouillol did not ask us to pay for it.

Arriving in England, we made a visit with the Bertrand Russells at their summer house in Porthcurno, Cornwall, and saw that they were causes of more Russlings in England: John and Kate.[1] You can't like a place without suitable introductions, and even introductions are not so good as old friendships. Over the hills of Land's End, I did more hill climbing than I had ever done. We also had access to a nameless beach there, which Russell called the Inaccessible Beach, because the road passed a place where there was no road.[2]

We had not bothered the Chinese Legation with our problems on our previous visits to London, as we wished to stay away from everything official. But as my earlier ideas of London and England had a good deal to do with the Legation, we made a call there this time. When we came to 49 Portland Place, we saw a boarded front, apparently with repairs going on, with a sign "Drink Bovril" on the

---

[1]She was a contemporary of Iris and Nova at Radcliffe College.
[2]Is that what I have said, Translator?—B.Y.C.

board. Yuenren said to the man at the door, as he started to turn back: "I am sorry. I thought this was the Chinese Legation."

"This *is* the Chinese Legation," the man replied.

So we went in and had our disappointing first impression corrected by the finely furnished interior. Perhaps it was just as well that the exterior of the legation representing a republic should match in drabness that of the palace of a constitutional monarchy. I had thought that it was an old apartment house when I first approached Buckingham Palace from the side.

While Yuenren went to University College in the day time, I tried to study some English by reading up the plays I was going to see in the evenings. I did not make much headway with my reading. When I found that I could understand a play much better when Yuenren read it to me, and still better when I saw it acted, I decided that plays were to be seen and not read, and that the best preparation for going to a play was to have your husband read it to you beforehand. It was so much more convenient to have words explained to you than look them up in a dictionary. That was another reason why I never learned to read or write English.

The plays I remember best were *White Cargo, It Pays to Advertise,* and *The Great Adventure* (dramatic version of *Buried Alive,* by Arnold Bennett). I liked the last one so well that I saw it three times. I did not understand *St. Joan* and did not like *Getting Married,* and it was only after I went to France again that I began to like Shaw's plays.

Yuenren registered at the Sorbonne, but actually went to classes all over the place. They run things very differently there. In America, students seem to play in high schools and study in college. The average college students are helped along and have to learn something before they can graduate, while the best students feel the restricting influence of regulations and requirements. In Europe, they study hard in the high school, or rather the equivalent of the Japanese Junior College. When they enter a university, they do what they like and come out good for nothing or first-class scholars. The Chinese students who have studied in Europe and America seem to reflect the same conditions as the native students of those countries.

While Yuenren was getting "glazed" with the title of "European-returned," I contented myself with going to the Berlitz School for my English and French. I had been doing my shopping with pocket dictionaries and always managed to be one or two countries out of date with my languages. Going from France to Germany, I would say, *"Oui, monsieur,"* to the annoyance of the Germans. After having learned to say, *"Ja, danke schön,"* I would say it in Paris and annoy the French.

As a woman, I was of course attracted by the Parisian stores, with their window signs which I misread as "English Broken Here." Yuenren had shed his American pronunciation the moment he landed in England. But I had enough American accent coming through my Chinese accent to make things more expensive. In places where there was bargaining, they actually told me that, since I came from America, I ought to be able to pay more. So I went more to the *grands magasins*, like the Bon Marché, where they had standard prices. Once, when I was trying to buy socks for Yuenren, the English speaking clerk was out to lunch. So I pointed at my stocking and said, *"Monsieur bas,"* and got what I wanted.

In Paris I went to many more English plays than French plays. The MacDona Players gave a series of Shaw's plays, the Three Pleasant Plays, the Three Unpleasant Plays, and ten other plays. Yuenren and I went to all of them. It was the Pleasant Plays that converted me to Shaw's plays, though not to his prefaces. I usually stopped Yuenren halfway when he tried to read those prefaces to me. Sometimes he stopped of his own accord. Then the Old Vic Players came to give a Shakespeare series and we went to all of that. My previous acquaintance with Shakespeare had been limited to Lin Shu's translation of Lamb's *Tales* in literary Chinese. Even Yuenren found it hard going when he tried to read Shakespeare's lines to me. But when I saw the plays on the stage, everything began to mean. I could not of course follow the long soliloquies, but I fully understood that "the play's the thing." Without realizing it, I was preparing myself for activities in the Little Theatre movement in Peiping.

Came spring, 1925, and we prepared to go home, after having been abroad for four years. We went to St. Aubin to take the children back from the country. They got used to us again very readily and seemed to pick up right where we had left them, except that they both talked French. Nova had not been talking much so far. But on the way, when the train stopped, she stood up and asked: *"Qu'est-chéque ch'est que cha?"* and was generally interested in things.

We bought tickets for Marseilles just before Iris was old enough to pay increased fare. It was still before her hour of birth when the conductor punched her ticket and asked her age, which we gave quite correctly.

We got excellent third-class accommodation in an end section on an upper deck of S.S. "Porthos." Except for a choppy Mediterranean Sea, I was an unusually good sailor for most of the voyage. One morning I got up to find the ship sailing smoothly on land. I was sure that it was too clear and sunny to be one of those dreams I had of sailing on land. Not until I looked over the railing did I see the narrow strip of water of The Suez Canal. At Port Saïd, one of the Chinese passengers bought a mahjong set. From there on, we did not find the days and the voyage so long.

Singapore, almost on the equator, was the farthest spot south I had been on earth. But Saïgon was the hottest. Between the mosquitoes and bed bugs and two crying children, I found it more distressing traveling than when I was a refugee during the Revolution. After stopping briefly at Hongkong, a cool breeze from the coast of Fukien, now visible in the distance, made me forget even the choppy coastal sea. After thirty-five days on the sea, I had become a fairly good sailor. But I still preferred the terra cotta on the floor of our Chinese-style hotel in Shanghai. Although I had my family close together around me all the time, there was no place like China for home.

Part V
"PEACEFUL" YEARS

44

PROFESSOR'S WIFE

I RETURNED to Peiping and found it very much the same—and yet not at all the same. For one of life's surprises is that, though you may see what you expected to see and live the life you expected to live, the actual details are never what you pictured them to be. Whether you like them or not, they are all new and different. You say to yourself, "Well, I never imagined it was going to be quite like this!" It is part of being a good sport in living to take your surprise pleasantly, especially in cases where you looked forward to going back to an old place and living the old times again. Times move and children grow. The important thing is that you remember old friends and make new ones. For it is only through people that the past lives in the present.

That was why I was so happy to be able to see Auntie once more when I returned to Peiping. That was why I felt so lost when she died shortly afterwards. Looking back now at those days, I am ashamed that my grief, heavy as it was, passed away so quickly. It was soon diverted by preoccupation with something else.

Nova was down with pneumonia. A sudden change of diet after returning to China and sudden changes of heat and cold had affected all our family, and, what with our Shanghai-Tientsin boat turning back and forth between the sun and the wind, as it entered the winding Pai Ho, the baby took it the hardest. Then, after being busy with settling down at No. 1 South compound, Tsinghua Yuan, and making a number of the six-mile ricksha trips to and from the city, Yuen-ren came down with something like the influenza. It took all of what was left of the summer vacation to gradually get the feel of the comforts of a Chinese household again. Since Yuenren practically had had sabbatical year before he started to serve, we had nothing to complain of.

While the men were changing Tsing Hua into a more Chinese institution from the academic side, I took the cause of the Chinese ladies and tried to change the social life into that of a more Chinese community. Hitherto, the emphasis on English had given a superior position, not only to the English-speaking teachers and their courses, but also to the English-speaking ladies, whether they were foreigners or foreign-educated Chinese. Wives of the faculty members who did not speak English were rarely invited to the most important social functions on the campus. Here was a fine opportunity for me to champion the cause of nationalism. As the America-returned wife of a doubly America-returned professor of Chinese, I could hold my ground in insisting on talking Chinese with the foreigners.

At first, most people missed the point, since the inferior position of those who did not speak English was such an established fact that they accepted it without even a complex. But I did have an inferiority complex about my English, and it took the form of righteous indignation. In the course of time, as the personnel of the faculty gradually changed from that of a preparatory school into that of university caliber, men like Robert Winter and I. A. Richards began to set a new tone for the foreign community and prided themselves on how much they knew of Chinese and China, and there was one social life at Tsing Hua instead of two. I did not change it all. I may have been slightly ahead of the times, but the times were going my way.

Tsinghua Yuan was something like two hours by ricksha from the center of things in Peiping. There were trains for the suburban part of the way, but they were few and far between, and slow. So I had to find ways to keep myself occupied in the small place.

As the college physician often had more cases than he could give adequate attention to, families of the faculty often came to me for treatment. As usual, the reward took the form of presents, dinners, and goodwill.

As the families grew up, the education of children became a problem. A private school committee was organized. Because of my outspokenness and readiness to interrupt when someone else was speaking, they elected me spokesman to approach the college president for subsidy to a kindergarten and primary school, and I helped talk him into giving a substantial appropriation for the school.

We started to organize a San T'ai Company, or Company of Three T'ait'ai ("Mrs."), to get the original local women to make handicraft goods. I had brought back from abroad a lot of pattern books, which Peiping stores, such as the "Clock Store," had been borrowing from me. We thought it would be a good idea to apply the local talents to new designs and improve their livelihood. Before the company was actually organized, however, I got switched off to something else.

Eating at Tsinghua Yuan had become monotonous from the inbreeding of culinary ideas. Why not get some first-class chefs from Peiping and organize a community kitchen? That was the drift of an afternoon's gossip at my house. A three-room house across a five-foot bridge just outside the campus was rented and the place was to be called "The Little Bridge Eating Society." But we could not agree on the exact way in which the thing was to be organized. So I offered to start it on a small scale entirely at my risk and on my own responsibility. When the remodeling was going on, students gathered around the place and wanted to become "customers." When told that this was to be a faculty kitchen, they appealed to President Ts'ao. The president said, at a meeting of the University Senate, that, since Mrs. Chao was opening a restaurant, he had permitted students to choose freely between the dining halls and her restaurant. This angered Yuenren so much that he told me to stop the whole thing. But there was already too much momentum to stop.

The business was a great success. Even people in the city sent for take-out orders for dinners. Some families and students boarded there regularly. In two years, I had my investment of a few hundred dollars charged off to bad debts and invisible commissions and turned it over to some real businessmen successors. Like many another enterprise, it took a failure and a cheap sale to another hand to make it a subsequent success.

The urge of the big city for a city woman like me was too strong to be content with a ricksha trip once a week. There was a bus line between Yenching University and Peiping, but that was almost a mile away from Tsing Hua. So I talked with Mrs. L. Y. Ho about organizing a bus line. Before any of us ladies wasted any more of our husbands' money, the Continental Bank took up the idea and started to run a bus between Tsinghua Yuan and the Y.M.C.A. in eastern Peiping.

The improved communications made it possible for me to set up in Peiping a Birth Control Clinic, to which I had given a good deal of thought while abroad. Now that I could go to the city several times a week, I rented a three-courtyard house on the East Main Street at the foot of the Coal Hill. My Third Brother, who was working in the government archives, moved into one of the courtyards. I sublet another courtyard and used the third. I tried to carry out a scheme of encouraging the use of contraception by the underprivileged classes by giving them free service and charging others enough to cover expenses. Each paying patient was also given the chance of bringing five others who could not afford to pay. Actually, however, few availed themselves of this opportunity, and my scheme of social equalization did not work the way I had hoped.

The bus line brought Yuenren closer to his fellow linguists in the city. He could now attend more frequently the meetings of the government Committee on Unification of the National Language. Some of his close associates formed with him a "Society of a Few Men," based on an idea from the preface of Lu Fayen's dictionary *Ch'iehyün* (601 a.d.), which says: "Let us a few men decide on things and things will be decided. "The Few Men were Ch'ien Hsüant'ung, Liu Fu, Lin Yutang, Li Chinhsi, and Wang Yi. They met at our house on

Coal Hill East Main Street every week or so for a meal and argued about phonetics and romanization, usually with several persons talking at a time. It was here that the system of National Romanization was first drafted (which became official in 1927). People often speak of it as "Chao Yuenren's system." While Yuenren does not disclaim responsibility for its defects, he does attribute to Lin Yutang the idea of indication of tones by variations in spelling, for better or for worse. For instance, *mha* (high level) "mother," *ma* (high rising) "hemp," *maa* (low rising) "horse," *mah* (high falling) "scold." But I have never learned the National system, or any system of romanization of Chinese. The characters are so much more simple and direct.

Restless Yuenren and restless I could not stay put, and found our frequent visits to the city too unexciting to satisfy our love for travel. After two years of Tsing Hua, we started to make more trips. After another year, we made more trips and Yuenren changed his job.

45

TRIPS TO "THE SOUTH"

MY HUSBAND LEADS a double life, that is, academically speaking. On the one hand, there is Chao Yuenren the reformist and innovationist. He joins Esperanto clubs, writes in Basic English on Basic Chinese, sits on Committee on Unification of the National Language, writes Chinese-style melodies with Western harmony, and tries out E. V. Huntington's "normal notation" of music, with one staff to an octave. Because of his fondness for using strange symbols and signs, Fu Szenien calls that side of him "the Cult of the White Lotus," which was the name of one of those secret societies associated with the Boxers of 1900. The other Chao Yuenren, who maintains his academic respectability from 9 a.m. to 5 p.m., is the college professor, whose chief concern is the search for "truth for its own sake." To him, whatever is *is*, and that's the end of it. Classical Chinese is not something to be fought against, but something to be understood. Dialects are not something to be abolished, but something to be recorded and compared. That atoms split in a chain—whatever that means—on December 2, 1942 was a bigger event for him than that one bomb destroyed a city on August 5, 1945.

It was in the latter capacity, in the capacity of a research professor, that Yuenren set out in the fall of 1927 for a survey of the Wu dialects, the dialects of southeastern Kiangsu and northern Chekiang, where people call themselves southerners. While in Cambridge, Massachusetts, Yuenren had had frequent talks with the anthropologist-archaeologist Li Chi about plans for making field trips in China, and I had appointed myself field doctor. This time, when the Tsing Hua Research Institute sent Yuenren out for the survey, I took office—from that previous appointment and at my own expense. While

Yuenren interviewed the "informants" of various dialects and transcribed their speech, I took time out for side excursions, and even went to Nanking[1] to visit my relatives.

Soochow is the city of the Wu dialect par excellence. In fact, the official *hsien* name for Soochow is Wu. Soochow women are supposed to be specially charming because of the melody of their tones and the ingratiating qualities of their vowels. The story has it that when a new northern sergeant at Soochow called gruffly in Mandarin, "Forward—MARCH!" nobody stirred. But when a local man commanded in the Soochow accent, "*Do* let's all go forward, *please!*" the company responded at once.[2]

But there was another side of Soochow which was quite an eye opener to me. Our party made an excursion to the T'ienp'ing Hills of Soochow, famous for their scenery and temples. When we reached the foot of the hills, a lot of women came to solicit fares for sedan chairs to go up the hills. Some of them had just been doing embroidery. One was nursing a baby. When she saw me, she quit nursing, tied the baby to herself, and carried the chair with another woman to solicit my business. I told her to finish with the baby, but she wanted to do as much business as she could for the day. The baby could wait. The men of our party, being mostly foreign-returned, were very reluctant to be carried by women. They walked on and on, but the women followed them with their chairs. Finally, the Soochow tones and vowels grew so importunate that they had to give in and decided that the better part of chivalry was to give them the much-needed business. For the women had too much pride in their trade to accept any payment unless the men actually rode in their chairs.

Hangchow, with its West Lake, has been called the beauty spot of China. Next to Heaven, Hangchow and Soochow are said to be the best places to go. The Hangchow dialect interested Yuenren

---

[1] Just outside the western boundary of the Wu dialects.—Y.R.C.
[2] See Lin Yutang, *My Country and My People*, p. 21, for the original Chinese words.

because Hangchow was the capital of the Southern Sung dynasty, thirteenth century a.d. They speak with a Mandarin vocabulary in a southern pronunciation. Yuenren says that if you give a native of Soochow a copy of any novel in Mandarin and ask him to read it aloud, the result will be something like the Hangchow dialect.

Both Soochow and Hangchow are known for their silks and between-meal foods. I often stopped to peep into the small home-industries in sericulture and weaving. The Hangchow crêpe, which is liked by foreigners for its rough texture, combined with a flexible body, is regarded by the local people as inferior material, as it is made from defective cocoons with knots in them. With the broken cocoons, bitten through by silkworm moths which are kept for eggs, a silk cotton is made for making ink pads and wadding for winter gowns. Silk wadding is warmer than fur. Once, I had such a gown on while walking in front of Schumann's on Fifth Avenue and a man said to me, "Lady, you will catch pneumonia, walking in this blizzard without a coat." I said, "This *is* my coat."

You can live in Soochow or Hangchow without eating any meals. They not only have all kinds of sweets, such as lotus-starch pudding and rose candies, but meat and shrimp things, made into fancy pastries in all sorts of flavors. They call those things *"tienhsin,"* literally "something to dot the heart." But you can eat them to your heart's content, if you like. Fresh bamboo shoot you see them dig out from the grove is a Hangchow specialty. By the time the pulp reaches America in cans, all the flavor will have gone out of them. Another delicacy of that region is the drunken shrimps in liquor and sauce, which jump in your mouth as you shell them with your tongue and teeth. And, of course, the tea from Dragon Well, Hangchow, is so good that any high-grade green tea gets to be loosely called "Dragon Well."

Soochow is a typical residential city. The first sight of the residential sections of Soochow and similar cities is a little forbidding to a foreign visitor, since the richer the interior, the higher the fence walls are built, to guard against theft and possible spreading of any fire in the neighborhood. Along the narrow streets of central Soochow, you just see great stretches of dark, high walls on both sides. But if you have introductions, as we did on our visits, you will find many Shangri-las in the city, each having its gardens, pavilions, and artificial hills, among goldfish ponds. One of such places I visited was the Garden of Cranes. It belonged to Mrs. Pang, Yuenren's maternal aunt and mother of Pang Tunmin, in whose Peiping house I had first met Yuenren.

But Yuenren claims that his hometown Changchow, not Soochow, is the Venice of China. He had lived in Soochow for one year, but he liked the bean oil of Changchow for cooking better than the vegetable-seed oil of Soochow. Nothing could equal the favor of the flat, soft kind of sesame-sprinkled hot biscuits of Changchow. That was why one of the cooks of my Little Bridge Eating Society at Tsinghua Yuan had to be able to make Changchow-style hot biscuits.

"How would you like to be the wife of the Mayor of Changchow?" Yuenren had once asked me. I said it would be a good idea, judging from the skill of the cook of the Little Bridge Eating Society. But when I entered the city wall of Changchow for the first time and found that the streets were even narrower than those of Soochow, I said I wanted to think it over before letting him accept any offer of mayorship.

Yuenren's Changchow home was a nine-courtyard house on Olive Lane, built by his great-grandfather in the early 1800's. It still had mother-of-pearl instead of glass in the latticed windows and doors. We were entertained by his aunt Amniang at her own house in a different part of the city. I had been married for six years. But as this was the first time I "returned home," I was feasted as a bride. It was the season for fresh-water crabs, compared with which sea crabs as you find in America would be as prosaic as corned beef. I requested, in my un-bridelike manner, to be given a crab party. Dean Y. C. Mei and Mrs. Y. T'ang, who were also traveling with us then, joined the request. Amniang agreed. But after we had had the wonderful crabs, still came a complete banquet, fit to set before a bride.

Amniang took me to the house on Olive Lane to show me Yuenren's mother's things. Besides the little box of jewelry he had brought to me, Yuenren had spoken of books, paintings, and scrolls of calligraphy which he had left in Changchow, but forgot about the sixteen trunks full of furs and embroidery, which his maternal grandmother had given to his mother. Now that we were getting settled, Amniang told us to take the things with us. We took only a part of them, as it was quite a job to move so many things to Peiping. We made another trip in 1936 to move all the old books and the art things to our house at Nanking, where we lived later. When the war came, our Nanking house was burned to the ground, including all its contents, but we heard that, on Olive Lane, both the house to the right and the house to the left were destroyed, but Yuenren's great grandfather's house was, and still is, intact.

46

THE NATIONALIST REVOLUTION

I NEVER ENTERED politics. Anyway, I certainly got out of it when I went to Japan in 1913 after the failure of the Second Revolution. Since then, I have been interested in political happenings in China only in so far as they have to do with the fortunes of my personal friends in the Revolution (such as the Pos and the Lins), and, of course, with the prospects of a free and democratic China, as who wouldn't be?

While the Nationalist Government was for years confined within a small region around Canton, revolutionary movements were alive and vigorous even under the successive regimes of the warlords in the rest of the country. Hu Shih's Literary Revolution, though it had no official connection with the Kuomintang, was a movement in the same general direction. The May 4, 1919 Student Movement was an effective protest against the country-selling acts of the government in the North. The death of students in the May 30, 1925 incident in the Shanghai concessions was part of the birth pains of a new nation wanting its freedom back. When the Nationalist army marched through Kiangsi in 1926-27 and reached Peiping in 1928, the country was more or less ready for it. Many of us felt that the Revolution had finally succeeded.

As a plain naïve citizen, living in over-privileged comforts, I did not anticipate that the Kuomintang-Communist split to last for more than nineteen years. True, I was more Japan-conscious than most people at that time, but I did not expect that Japan would start serious trouble very soon. All in all, the sight of the new red, white, and blue flag flying in Peiping[1] in 1928, in place of the old five stripes, gave us all a very bright picture of things. If the Nationalist slogan displayed in every public hall still reminded us that:

> "The Revolution has not yet succeeded,
> We comrades must still continue our efforts,"

nevertheless the Revolution was succeeding to a substantial degree.

The Nationalist front extended to Tsing Hua University when Lo Chialun came as Wartime Commissioner on Education, to take over the educational institutions. Gossips were making the rounds on the campus as to what Kuomintang member would be appointed new president of the university. Yuenren's name was mentioned among the wild guesses.

"But is Chao Yuenren a member of Kuomintang?" someone wondered.

"Doesn't he look like one, though?" someone else insisted.

I don't know what a Kuomintang-face is supposed to look like, but I do know that, compared with me, my husband has about as much to do with Kuomintang as he has with embroidery—I don't embroider very much myself, you know. However that may be, the fact was that Lo Chialun came with an errand, on behalf of the new government, to offer the Tsing Hua presidency to Chao Yuenren.

In 1925, just as we were stopping over at Shanghai on our way from Paris to Peiping, Yuenren had already escaped once from the burden of an administrative job. At that time, the Southeastern University (which had asked him to be professor a year before) was in need of a president, and, the moment he was approached on that subject, he advanced his date of departure and hurried north. Honestly, I am not absolutely averse to be a college president's wife, if my husband liked that sort of thing. Now don't get me wrong. I may

---

[1]The name "Peking" was actually changed into "Peiping" in 1928. In this book, I have made the change from 1911 on, which seems to suit me better for continuity in my story.

like the idea of being a college president's wife, a little. But I do like the idea of having Chao Yuenren for a husband, much. Since I know that Chao Yuenren will never want to be a college president, therefore, when any such offer came up, I always helped him get out of it.

The next president of National Tsing Hua University was Lo Chialun. During his brief and somewhat stormy tenure of office there, he added several buildings to the campus, and, above all, brought up the level of the faculty by adding to it a number of first-class scholars. Socially, I find Mr. Lo a little fond of repeating that story about Dissertations on the Elephant by Writers of Various Nationalities, but what's a story or two to hold against a man who left a university better than he found it?

One of the greatest liberals in recent China was Ts'ai Yuan p'ei. As President of the National University of Peking, he built it up into the leading institution of the country for free inquiry and liberal thinking. When the Nationalist Government was established at Nanking, he was called upon to reorganize the education of the country. Himself a holder of the pre-Republic degree of Hanlin, he fully supported the vernacular-literature movement, which he and his successor Chiang Monlin advanced by a series of educational acts. As a believer in the importance of research, he organized in 1928 a central research institution known as Academia Sinica (i.e. Chinese Academy), consisting of ten (now thirteen) institutes, representing all branches of science and learning.

In the fall of 1928 Yang Ch'ien, the Academy's Secretary-General, and Fu Szenien, Director of its Institute of History and Philology, invited Yuenren to join the Institute and organize a Section of Linguistics. Yuenren is normally a great hesitator. But this time, he concluded very quickly that this was the place for his life work. I chorused approval, because there would be a chance for me to do more traveling with Yuenren and to move to a large city like Peiping or Nanking, instead of living in a remote suburb.

Yuenren took office by starting a survey of two more provinces, Kwantung and Kwangsi. I accompanied him as far as Canton and had a good time there, but it turned out also to be our longest period of separation from each other since we were married.

47

VISITS TO CANTON AND SHANGHAI

IF RETURNING to Peiping after an absence of four years did not quite give me the feeling of returning, returning to Canton after an absence of thirty-six years was almost like going to a new country. I never learned to speak Cantonese when I was there as a child, because my amah Huang Ma was from Yangchow and spoke a dialect like that of Nanking. Ordinarily, when I fake a smattering of various dialects, what I usually do is simply to shift a gear, so to speak, and guess at the pronunciation of words. Though the result is as often wrong as right, and the effect is sometimes amusing to the native listener, I can at least make myself understood. But Cantonese is too difficult even to fake. Yuenren insisted that I had to make a separate effort of memory for each word I was to learn. I had to memorize that the word for "six" ended in k, the words for "seven" and "eight" ended in t, the word for "ten" ended in p, and so on without graduation.

"But," I objected, you are being paid for your 'separate efforts of memory.' Who is going to pay for mine? It's no fair to expect me to pay for my traveling and work for it, too."

However, that was only my lazy excuse for preferring to speak Mandarin, my kind of Mandarin. In fact, those were the years when Mandarin, or the National Language, was being promoted in the South.[1] When we passed Singapore three years before that, we were

---

[1] That is, the real South, not "the South" in the sense of Kiangsu and Chekiang. In talking to people in Canton, I often made the mistake of saying, "You Cantonese

met by Chinese residents there who had learned Mandarin from Yuenren's phonograph records. In Sun Yatsen University at Canton, which Chu Chiahua and Fu Szenien were reorganizing into an institution after the liberal tradition of the National University of Peking, even the professors from Canton began to give their lectures in Mandarin. Because of this interest in the standard speech, Yuenren sometimes had difficulty in making it clear that it was in his academic personality that he was making these surveying trips. People expected him to be a sort of inspector of education in the National Language. Instead of telling him how they did speak, they were more interested in asking him how they ought to speak. They could not see why a professor was sent out to the provinces to learn and not to teach.

My excuse for not speaking Cantonese, because I was paying my traveling expenses (out of my husband's pocket), proved to be a rather weak one, for we were being entertained all the time. Yuenren and I were guests at Fu Szenien's house. We were feted at various dinners, which reminded me of the Cantonese dishes I had seen but had been too young to eat much first stay in Canton. At a dinner given by the university, one of the guests was on a diet. Each time a particularly good dish came on the table and this guest started to poise his chopsticks, his wife would call his name and remind him, "You know you can't eat that!" So I was able to eat more than my share.

After I had visited a number of eating places, Mr. Chuang Tsehsüan, one of Yuenren's Cornellian friends, asked us what new things we would like to eat. I said I had heard so much about snakes as a Cantonese delicacy. So to a snake restaurant we went. The shreds of snake were cooked together with shreds of chicken, sprinkled over with petals of white chrysanthemum. I liked the dish so well that I ate seven bowls of it. I did not know until later that a snake dinner cost fifty dollars, that is, when fifty dollars were fifty dollars.

---

do things this way, but we 'Southerners' do them differently," and I was usually puzzled why they were so puzzled over my remark.

After knowing Cantonese cooking at first hand, I realized how people had wronged the Cantonese by judging it by the great quality of American chopsuey. The virtue of Cantonese cooking lies mainly in the right and simplest treatment of the best material, as contrasted with the use of elaborate seasoning of some other provinces. It was only in quite recent years that genuine Cantonese cooking found its way into a few restaurants in some of the larger American cities.

I tried to pick up what I could remember of old Canton. But it was a new Canton, with a somewhat modernized waterfront. As I knew the old governor's yamen best, I went there to see what I could recognize. It had been changed into Chungshan Park. There were few buildings left there. After I had wandered around for some time, a feeling of familiarity seemed to come out of the air, which, for a moment, I could not attach to anything in particular. Then it came into focus in front of me in the form of a big banyan tree. That was the place where I had played and climbed in and out of those aerial roots. Thus, after several days of a busy social life in a strange city, I finally came back to Canton.

When Yuenren started on his extensive trips in Kwangtung and Kwangsi, I left for Shanghai, where I had left Iris and Nova with a Peiping amah, Little Li Ma, in one of those *lungt'ang* style apartments on Scot Road in Chapei. We had given up our house at Tsing Hua and brought the children to Shanghai, where I waited for Yuenren's return before settling down again. When you think of wives waiting for their husbands gone to war "for the duration," and, in unfortunate cases, forever, it ought to be nothing to wait for a husband on a field trip for two or three months. But you mind it just the same when it's your own husband.

Yuenren wrote to me very scientifically by writing more often on his way out and less often on his way back. He called it "Doppler's Principle," which he explained to me by a complicated diagram. But I never understood what Doppler's Principle was; for it never worked the way he said it would. Sometimes several letters would arrive in a bunch; at other times, letters of consecutive dates would arrive a week apart.

There is something about writing that you don't get when you talk to each other. You sit there alone and try to imagine yourself not alone. Your thoughts ramble out, sometimes in directions which they do not usually follow in conversational situations. You are not always addressing the person of the moment. You feel the presence of the whole person because no part of him is actually there. I am not as much of a letter writer as Yuenren. But I do notice that I write differently from the way I talk. Not that I write in a literary language, for I write more colloquial Chinese than even Hu Shih advocates, but when I write, my thoughts seem to have longer threads.

Wonderful as love letters are, they are at best only substitutes for love. Cursive Chinese may be a faster-writing language than English, but it never goes as fast as you can think. By the time you have put your first thought down on paper, your next thought has already got altered while waiting to be written. Besides, you miss the experience of immediate response: When Yuenren referred to my "last letter but two" (for I never number and rarely date my letters), I had forgotten what it was all about.

It was on a spring-like February day in 1929 when the S.S. "President Lincoln" sailed into the port of Shanghai, with Yuenren standing on the deck. I went on board with Iris and Nova to meet him. After we returned to our apartment, Yuenren asked: "What was this about our chance to lose a daughter you wrote about?"

"I am still too scared to tell about it," I said. "But, as I told you, nothing serious really happened—Little Li Ma, you better tell Hsiensheng about it!"

"Well, Hsiensheng," Little Li Ma said, "we were all on the third floor that day. I was holding Miss Iris and T'ait'ai was reading. And before I knew it, I saw Miss Nova standing on the table by the window and she walked right on the window sill and she had both her feet on it."

"Did you tell her to come back?" Yuenren asked.

"No, sir, I was afraid to scare her, you see, there was nothing between her and the courtyard—and it was forty feet below, you see. And I talked very quiet-like, and I said, 'Where do you think you are still going Miss Nova?' But I couldn't do a thing, 'cause I had my hands full, you see?"

"And then?"

"And then Tait'ai heard me and she saw where Miss Nova was going. She sort of eased towards her from one side, and, thank Heaven! she just grabbed her into her arms!"

Thus Nova was saved from a fate which, only a few days before, had overtaken another child in the same neighborhood in those *lungt'ang*-style houses, in which all windows opened outwards. But, soon afterwards, this amah had another occasion to see Nova pass from danger to safety.

Meanwhile, I told Yuenren that I had a good little news for him.

48

LENSEY IN A LONG HOUSE

WHEN YUENREN ACCEPTED the job in Academia Sinica, I had looked forward to the prospect of living in Nanking. For the constitution of the Academy specifies that its location should be where the capital is. But there were as yet no suitable buildings for it in Nanking, and the various constituent institutes had to be scattered in different cities. The institutes of the natural sciences went to Shanghai, for its material facilities, and the Institute of History and Philology to Peiping, for its rich historical and bibliographical resources. So to Peiping we moved.

We found a large, elongated house, consisting of four courtyards arranged in depth, at 40 Yangyi Hutung, Tungtan P'ailou, near the center of practically everything in Peiping. But I did not like the house at first. Soon after we moved into it, Nova had another attack of pneumonia. It got so bad that the doctor had to give her seven hypodermics a day to keep her heart going. After many nights of vigil, chiefly kept by Little Li Ma, she was nursed out of danger.

But hardly before Nova was able to sit up in bed, Yuenren came home with a sprained wrist. Coming out from a meeting one evening, the absent-minded professor suddenly remembered that he had passed his stop and stepped out of the street-car onto a moving street. The sprain developed into arthritis, which kept his right arm in a sling for several months. He could not even use his left hand very much, because of the sympathetic innervation of the corresponding muscles in the right hand.

During all those anxious months, I was kept busy with making and renewing friendships in the great city, and was even charged with the duty of promoting social life between young men and young women. I rarely accept the job of introducing a specific individual to meet another specific individual from a specific point of view, as was, and still sometimes is, done in so-called new-style society. I believe in providing opportunities for young people in general to meet in general, so that they can take a "bystander's," and therefore an objective, point of view. As a result, I always had to arrange my parties on a large scale. It did me good to be so busily occupied, as it kept me from my worries. But the results of my efforts, if any, were largely invisible. Anyway, they were not supposed to be part of my system. People like to speak of Chao T'ait'ai as an active match maker. Nothing is further from the truth. I have not succeeded in making a single match to my credit. Even with Chao Yuenren, I began with trying to make a match for him with somebody else.

With the dust storms settling down to the warm breeze of late spring in Peiping, everybody in the family got well again. Now I took my turn to be confined in bed. The good little news which I had hinted at to my husband while we were in Shanghai was now announced to all friends as the birth of our third daughter Lensey.

There is no such name as Lensey, that is, not until she was so named. In finding a name for our child, Yuenren looked over the chart of possible syllables and found that the syllable *len* (2nd Tone, implied in the spelling) and the syllable *sey* (4th Tone, implied in the spelling) had never been used before, and so "Lensey" she should be.

Lensey grew up as the family philosopher. At one, she discovered personality in chairs. When her sweater got caught in a little chair as she tried to stand up, she said: "You want Mei[1] to sit down?"

---

[1]She called herself "Mei," that is, "Little Sister."

And she sat down. When she tried to stand up again, her sweater was still caught in the chair and she said again: "You still want Mei to sit down?"

And she sat down again. She repeated this three times until her amah Chang Ma could control her laughter enough to disentangle the sweater.

At five, Lensey stumped her philosopher father by asking: "Daddy, of all things in the world, why should they be?"

Then she started to count how many things there were in the world, such as "rouge and powder, pots and pans and things." But she could not decide whether her doll, one head, one body, two hands, and two legs were six or seven things.

A few years later, she asked: "On the whole, are people's affairs getting better or getting worse?"

My husband says that there are two kinds of people—those who are interested in things, like himself, and those who are interested in people, like me. Now he has to recognize a third kind of people, those who are interested both in things and in people, like Lensey.

As housekeeping with a baby was less of a job for me in Peiping than in Cambridge, I started soon to look for outside activities. Not that I wasn't going out every day, but I wanted to do something not connected with the household. There was a Little Theatre movement in Peiping, started by a few people in academic circles who were interested in promoting the spoken drama, which was a totally foreign art form. Yuenren had been doing some research in the expressive intonations of Chinese and English. For collecting examples of intonation, he translated two English plays into Chinese. The Little Theatre produced some of his translations on the stage, together with other plays written by contemporary writers.

With my interest in the spoken drama thus revived, I joined the activities of the Little Theatre by helping with the directing, makeup, and scene-setting, while Yuenren interfered with me and with the chief directors all the time by insisting on everybody's using the intonations he had worked out for each line. One of Yuenren's translations and an original play by the physicist Ting Hsilin were among the most successful productions. Hu Shih remarked after the show: "I have heard of 'Physics and Politics' before,[2] now there seems to be some connection between 'Physics and Dramatics,' too." This pleased Yuenren very much, because, having become a back number as a physicist, he always feels flattered to be still called one.

After having left the Ch'ungshih School of Nanking for seventeen years, I took another crack at teaching at the Women's College of Liberal Arts and Sciences of the National Peiping University. Now get this straight. The National University of *Peking* is a very old institution. It is the university which President Ts'ai Yuanp'ai built up, President Chiang Monlin kept up, and now President Hu Shih is taking up. The National *Peiping* University was an amalgamation of a number of independent undergraduate professional colleges, plus the Women's College. After the amalgamation, it became a unique university, in that all its colleges were coeducational except that the College of Liberal Arts and Sciences had only women in it. It was non coeducational in reverse, so to speak.

I taught anatomy and physiology at this college. The facilities for my subjects there were somewhat limited, but I had the good luck of being able to secure the cooperation of the Peiping Union Medical College, to which I was able to bring whole classes of students for demonstrations.

One of Yuenren's fellow members in the Society of a Few Men was Liu Fu. Besides being a phonetician, Liu was also a lyric poet. Yuenren had set a number of his poems to music,[3] among which one has become one of the most popular songs among college students all over the country. The title cannot be translated into English, since it contains the word *t'a*, which means "him or her, as the case may

---

[2]Walter Bagehot, *Physics and Politics*, New York, 1902.
[3]Chao Yuenren, *Songs of Contemporary Poems*, Shanghai, 1928.

be," and you can't very well sing "How can I help thinking of him or her, as the case may be?" At the Women's College, the girls sang day in and day out the refrain, "How can I help thinking of t'a?"

Then there was a change of administration at the college. When I learned who the new head of the college was, I told my students: "You are singing of *t'a* all the time. Now *t'a* has come. Mr. Liu Fu has been appointed to be your new president. "

But I had quite a problem of my own as to what *t'a* was going to be. My question was:

"Will it be a he or a she?"

49

BELLA IN A BIG HOUSE

AUSPICIOUS AS THE Yangyi Hutung house finally turned out to be, I still did not quite like its early associations. So, as soon as there was a bigger and better house vacant at 724 Hsi Kuanyinser, almost next to the Yangyi Hutung house, we moved in there. It was an enormous three-story foreign-style house, on nearly one acre of ground. In the winter, we filled the yard with water and made a skating rink out of it.[1] The hall on the first floor was big enough to set five tables in it and still leave a lot of dancing room—though none of our class of people did any dancing. We rented it at a very reasonable price. But when V. K. Ting, Yuenren's best scolding friend, came to see us, he remarked: "Yuenren, this is not the kind of house for people like us."

Fortunately, we did rent such a big house. For we soon found it not big enough.

I believe in spacing out one's children. That was why Nova and Lensey were several years apart. But I also believe that every child should have a companion. That was why Iris had Nova. Since Lensey was alone, Bella came to keep her company. My question about "*t'a*" was finally answered—"*t'a*" was Bella.

Bella's name is not Bella. When Bella was born, we asked Lensey what she was going to call her little sister. She had just begun to be interested in the characters on our hanging scrolls. The only two characters she knew were 小 *hsiao*, meaning, "little," and 中 *chung*,

---

[1] The rink was so big that even tall and athletic Professor Thomas L. Yuan could fall, slide on it, and still lie entirely within its boundaries.

meaning "middle." So she gave her baby sister the name "Hsiao-chung."

Bella has a more rounded-out personality than any other member of the family (not excepting Daddy and Mammy, of course). Because I was quite ill for a time after her birth, I had to get a wet nurse for her, as fresh cow's milk was unsafe and powdered milk would be both less satisfactory and more expensive. Bella's nurse had a very sweet disposition, except that she had fits of temper once in a while. Bella acquired both her sweet disposition and her fits of temper, but as she grew up, she kept her disposition and lost her temper, which she has kept ever since.

We did not quite need a three-storied house on an acre of ground to accommodate one small baby, even with the addition of a nurse. But did need a lot of space when fifteen or twenty more people came to live with us.

On September 18, 1931, as everybody knows, Japan marched on Mukden and took Manchuria. A number of our friends, Hoh Gun-sun, Ting Supao, and others, had been teaching at the Northeastern University there and had to leave in a hurry. Some of them caught the last train out of Mukden for Peiping. We met them at the East Station.

One of them remarked, as they saw us: "We are just like a bunch of refugees."

"What do you mean, 'just like'?" I said. "You *are* refugees, aren't you?"

He looked at me, wondering why I was getting so familiar. Then it dawned on me that he was not his brother, whom I knew, but his brother's *brother*, whom I was meeting for the first time.

Three of the refugee families, with their children, were put up in our house. The big hallway could now be put to full use as a dining hall. I used my technique of increasing the quantity, instead of increasing the number of dishes, for an increased number of people.

Having grown up in a large household in Nanking, and even taken part in its complicated management, I did not find the job of entertaining three families too overwhelming. Instead, I rather enjoyed it.

There was another change of administration in Tsing Hua University. Y. C. Mei, who was Director of Tsing Hua students studying in America, was summoned back to be president of the university and Yuenren was called upon to take his job at Washington. Yuenren had been back from America for seven years and a furlough would have been due if he had remained at Tsing Hua. (Actually he had continued giving one course in phonology there after he joined Academia Sinica.) It was not exactly part of his plan to take a year off from Academia Sinica so soon after joining it. But he reasoned that it was a time of rapid progress in electronics and acoustics, and it would help his work to make new contacts in the field by going to America. With this rationalization, we were able to satisfy our recurrent urge towards America with an appeased conscience. But other difficulties came up. Bella was too small to travel. Besides, she had a wet nurse. Fortunately, the Y. T'ang's, very close friends of ours, would like to have her and the nurse at their home during our absence. Thus, Bella became richer than all her sisters by having not only a Mammy, but also acquiring a Ma and a Niang.[2]

After the five of us waved goodbye to Bella and "Ma," got into further difficulties when we reached Shanghai. From our top-floor room at Huichung Hotel on Hankow Road, we saw, in the direction of Chapei, a skyline of continuous conflagrations. It was the time of the "Shanghai incident." This was the first time that China showed any sign of active resistance to the step-by-step advance Japan had been making on the continent. In that solid sheet of flames we were watching through the night, one flicker may have come from the manuscript and the final proofs of Yuenren's translation of *Through*

---

[2] "Ma," unprefixed by a surname, is the term of direct address for one's mother or for one's wet nurse. "Niang," used by the children of the T'angs, also means "mother." "Mammy" (pronounced with Chinese Tones 3 and 1) is the way all my children call me.

the Looking-Glass and What Alice Found There. The Chapei works of the Commercial Press were burned to the ground, and *Through the Looking-Glass*, which Yuenren regarded as the best piece of work he had done in any line, was never published.

Came the armistice, and we resumed our plans for going abroad. I had not been well after the birth of Bella. Now I was getting worse. On the morning on which we were to sail, the doctor advised a major operation. I could sail if I insisted, but he would not recommend it. I did not hesitate in deciding what to do. I told Yuenren that it would be all right.

50

SECOND SOJOURN IN AMERICA

I ARRIVED AT San Francisco in much better spirits than when I left Shanghai. It had been a trying voyage, during which we ran into the tail end of a typhoon. But when I landed and got over my seasickness, I also got over my sickness. I did have to have some minor treatments afterwards, but as compared with having a major operation, I would rather have the tail end of a typhoon any day;

One of the regrets I carried with me when I left America in 1924 was that I left without having visited Washington. This time, I came back and lived at Washington for a year and half. I said that New York was a place you would like to visit occasionally and that Cambridge was a place where you would like to live all the time. Now Washington was a place you would both like to visit occasionally and like to live in all the time. For you cannot get tired of visiting the Lincoln Memorial or living by the Rock Creek Park. The Washington of that time was of course not the Washington of the early 'forties, where there was a shortage of everything except people. For I arrived there in the midst of the depression after the 1929 crisis, and, with fresh pork shoulder selling at nine cents a pound, you can see how little we salaried people appreciated the meaning of the word "depression."

But one fine morning, I woke up to find myself penniless. So did everybody else in the household. I had been very rich on the previous Thursday. I had collected more than a hundred dollars' worth of assorted gold pieces, from tiny two-and-a-half dollar pieces to big twenty-dollar pieces. But because the children almost lost a big one while playing with them on the floor, Yuenren had them all deposited at the bank. On the same Thursday, he had also deposited a large check without taking out any part of it in cash. On Saturday, March 4, 1933, we went to see the first inauguration of President Roosevelt in front of the Capitol, and heard him speak of the failure of the "money changers." True enough, by Monday, they were unable to provide me with change. The general "bank holiday" was on throughout the country, The Tsing Hua students under Yuenren's care wired that they were "broke," and Yuenren wired back, "Same here." After a few days, during which the government sorted out the good banks from the bad, Yuenren was able to take a little cash out to send some relief to the students by money order, on the theory that they were on his "payroll."

When I said I lived for a year and half in Washington, I meant I lived for a year and half in the United States. For, during that period, I spent almost as much time in the states as in the District of Columbia. Yuenren's job required him to make inspection trips to various institutions to meet the students and to find out from their teachers how they were getting along. He made his trips by driving in an automobile. In the early days of the Chinese Educational Mission—that was the name of the office of the student director—there had been a chauffeur to drive the director around. But democratic-minded Y. C. Mei abolished the chauffeur and drove the car himself. When mechanical-minded Yuenren inherited his job and car, together with a couple of unanswered tickets for over-parking, he had to learn to drive. He made both a hobby and a science of driving. I made a few false starts at driving, too, but could not follow Yuenren's grammar of science, and so settled down as backseat driver on the right front seat.

Thus I got a different view of America, not only from living in Washington, but also from living in cabins and going through country places. Even on renewing my acquaintance with good old Cambridge, I was able to see people and places in ways I had not been able to during my first visit. Previously, if I called on Mrs. W. E. Hocking and she was not at 12 Quincy Street, I just walked back to

3 Sacramento Place and that was the end of it. But with an automobile, we could see the Hockings at their Madison, New Hampshire farm, only five hours away. You really don't know all sides of your friends without having been with them in all sorts of places and activities. When a professor worked in overalls and the professor's wife busied around in her sneakers in a half-built house, with Mount Washington framed in its yet glassless window, conversation was not likely to flow in grooves in which tea with or without lemon or sugar was likely to flow. In fact, I sometimes wonder if social life would not be much more interesting if there were no social life at all and people would just meet as they work and play.

One of our driving adventures which Yuenren is fond of telling about was a wild chase after the shadow of the moon. In the summer of 1933, there was a meeting of the U.S. branch of the Science Society of China at Cambridge. Part of the program consisted in a trip to Freiburg, Maine, to see the total eclipse of the sun. The party went there in several cars. In our car was our family of five and Sophia Han (now Mrs. Wei Lihuang). When we reached Freiburg, Maine, the streets were lined with people watching the partially eclipsed sun with smoked glasses selling at a quarter a piece.

Some thick clouds were coming up. Judging from the way they were moving, Yuenren made a U-turn and drove toward New Hampshire in the direction of Conway. But as we went northwestward, the clouds became thicker and thicker. So we whirled back toward Maine again. Discovering in Maine that we had dropped a suitcase from the trunk rack while making one of those U-turns, we returned to New Hampshire, to pick up our suitcase, which was still lying on the highway. The day was getting sensibly cooler before it got darker. By the time we were in Maine again, we thought it was time to stop making any more U-turns, clouds or no clouds.

As we watched the disappearing golden crescent, birds started to roost. "Evening" clouds changed colors in seconds instead of minutes. Then, with a—I wish I could find a word for it, but you can't speak of an absolutely quiet event as a boom! or a swoosh! or a woof! And yet, the event was so big and overwhelming and so sudden, that you can't help feeling that it was with some sort of a m—!! and the whole sky was darkened over under the moon's nightcap.

"The corona, the corona!" Yuenren shouted, as he jumped up and down like a school boy. There were enough clouds in that Freiburg suburb to spoil the scientific value of the astronomer's photographs, but not enough to make any difference to the view, except that they made it more wonderful. "Wonderful?" That was what Yuenren and I said, having hoped to be at such an event for more than forty years and just barely hit a near-miss after the wild chase. But Sophia Han, more than half a generation younger than we, remarked that the show was over too soon to be very impressive. Iris and Nova, of another generation, asked: "Is that all? We haven't seen anything yet."

And Lensey, the baby, said: "The sun looks so ugly! It's got a black face and white whiskers."

Now Lensey wishes she could have the show repeated.

With the number of Tsing Hua students in America decreasing, there was no longer need of having a whole office of the director at Washington. So Yuenren turned the job of taking care of the few remaining Tsing Hua students over to Chih Meng of China Institute and packed up for home. We drove from Washington, D. C., to Seattle, Washington, taking in the Yellowstone Park on the way, and almost taking in a little bear, on the way, too. "Don't feed the bears!" the tourists were warned. For the behavior of animals is as unpredictable as that of man.

We drove our car right alongside of our steamship, on which it was to go as baggage for the price of a third-class ticket. We left the States with a very nice Seattle hotel as our parting impression. By this time, Yuenren and I had begun to feel like commuters between America and China, and the departures and arrivals seemed to have less of the feeling of eventfulness than on our first trips.

As usual, I prepared the children's minds (as well as my own) for a new condition of living by talking about it before hand. While on board the S.S. "President Jefferson," we talked about the delicious puffed fritters and stuffed dumplings we were about to have. But Iris and Nova were more concerned with having to change their language in school again. Starting life in English-speaking Cambridge, then changing over to French-speaking "Maman de St. Aubin," then to Chinese at the Tsing Hua Primary and the Auguste Comte School in Pei ping, then to English at Oyster and Brightwood Schools at Washington, now they had to change back into Chinese again. We had always spoken Chinese at home, which was a great help. But when the children went to school, they had to speak in one more accent. For, instead of going back to Peiping, settled down in "the South."

51

A "PERMANENT" HOME IN NANKING

OUR FAMILY was reunited at Shanghai when Bella met us at the Whampoo Wharf, accompanied by the T'angs and her nurse. Lensey wanted to take her home at once.

"Mei want Bella to play with Mei," she said, speaking of herself in the third person, as usual.

I was awfully disappointed that Bella looked at us with a blank stare—though that was only to be expected. But the T'angs had been very thoughtful in often speaking of Daddy and Mammy and all the sisters, and showing her our photographs. So it took only a few days for Bella to feel as one of the family again. Her homecoming was also made easier by her nurse coming over with her. But it gave us another problem. She lived her world through her nurse's world. If someone gave her something to eat, she would turn around and ask: "Ma, do I like this?"

And it took a lot of tact and love to make her discover a world for herself at first hand.

Lensey's prestige as the baby of the family for a year and a half was lowered when Bella returned home. It suffered another setback when "Mei" noticed that Bella already knew how to use the first person pronoun *wo*, that is, "I." One day, she decided to talk like a big child and started to say "I" instead of "Mei." She was so elated over her accomplishment that she exclaimed: "I have learned it, I have learned it! Mei can say 'I' now. Mei don't say 'Mei' any more.

We lived at Shanghai for nearly a year before finally moving to Nanking. The Institute of History and Philology of Academia Sinica had moved in 1933 from Peiping to its temporary office at the Little Hall of Ten Thousand Willows, near St. John's University. We took a house on Edinburgh Road, which was conveniently located near Yuenren's office and the children's school—the primary department of McTyeire's, in fact. Iris and Nova were in the grades and Lensey in the kindergarten. They had lessons in Mandarin, which they already spoke better than their teachers. But most of the people they met in school talked the Shanghai dialect.

The house we rented was a large, modernized *lungt'ang* style apartment. It was comfortable enough, but I took little interest in it, since I was looking forward to going back to Nanking, where Academia Sinica was having its permanent headquarters built on the southern side of Peichi Ko, about one mile north of Yenling Hsiang. While Yuenren made frequent trips to Nanking to see about the wiring and soundproofing of his phonetic laboratory, I made plans for selecting a site and building a permanent home there.

It was a time of real estate boom in Nanking. Besides the Institute of History and Philology, other public buildings were going up. The Central Hospital and the Civilian Airport were filling out the ruins of the Ming palaces. The Observatory of Academia Sinica was placed high up on the Purple Mountain, with the city wall running along below it like the Great Wall. The Mausoleum of Dr. Sun Yatsen, the open-air Amphitheater—bigger than that of Arlington behind the Unknown Soldier—and many landscape projects outside the Chaoyang Gate promised to make the suburb continuous with Nanking itself.

It was not only the government that was lavishing money on making external shows, but the bankers, too, went heavily for investment in mortgages on houses and residences. People like ourselves were of course not unaware of the uncertainty of the times under worsening national and international conditions. But what was our judgment worth against that of the hard-boiled businessmen, who were ready to put up real cash for good, solid earth? Business must have been business.

So, after selecting a nice one-third-acre lot at No. 24 Lanchia Chuang, about seven minutes' walk from Peichi Ko, where were Yuenren's office was built, we borrowed enough money from a bank to buy the land and build a big, comfortable house of ten spacious rooms. As an afterthought, we enlarged our plans by adding a smaller house for the use of one of Yuenren's schoolmates and his family.

"With your ability, Mrs. Chao," said my banker Mr. T. T. Zee, "all you have to do is to draw your plans and I will let Mr. Chao sign on the dotted line. You are as good a risk as I can find anywhere in town."

This flattered me so much that, when I inherited from my family a small lot at 9 T'ienyin An, near Cousine Chinghua's[1] house, I recklessly borrowed some more money and built a little six-room house, "just for fun," I thought. This caprice of mine turned out to be an act of great prudence and apparent forethought. However, that is anticipating by eleven years.

The Institute building was completed first. So we moved from Shanghai to Nanking and lived temporarily in my old home on Yenling Hsiang. There was one small courtyard of two deep rooms, in which nobody had lived for many years. They were afraid to go in there because Big Sister, Second Sister, Big Sister-in-law, and one niece had died in them. I went in and had the rooms completely renovated and a kitchenette and a bathroom added. When we moved in, Yuenren wrapped two copper coins in a piece of red paper and handed the package to Third Brother as "rent." For a married woman is not supposed to have her husband stay with her in her own house, but if part of it is rented, it will be all right.

---

[1] Cousine Chinghua is Aunt Ch'eng's youngest daughter, for whom I have a special partiality, in spite of her being my late ex-fiancé's sister.

After we moved into this cozy little corner, I watched the building of my house at Lanchia Chuang. I had no architect, but drew my own plans—since I did not know how to draw elevations or perspectives. My contractor interpreted my ideas in the form of blueprints. But under the pressure of my constant hurrying, something went out of joint which nobody had noticed until they came to it. As there is a saying that a house is right so long as all staircases are right, I was careful not to have any upstairs without stairs leading up to it, or any stairs without a landing to lead up to. But surely you ought to be able from any room to the next on the same floor so long as you had a hole between them. I discovered, however, that that was not necessarily so. I found the study on the second floor several feet lower than the adjoining bedroom—I had forgotten that, while the garage under the study was almost level with the ground, the main first floor was several feet higher, as they should have been. The remedy was simple.

One of the reasons for which I was anxious to have a permanent house was to have a place to store our things. I like to travel, but hate to move house all the time. When I discovered my mistake in my amateurish architecture, Yuenren had a brilliant idea. Why not raise the floor of the study by adding a mezzanine floor between the garage and the study and make a stack room out of it? Thus, we gained something new as a result of a mistake. When all of Yuenren's books were finally on the shelves, I said, more prophetically than I knew: "If you ever have to move house again, Yuenren, I would rather put a torch to this and have the whole thing burned."

My feeling of settledness was shared by my relatives. On moving day, April 10, 1935, Cousine Chinghua sent us a batch of steamed prosperity cakes, made of very fluffy raised dough. Cousine Lang had a seventeen-year-old monthly-blossoming rose transplanted from her courtyard to Lanchia Chuang. Second Brother gave me his thirty-three-year-old wax-plum tree in like manner. Sixth Brother, who was living in a separate house, gave us two kittens, each sleeping in one of Lensey's slippers. Nephews and nieces, from Shihfeng and Lucy down, roamed over the new garden and in the new house. When Iris and Nova, Lensey and Bella entered the rooms of their own and looked out at the Hill of Peichi Ko to the west and the Purple Mountain to the north, they said they were so happy they wanted to cry.

I am an early riser, and early rising fits well with gardening. Besides the flower trees transplanted from Yenling Hsiang, I bought pines from the Ling Yuan nurseries. I collected roses and had more than thirty varieties of yellow roses alone. Yuenren was especially interested in keeping me supplied with chrysanthemums in the autumn. For he still felt apologetic about having stepped on and broken my pot of chrysanthemums the second day we met.

Now that we had a permanent home, we started going places again. For one of the pleasures of travel is to have a home to come back to.

My excursions from Lanchia Chuang ranged from an afternoon's drive to the Yentzu Rock on the Yangtze—where the signs said to would-be love-suicides: "Turn back and think how beautiful a world you are leaving behind!"—to a week's trip to the Yellow Mountains. If the gravel highway had not caused eight flats to the tires, I could have made a one-day trip to the strange formations of stalactites and stalagmites in the cave of Yi-hsing, near Yuenren's hometown. I had always maintained that my province had better highways than Yuenren's had. The proof of that was that on my second trip to the Yellow Mountains in Anhwei, Yuenren was able to drive in one day to the foot of the mountains from Nanking without a single flat tire.

The Yellow Mountains of southern Anhwei were alternately famous and forgotten once every few centuries. Our time was the beginning of another comeback. On my first visit, when Yuenren was making a survey of the dialects, together with Lo Ch'angp'ei and Yang Shihfang, we had had to ride in sedan chairs or wade in mountain streams. The second time, we arrived by car to a China Travel Service hotel and were able to start a three days' climbing with untired legs.

In spite of lack of waters and color effects, the formations and vistas of the Yellow Mountains surpassed anything else I had seen. I had seen the Yellowstone and the Alps. Yuenren had seen those, plus Grand Canyon and Yosemite. But he still preferred the Yellow Mountains. He said it was least unlike Yosemite, except that it was even more varied. One moment, you were on a precipice, facing a single piece of rock, three thousand feet tall, rising from the abyss under your dangling feet. At the next turn, you had to cross a "Perch's Back,"—a very natural and long ridge, with a drop of a couple of thousand feet on both sides. The guides told me that I was the first woman to have crossed the "Perch's Back"—unless they counted the female monkeys. You had to cross that ridge to get to the top of the City of Heaven. The City of Heaven was rightly called, for before you reached that 6,000-foot peak, you had to pass a cave with the architectural effect of a great temple or palace. Coming down from the peak, you would cross an open space of smooth rocks on which you imagined you could lay a couple of crossed airstrips.

Not all views there are of the mountains. From the Lion's Forest, where visitors usually spent a night at the temple, you got up to see sunrise over the sea of clouds. I called one of the rocks we climbed "The Homeward-gazing Terrace." For from there, about fifteen miles to the northwest, I could see the houses in my ancestral home city of Shihtai.

"Look, Yuenren!" I said, with more imagination than history "That's the house in which my grandfather was born!"

Yuenren tried to keep up with the ever-changing vistas with his camera, but the trouble with photographs is that they precisely miss the effect you most want. They always have a narrow point of view, whereas the main effect of those mountains is the rich variety of total scenes, of which you feel you are a part.

Neither Yuenren nor I had been to Taishan, Huashan, Omei, or any of the other famous mountains of China. People blamed us for having seen the Yellow Mountains first, because, they said, after the Yellow Mountains, there would be nothing left worth seeing.

Since we had to see some mountains, we planned a third trip to the Yellow Mountains. The trip did not come off. For it was later than we thought. The peaceful permanent home, to which all our trips were to return, soon became a dream and a memory.

52

A REALISTIC VIEW OF THINGS

BY THE SO-CALLED "Ho-Umezu[1] Agreement," the Chinese government troops were barred from going anywhere within a large chunk of their own country, including the Peiping region. People were incensed over the weakness of the government for making one concession after another to the advancing Japanese. Sporadic resistance arose against some of the puppet troops. Fu Tsoyi's fighting in Suiyuan caught everybody's imagination.

"We ought to be ashamed of ourselves playing mahjong all the time," some of us ladies said. "Why not let's get together and do something for the boys? It will be much more useful and just as much fun!"

So we formed a sewing circle and made hundreds of wadded jackets and had them sent to the cold North in the name of "the women of Nanking."

The lack of resistance on the part of the government was of course easily understood in the light of after-wisdom. But at that time, it led to a national crisis.

I happened to be called to Shanghai because of Ts'ai Yuanp'ei's illness. There had been great confusion over doctors. His family believed in herb medicine. Others attending him, mostly members of Academia Sinica and Ts'ai Hsiensheng's former students, believed in

---

[1]The same Yoshijirō Umezu who signed the Japanese surrender at Nanking in 1945.

Western medicine. They claimed the right to decide, because, they maintained, Ts'ai Hsiensheng belonged to the nation and was not the property of the family. I had the delicate job of trying to harmonize the conflicting views, in order that the patient could get some consistent treatment. I had to appear not to take any sides, although, naturally, I was partisan to the extreme. With moderate use of tact, helped out by the loudness of my voice, but principally through the influence of elderly Chang Yuanchi and the pleading of faithful Chiang Monlin, the situation was cleared up, and the patient started way back to health.

I had not looked at a newspaper for four days. While I was riding with Ting Hsilin in a street car, I heard the motorman swear in a violent Tientsin accent against the villain of a Chang so-and-so. What's this about Chang so-and-so? What's he done? The motorman pointed at the headlines of one of those tabloid "mosquito newspapers" of Shanghai.

"It's preposterous!" I said to Mr. Ting. "These cheap, irresponsible papers would stop at nothing to make sensation."

"But it's true," insisted the motorman.

Mr. Ting and I could not quite dismiss the mosquito paper from our minds. When we came to the Ts'ai residence, we met Lo Chialun arriving at the same time in a car. We commandeered his car and drove with him to the office of the sixty two-year-old respectable *Shun Pao* and got a copy of its morning issue. It was true. The Generalissimo had been kidnaped by Chang Hsuehliang at Sian!

It was not only Lo Chialun the party member who was greatly perturbed. So was I. So was everybody else. The people of the country surprised themselves with such spontaneous expression of loyalty. The events of those days have of course become familiar history today. We all know now that the government had been trying to mark time in order to make better preparations for resistance, that the young marshal forced the issue of resistance now, and that a united front was formed, which later hastened the inevitable Japanese attack,

While we were having supper on Christmas evening, back in Nanking, our rickshaman came in and said excitedly: "T'ait'ai, Chiang Kaishek is free!" Those were his exact words.

Yuenren turned on the radio and the news was broadcast every few minutes. There were wild celebrations everywhere. We went to Huap'ailou to see the lantern processions. The crowd and the firecrackers fairly warmed up the winter night. That was how a united front felt if you ever were at one.

Spring of 1937 was the calm before the storm. It seemed calm at least in our kind of environment. An unusually late snow blanketed the whole city, and I went out with Yuenren to take dozens of photographs of rare snow scenes. It was also a season of great revival of interest in art. In the magnificent hall built for the People's Congress, to be convened in November, exhibitions were held of art treasures which had just been brought back to China after having been shown in London. In the same building, festival concerts were held, to which a chorus from the National Conservatory of Music came from Shanghai to give Haydn's *Creation* and the Yenching University chorus came from Peiping to give Handel's *Messiah*. Another big chorus from Shanghai sang Huang Tzu's *Ch'i Cheng P'iaop'iao* ("Banners are streaming") in the open-air Amphitheater. A group of charming American women teachers came to visit China and Yuenren was drafted to entertain them. Niels Bohr came from Denmark and lectured on atomic structure, emphasizing the logical and methodological aspects of physics.

The calmest of calm scenes I remember of that spring was that of one evening when we were having supper in one of those refreshment tents on a low cliff, just above the open-air Amphitheater, in front of the Mausoleum grounds. The moon was sailing idly through one transparent strip of cloud after another without getting anywhere. Nobody talked. For Y. C. Mei and the Y. T'angs were not the kind of company we needed to keep up a conversation with. Yuenren broke the silence.

"I wonder how often we shall be able to enjoy this kind of scene again."

Nobody made any remark to that.

The next morning, I picked up the *Central Daily News* and read that Japan had attacked Marco Polo Bridge.

A Chinese proverb says: "Good fortune never arrives in pairs, but bad luck won't travel alone."

As the war came nearer and nearer, Yuenren came down with malignant malaria, with a delirious fever of 104° Fahrenheit. When the high fever finally subsided, the temperature would not return to normal, because the weather was too hot. He could not stand noises, and the war had already come to Shanghai.

The government had already planned to move to the interior, and ordered those departments which were not needed for rear guard services to move inland first. Educational institutions stood high in priority for transportation. I asked some of Yuenren's associates what could be done with the transportation of things, and learned that so much public property had to be taken care of that one could not begin to talk about personal belongings. Fortunately, big worries have a way of being forgotten because of bigger worries. My uppermost thought was how to send my sick husband inland. After much difficulty, with the help of Y. T. Tsur and Y. S. Djang, I got two up-river tickets and sent Yuenren from bed to ship, accompanied by Iris as nurse.

Friends scolded me for not going with Yuenren at such a time. My plan was to get Yuenren in a place where there would be less danger of a relapse. We had friends in Hankow, like Sherman Wang, and friends in Changsha, like K. Chu, to take good care of him. I would follow along with the rest of the children as soon as we could get steamship accommodations. Meanwhile, I attended to my affairs in as rational a way as I knew how. It helped my morale. I had asked

Yuenren what he would most like to save and he had said that his diary and photographs were his most important possessions—other things could be bought with money. Standing in line for several hours at the post office, I caught one of the last mails going abroad and sent away his diary of thirty-one years and some four thousand snapshots he had taken over the past twenty years. (A few weeks later, R. W. King cabled from New York to Changsha, "Packages received.")

It was due day on the mortgage. When I went to see the manager of the bank with my installment, he said: "Why, Mrs. Chao! You would do this now of all times!"

Then the sirens wailed and bombs fell. I found myself repeating: "*Hao le, hao le!* What a relief! What a relief!"

The servants thought I was talking nonsense from fright. What I meant was what a relief it was, now that my husband was safely at Changsha when Nanking was bombed.

Nobody appreciated the meaning of an air raid. We had previously had blackout drills and admired the beautiful colored lights dropped as dummy bombs. We had passed models of 1000-pounders exhibited at street intersections and parks every day without giving them much thought. When sixteen enemy planes flew over Lanchia Chuang in perfect formation, everybody stood in the courtyard to watch. Nova sat on the top of a slide with a volume of a translation of Sherlock Holmes. She would not have been any more afraid if those planes had had atomic bombs in them. I was certainly foolish to have allowed anybody to stay outside, as machine-gun bullets from any of those planes would have been just as bad for us as bombs.

Telephones were busier than usual. Hu Shih, who was visiting at Nanking, called up and told me that Mrs. Hu and Mrs. Chiang Monlin were coming down soon from the North. I offered them the use of my house, as I was planning to go away. Then an American friend from the Embassy called up, asking us to dinner. I said Yuenren had left. Why didn't the rest of the family go? Because I had no tickets. So he kindly offered me some tickets he had got for his mother, as it was relatively easy for him to get more.

I had the beds made and flowers arranged in vases for the coming guests. I got ready a few bundles and a couple of suitcases and waited for the tickets. I took a look at each part of the house to see if everything was all right. A fleeting thought came and went: Will this be my last look at this home?

The day before our up-river steamer was to sail, I discovered that the man who was to bring me my tickets from my American friend had made away with them for himself and his family!

Part VI
WAR YEARS

53

REFUGEES TO CHANGSHA AND KUNMING

ONCE MORE I was reminded of the Chinese proverb which says: "Heaven never puts man on a deadend road." For I had not lost my tickets for many hours before I got some again for the same boat. It was C. T. Huang, a relative of Cousin Chungying's, who got them for me and the three children. I telegraphed to Yuenren and Iris at Changsha about our departure, and the four of us took leave of Lan-chia Chuang.

There was such confusion and crowding at the Hsiakuan wharf that we had to wait for seven hours before we finally got on board. The tickets were "for admission only." We had no space except crouching room. The air-raid alert sounded. The captain decided to cast off without waiting for the scheduled hour. This caused some ticket-holders to miss the boat, and we were thus able to get some berths to sleep in. Night fell, and, as our boat passed the bend of the river near the great antenna towers of the Central Broadcasting Station, we saw a great display of fireworks from the bombing and antiaircraft batteries. It was the worst raid Nanking had had so far. I hoped that my telegram had reached Yuenren, so that he would know that we were on our way.

The war was apparently farther away during the three days we went up the river. But when we arrived at Hankow, it was like Nanking over again, except that the air raids were a little less frequent. Our next problem was to find a place to sleep and to find some railroad tickets for going on to Changsha. We were lucky to find much friendly help in Hankow. The director of the Hankow Broadcasting

Station was Yuenren's former student. The Mayor was my relative's relative. They could get an additional car attached to the already filled train. But the rule required that there had to be a minimum of thirty passengers before a car could be added. So I got busy going around Hankow and rounded up Mrs. Y. Tang and her children, and three generations of the Li family, all of whom were needing railroad tickets as badly as we. Including their servants, I counted twenty-eight people in our party. In such an emergency, it was not much of a strain on my conscience to stretch it by two parts in thirty. So I told the man in charge of traffic that we had the necessary number of people and paid for the thirty tickets. Then I had the job of making special arrangements to get immediate transportation for forty-odd pieces of their baggage out of two different warehouses, get them ferried across to the station at Wuchang, and have them checked—all of which had to be done between air raids or air-raid alerts. In the final rush against time, Senior Mr. Li missed his traveling basket in which he had left a lot of cash. A frantic search, with the train ready to start any minute now. Finally, the basket was located, and I marched everybody onto the train, as I called the roll, to make sure that no child or servant got left.

Yuenren did not get my telegram from Nanking until after I arrived. But he did get my second telegram, from Hankow, telling him how many there were in my party. As he had anticipated, I arrived at Changsha quite hoarse from directing such a campaign. It was good to see him up and about. It was good to have our family together again. It was good to have helped people and to have been helped by people.

I am not a Buddhist in any fundamentalist sense. But I grew up in a Buddhist-minded family and believe in ultimate retribution and reward, or would like to. More than once, things have happened to me, when I have felt like giving up and saying: What's the use of doing good? But then something has always kept my spirits up, and so I continue to go out of my way to help others. As I still tell my children, do to others what they have failed to do to you, and you will feel better toward those who have failed you than if you failed them in return.

In the relative safety of Changsha, we faced an uncertain future. How was the war going to come out? How were we going to live? Group after group of people came from the North and from down river and set up refugee offices or institutions at Changsha. Together with some of the other early arrivals, Yuenren went about getting quarters for Academia Sinica, National University of Peking, National Tsing Hua University, and Nankai University. All the four refugee institutions were housed in the American Bible School building and soon started instruction and research the best they could.

Living was cheap and inflation had not yet begun. We rented a one-room-width second-floor apartment, with a bed-dining-living room, a veranda, and the use of a kitchen. Nova was sent as a boarding student to Fuhsiang School and Iris and Lensey as day students to Chounan School. With our salary cut from 500 to 180 dollars a month, we were able to actually save money for the first time in several years. With the rich variety of wonderful fresh-water fish of Changsha, I even entertained quite a lot.

My nephew Shihfeng, who arrived later from Nanking, brought from our house a few fur coats, a radio, five tablecloths (mistaken for sheets), and a big bag of old shoes (mistaken for new). With the radio connected, we tried every night to get the Hongkong rebroadcast of the BBC news through two stages of statics.

There were frequent air-raid alerts, at which everybody took whatever shelter he could find. At the Bible School, all the professors and the few students who had arrived would gather in the spacious basement of the main building. Air-raid alerts were getting to be quite a social affair for members of the four institutions of learning. Friends from different cities who rarely saw each other during peace years now had a chance to meet at these hours of enforced leisure.

"Do not put all your intellectuals in one basement," Yuenren remarked at one of these "socials."

On November 24, 1937, without a single siren sounding, I heard the crash of bombs and saw from my house dust rising in the direction of the Bible School. The bombs had been aimed at the railroad station and one of them fell only a quarter of a mile from the school. As we had no telephone, it was more than two hours before I was sure that all members of my family were all right. Lensey had been marching with her class of school children to visit the wounded soldiers. A bomb fell so near that the dust fell on her clothes—it had been a dud!

Then the sack of Nanking that shocked the world. True, most of my near relatives and friends had left. The national capital had moved to Chungking.[1] Nobody had expected that Nanking could be defended. But it was my Nanking. The fact that Nanking was lost weighed so heavily on me that it absorbed most of the shock of the subsequent news that my Lanchia Chuang home had been burned to the ground. I surprised myself with the calm with which I took the little news. I had left my home in such good shape that I often have the illusion of still having such and such a book on such and such a shelf before I remember that that was at Lanchia Chuang, Nanking, and not Walker Street, Cambridge.

The war came closer. Hankow and Canton were in peril. The educational institutions were ordered to move further inland. With the Y. S. Djangs, the Ting Supaos, the Yang Shihfengs, the Chang Shaohaos, and Ting Shengshu, twenty-eight of us got into two buses and started on our westward trek from Changsha to Kunming.

It's a long way to Kunming City. The shortest and hardest route across would be something like one thousand miles. The easiest, but most expensive, route would be to go through Hongkong and Indo-China. We took the intermediate route, through Kwangsi and Indo-China. The highways in Hunan were the best in China. They had better be, as our buses burned charcoal instead of gasoline and had

---

[1] Moved back to Nanking on May 1, 1946.

to go into low gear on the slightest excuse. When the driver stopped at a station and said, "Fill it up!" he meant he wanted to have a bag of pebble-sized charcoal fed into his barrel-shaped burner for making gas.

Life on the highways was pretty hard according to our soft standards. But it was great fun. Sometimes, we four families would spread our beddings on one large attic floor around a dim kerosene lantern and exchange ghost stories. Entering Kwangsi, we changed into gasoline buses, driven by student-like 'teen-age boys singing modern songs, to Ah Ting's accompaniment on a mouth organ. While we were having some *kuotzuli*, a kind of wild cat, at a Lungchow restaurant, six-year-old Little Szumei (Chang Shaohao's adopted daughter) remarked: "This is not traveling like refugees. This is just traveling."

As we passed the border town of Chennan Kuan, there was a sign which said: *"Guardez Votre Droite,"* and the bus changed from the left side to the right side of the road. In a few moments, we were at the customs house of Langson, Indo-China.

There was something depressing about the glum expression on the faces of the Annamites. Maybe it was something I put into them from reading what had been written about them. But most of our party shared my impression. Another impression, which was strongest with the men, was the great beauty of the Annamese women.

We occupied a fourth-class section of a train from Hanoï to Kunming. It had openings, but no windows. We piled our things in the middle and sat on both sides. Some farmers tried to come in with a big cage of live poultry.

"No room, no room!" the children of our party shouted.

"Is this section reserved?"

We could not answer yes, so the rest of us just repeated: "No room, no room!"

Which was near enough to the truth to be acceptable by our children's standards.

We entered China again when we crossed the Nanhsi River bridge from Laukai to Hok'ou. There was a noticeable change in the tone of life as we passed and stopped at various places in Yunnan province. I had heard of the poverty of the people and of the miserable conditions of mine workers there. Yet I got a distinct feeling of relief from the gloom of the last few days. Maybe the fact that we found a peaceful part of China cheered us up. Maybe the change from the oppressive jungles of Indo-China to the wide and deep gorges of Yunnan brightened up our outlook. Maybe it was the famous Yunnan—well, Yunnan is famous for many good things. After several days of indifferent fare and indifferent appetite, my nephew Shihfeng remarked idly: "I wish I had some soup noodles with thin sliced ham. I wouldn't mind if you put a few shreds of chicken on it."

"Silly dream!" his wife said scornfully. "Don't you know there is a war going on?"

The train stopped at a small station. A vender came up with a pole-load of steaming food.

"Refreshments! Refreshments!" he called. "Anybody want refreshments?"

At one end of the carrying pole were boiling-hot noodles on charcoal fire. At the other end were dishes of thin sliced ham— the famous Yunnan ham—one-fourth fat and three-fourths lean. Sorry, he had no chicken shreds, but would legs of chicken do, ladies and gentlemen? Upper leg, together with drumstick. Only a dollar a piece. And one dollar in Yunnan money was ten cents in the money we were carrying.

That was Yunnan in January, 1938, which later, after seven years of war, became the most expensive place in the world.

54

LIVING AT 6,000 FEET
ABOVE SEA LEVEL

OUR TRAIN STOPPED because the rails of Compagnie Yunnan did not go any farther. The setting sun was shining on the inscription on the gable of the terminal station: "YUNNANFOU 1896"

Yunnanfou was the old name for Kunming. The station, however, was not built in 1896, but around 1910. The number 1896 is the height in meters above sea level. That makes Kunming about the same height as the top of Mount Washington. But with the fields, the lakes, and the eucalyptus-lined aqueducts in and around the city, you could not tell how high you were, except that you got out of breath very easily for the first month and that it was harder to boil hard-boiled eggs.

I arrived at Kunming with a sense of finality. If we could not stay put in this corner peacefully "for the duration," then there would be no use moving on to anywhere else.

I liked many things about Kunming. First of all, the climate is the best in the world. The sun shines practically every day. Even during the so-called rainy season, the rain comes in showers, usually followed by sunshine. It is rarely colder than 60° and rarely warmer than 80° Fahrenheit, but the whole range is often covered by the changes occurring in one day, and that makes it rather invigorating. The exception that proved the rule was a snow which covered the ground for several hours. It was so unusual that shopkeepers had to stay in bed until noon, because they had no clothes to go out in for such a cold morning.

Being among the earliest arrivals among the refugees, we were fortunate to be able to find a good house, in the southeastern outskirts of the city. It had been built by the International Famine Relief Commission as an office while it was building a highway to Kweichow. Our family used the spacious attic for bed-dining-living room, and Yuenren used the rooms downstairs for the office of the Linguistic Section of his institute, which was the first part of the refugee institutions to resume work after their second removal.

The material conditions were more primitive than at Changsha. Electric power had not extended to that part and we had to use kerosene lamps for light. A well in the backyard was the source of our water supply. We slept on wooden boards. You would be surprised how quickly you could get over the feeling of not being able to lie down flat. But after you used to that, you would be surprised what a sinking sensation you got when you changed into a spring bed again. (The stories about returning soldiers preferring to sleep on the floor must be true.)

To supplement the old furniture which went with the house, we bought wooden boxes from the airlines. If a flight of a Douglas plane used 2,000 gallons of gasoline, they would have 200 wooden boxes for sale, as each box contained two five-gallon cans. Bookcases and fancy modernistic furniture could be made out of combinations of these boxes.

Our radio got out of commission from damage during transportation—we had no electricity to run it even if it had not. There was only a piano or two in the whole city. So, in order to keep up the children's music and his own morale, Yuenren arranged parts for a number of songs to sing with the children. He said they learned more music during those months than in years when we had both a piano and a radio.

All was not nice and comfortable. But once you decided to like a place, you wouldn't mind many things. There was a moderate breeze all the year round. Our upstairs room was always drafty. With the children's mechanical construction set, Yuenren built a windmill and hung it in the room to test the draft. Sometimes it was so much fun to watch the windmill turn that he purposely opened the window to let the draft in.

Once there was an unusually heavy rain. The roof leaked at several places. After trying to hold all the drippings with pots and basins, Yuenren had to put on his raincoat and hat in the room to keep dry. Remembering that Robert Louis Stevenson was a source of optimistic feelings, he made the following parody of "Rain":

> "The rain is raining all around,
> It falls on field and tree,
> It rains on all my children here,
> And on my wife and me.

I have spoken of ham and chicken noodles we had on the train; 1938 was still a golden age in Kunming. Giant-size hen's eggs were a dollar and a half a hundred. Yellow peaches covered the sidewalks, selling for next to nothing. Goat's cheese was plentiful and good, but I did not stay long enough to learn to like it. The P'u'er tea of southern Yunnan used to be sent to the imperial court in the form of bricks of black tea. But in Kunming we actually had *green* P'u'er tea. Though it sounded to me like a contradiction in terms, it tasted delicious.

The southwestern provinces form a rich region for the scholars to study the aboriginal tribes and languages. But in a large city like Kunming it is sometimes hard to tell a Lolo from an ordinary Chinese, as most of them speak some Mandarin. Oftentimes you could spot the Lolo men by the embroidered sandals they wore. I admired them—the sandals—so much that I had many pairs of them made for myself and my daughters, but Yuenren refused to walk as a Lolo. The Lolo women have large beautiful eyes and clear features. There are many names for the languages and tribes in the Southwest, but, in popular usage, they are often called Lolo or Miaotzu indiscriminately.

My kind of environment made me notice, if not very much interested in, the linguistic and ethnological sides of Yunnan. If I was not naturally language-conscious, I had certainly become language-husband-conscious. For I could not help noticing things when Yuenren and his colleagues argued endlessly downstairs, separated by only one layer of wooden flooring from my attic.

But, in the course of a few weeks, things began to hum in less academic tones, and quiet and quaint Kunming changed into a busy bustling town of a wartime metropolis. A school of aviation was opened in the suburb on our side of the city. The three universities which had moved from the North to Changsha were now in Kunming and formed the National Southwestern Associated Universities. Uniforms were more noticeable on the streets. Automobiles tags reached the high number of "0066."

Faces, too, grew more and more familiar:

Here comes our epicurean logician Lao Chin, who tries to imitate my buying technique and chooses a worse sample of Yunnan ham, because it's smart to refuse the first offered, which is actually better—

Here is Chang Hsijo, champion of political liberalism. As well dressed as ever, he still remembers to tease Yuenren about having to be reminded by street urchins that he needs a haircut—

Physicists P. Y. Chou and C. K. Jen[1] call on us and offer suggestions about improving the construction of Yuenren's windmill—

President Chang Poling of Nankai, whose son has recently died while serving in the airforce, brings with him his ever contagious optimism about the future. No, Chang Hsiensheng, better not sit on that frail box, this chair is much safer for weight—

---

[1] Why does Mrs. C. K. Jen keep calling me *"chen bang, chen bang!"*?—*Lensey.* Because you like to argue and never give in.— *Mammy.*

Well, if it isn't Nyokzoe, my McTyeire schoolmate! When did you get back from Moscow? We haven't seen each other since Nanking—

And so they came, till I lost all sense of where I was. Then came the swelling sound of the footsteps of marching students of three universities. I spoke of three routes from Changsha to Kunming. One group of several hundred students marched all the way on foot for one thousand miles overland. Some ladies organized a canteen two miles out, at Chang Shao hao's country home, to welcome them. I organized a party to present them with a flower basket at the city limit. Yuenren improvised a parody of "Tipperary" and distributed mimeographed copies to them, which they sang as they entered the city. As we watched the formation file past our door, Nova was not aware of the existence of one of the boys who was to be her future husband.

We were all optimistic about the outcome of the war. We could not see exactly how victory was to come about, but the belief in final victory was what kept our spirits up. It was nice to see more and more old friends again. It was healthy to resume some of the activities of our kind of life.

But there were some things we could not fool ourselves about. Yuenren had been slow in regaining his health. He was more absent-minded than ever. I felt best when I was busily occupied, but, since Yuenren's illness, I had lost eighteen pounds, and my memory, which used to retain every essential thing in a book I had read once, began to play tricks on me. Starting as an absent-minded *professor's* wife, I gradually became myself an absent-minded professor's *wife*.

After finishing with his collaborators a 1700-page report on the survey of Hupeh dialects, Yuenren felt that he needed a rest. An opportunity for a rest came. Two years back, Director Gregg M. Sinclair of the Oriental Institute of the University of Hawaii had asked Yuenren to visit there for a year. With his hands full of projects and so soon after his 1932-33 visit to America, Yuenren did not feel like taking another leave. Now he was ready to accept the standing invitation. I thought of letting him take Iris and Lensey along, while I would remain with Nova and Bella, as Nova did not want to go and Bella, without her "Ma" this time, was too young to leave me. But Yuenren would not have the family separated. On August 1, 1938, with Nova crying, our whole family of six bade goodbye to our friends, as they waved to us at the station under the sign "YUN-NANFOU 1896" and we retraced the winding route through tunnels and gorges towards Indo-China, on our way to peaceful Hawaii.

As farewell gift, Mr. and Mrs. Chiang Monlin presented us with a beautiful vessel of pottery for steaming chicken, which Mrs. Chiang had carried in her lap while flying from Mengtze to Kunming. On the lid of the pot, was inscribed a motto, in gently chiding characters:

"The Old Country Can Be a Home."

55

A YEAR OF HAWAIIAN SUMMER

I WENT TO HAWAII in 1938 with nothing but summer clothes. It was only a one-year plan. Yuenren should be able to regain his health after a year on the beaches of Waikiki, and we would then return to Kunming, or, as I fancied, possibly to Nanking. I had little idea that this was to be my longest stay in America.

I shared the common impression of outsiders that Honolulu was not United States, but a United States military outpost in a country inhabited by aboriginal natives and a large Chinatown population. I have actually heard people from the States ask what kind of money they use over there and what their postage stamps look like. My previous one-day visits had not taught me much. But when I actually lived there, I found that there was much greater approach to harmony between racial groups than anywhere else.[1] I often did the tactless thing of speaking of the white people there as "Americans." But they are all Americans. The white Americans, as against the non-white Americans, are called *haoles*, a *haole*,[2] in the Hawaiian language, meaning a person who does not have to work.

One of my previous impressions which remained with me was the holiday air about the whole place. While the 60-degree mornings and evenings of Kunming stimulate you to work, the constant 75- to 85-degree days of Honolulu send you to the beach and make you feel like going barefoot all the time. We did have a few chilly days in

---

[1] See E. G. Burrows, *Chinese and Japanese in Hawaii during the Sino Japanese Conflict*, Honolulu, 1939, in which he reached similar conclusions.
[2] Pronounced *how lay*.—Y.R.C.

November, but we all went to have our regular bathing on New Year's Day.

Our house was one of a row of pretty bungalows on Lunalilo Street, with small but comfortable rooms. A tall tree in our neighbor's yard dropped ripe mangoes into our yard, while a still taller tree in our yard dropped ripe coconuts into the other neighbor's yard. When I gossiped with Mrs. Kam, our mangoes neighbor, and Iris called me up to say supper was ready, I could hear her both through the telephone and through the windows.

Being prepared to stay at Honolulu for a whole year, of course I never visited the Aquarium. I had already "done" the Aquarium as a tourist. I thought that the Hawaiian fish markets must be the richest in the world. I had heard of the fish called *homohomonukunukuapua*, a four-inch little fish, and the *o*,[3] a big, long fish. Would they taste as interesting as they sounded? But when I went to the fish market, I was greatly surprised to find that there was less variety of fish there than in Peiping or Washington, not to say Shanghai or Boston. They had only the usual things like tuna or flounder and, owing to some special conditions, all the seafood was expensive. Shrimps and lobsters had to be even imported from the mainland.

I found catching seafood more fun than buying seafood. Our neighbors the William Kams had a villa on the north side of the Oahu Island, on the opposite side of Honolulu. They used to take our whole family there in a car to do squidding. Each of us would wade over prickly corals with a glass-bottomed box, into which you could look through the shallow water. If a squid caught hold of you before you caught hold of it, the thing to do was to bite its head with your teeth and its tentacles would release their hold at once. But I never had occasion to bite a squid until after it was properly seasoned and cooked.

Crabbing at night was even more fun than squidding at day. For this I sometimes went with the Kams, sometimes with Mrs. Loo

---

[3]Pronounced very short, like *o* in *obey*.—Y.R.C.

Goon, who had a fishery near Pearl Harbor—the Pearl Harbor before "Pearl Harbor," of course. Mrs. Loo Goon is a remarkable Chinese woman. She was widowed young and had to raise a family of ten children single-handed. She put all her children through college in Hawaii or in the States, got them established, and found time to study Mandarin on the side. I used to meet her at some of the social-service meetings and was often invited to visit her fishery for picnics and crabbing, Once, four of us ladies caught one hundred pounds of crabs in one evening's operation.

I lived idly and a good deal out of doors because I minded the constant summer heat and had no mind for work. But Yuenren found that he had more to stay indoors for than he had expected, though it suited his sedentary habits very well. He had some good students in his language courses, but was bored by his own lectures on the History and Appreciation of Chinese Music. He is fond of "doing something with Chinese music," but frankly unappreciative of Chinese music as it is. In order to find what could be appreciated in the history of Chinese music, he went into such technicalities as Chinese scales and the Chinese discovery of equal temperament one hundred years before the Occidental discovery. That was of course over the head of most of the students, as it still is over mine.

The children had stiff schedules of their own. Iris and Nova entered Roosevelt High School. This was their third change of reading language, not counting their previous changes of spoken language from English to French and from French to Chinese. Each day for the first few days they would come home with six hundred new words for Daddy to tell them the meanings of. The school newspaper made much of the fact that their favorite subject was mathematics. The reason was of course that mathematics was the subject with the least number of new words.

Lensey and Bella did not even know how to speak English. Didn't Lensey learn to speak it while in Washington? She did. But as soon as she returned to China in 1933, she refused to speak a word of English. When urged to keep up such a valuable accomplishment, she would reply: "You are talking about promoting native goods all the time. What I am doing is just promoting our native language."

The war with Japan made the Chinese in Hawaii, both those of Chinese citizenship and those of American citizenship, more China-conscious. There was great interest in the study of Mandarin. The Chinese community organized a School of National Language for businessmen and students to learn to speak Mandarin. It fell on me and Iris to do the actual instruction. The students ranged from young men and women who knew no spoken or written Chinese, but only English, to elderly men and women, who knew no English, but only the Cantonese form of Chinese. As I had more experience with people and knew better literary Chinese, which some of the pupils already knew, and as Iris had a better Peiping pronunciation and better English than I, we divided our classes according to age. Some of my pupils were contemporaries and friends of Dr. Sun Yatsen at the Iolani School. Their enthusiasm encouraged the fifty- or even sixty-year-old youngsters to remember that "you are never too old to learn,"—we say that, too, in Chinese.

On my two previous visits to festive Hawaii, I had expressed a wish to stay at least "a couple of months" in order to enjoy it fully. But a perpetual summer was too much of a good thing. Like the others there who had lived in continental countries, I soon learned to be ship-conscious. I liked to meet people who passed there for a day and ask how things were on the mainland and how the war had been affecting our friends in China, for you couldn't get such intimate news about people from newspapers and letters. To those who had been born in Hawaii, that was the world; but to those who had been around, the whole Oahu Island was only one afternoon's drive.

Then, on summer solstice day, 1934, I had the great experience of coming into contact with the farthest end of the world from Oahu.

There was an amateur radio operator, Mr. Smith, who had a station at Kokokahi, on the north side of the island. He had contacted

Mr. J. S. Lee, Director of Institute of Geology of Academia Sinica, then stationed at Kweilin, Kwangsi. Learning that Lee knew us well, Smith arranged for us to talk with him. His hour was about six to seven o'clock in the morning. So I went with Yuenren to stay at Kokokahi the previous night, in order to get to his station in time for the rendezvous.

With that home-made set of crude-looking gadgets in a dilapidated shack, I would not believe that one could hear halfway around the world, not to say talk to such a great distance. I was right. After starting and stopping various switches, twisting this and turning that dial, and calling, "Hello, this is K6OQE, hello, this is K6OQE," time after time, Mr. Smith could find no Mr. Lee, no Kweilin, and no China. But he reached even farther than China. A voice from Livingston, Northern Rhodesia, the exact antipodes of Hawaii, came out as clear as from a table model receiver, "Good morning, Harold!" it said. We were asked to say "Good morning" in reply. It was certainly a great sensation to actually talk to a person on the opposite side of the earth. I was not unconscious of the carrying power of my voice, but had not realized that it would carry that far.

The morning wore on. The sun was well above the horizon now and Mr. Smith would soon have to sign off for the day to catch his nine-o'clock office hour in Honolulu, on the other side of the island.

"Thank you ever so much for such a wonderful treat, Mr. Smith," I was ready to say, when out came another voice from the loudspeaker with a distinctively familiar accent. Mr. Smith did not know who it was or where it was from. What was he saying?

"Calling Mr. Chao Yuenren! Calling Mr. Chao Yuenren!" he seemed to be saying.

"How would he know there was a 'Chao Yuenren' here?" we wondered.

The call continued: "This is Tsing Hua University Experimental Station, Kunming. Calling Mr. Chao Yuenren!"

There was no mistake about it.[4] We were more excited than even Mr. Smith, because Yuenren and I agreed in guessing whose voice it was. So we introduced the operators to each other. But it was slow work. To confirm our guess, Mr. Smith had to sign off by saying, "This is K6OQE, Kokokahi, signing off. Go ahead, Tsing Hua University Experimental Station!" and then switch over to the listening position.

For, according to regulations, amateur radio operators were not allowed to keep two channels open both ways all the time like a commercial radio telephone, but had to shut off when listening, in order not to waste channel time. When we were in the sending position again, Yuenren said ceremoniously: "Mr. Jen, this is Mr. Harold Smith of Honolulu. Mr. Smith, this is Mr. J. K. Jen of Kunming."

That, however, was not quite correct manners. For the rule among professional amateur operators was that, while on the air, they must know and call each other by their first names only.

We exchanged pleasant surprises and personal news and almost caused Mr. Smith to be late to his office.

That experience gave me at once a sense of freedom and a sense of restlessness. If ten thousand miles was so near, why couldn't I go thousand miles any day I wanted to?

On July 14, 1939, we were all packed up, ready to sail.

Yuenren's next-room colleague at Academia Sinica, Li Fangkuei, and his family had been staying with us. Li had been Visiting Professor of Chinese Linguistics at Yale University and they were now on their way back to China. As usual, the grownups had been telling the children how nice it would be to return home, and what a lot of

---

[4]While I was right in identifying the voice that was calling, I was wrong about the name that was being called. Actually, they were calling a station on Catalina Island, California and we happened to have tuned in on the Tsing Hua band.

good things there were to eat in China. Five-year-old Lindy and three-year-old Peter both talked perfect English.

"You are all saying what a nice country China is," Lindy addressed everybody in general. "If China is such a nice place, why does everybody want to go to America?"

The Lis sailed in the morning on their way to Kunming, Yunnan.

That evening, the Chaos sailed toward San Francisco, on their way to New Haven, Connecticut.

56

"YOU'VE COME A LONG WAY"

YUENREN OFTEN SAYS that there are three classes of Chinese citizens. The first-class Chinese moved into free China in the interior, shared the hardships of their fellow citizens, and helped win the war. The second-class Chinese went abroad when they could and sat out the war in safety and comfort. The third-class Chinese remained in occupied China and became puppets and collaborators. He considers ourselves second-class Chinese, exempting Iris and Nova, who are American citizens.

When Li Fangkuei wrote to Yuenren from New Haven that he was planning to return to Kunming and that Yale would like to ask Yuenren to go there as visiting professor, with few hours to teach and many hours in which to talk shop with the "Yale School" of linguists, Yuenren found the temptation too great to resist. So, instead of going westward to return to the Orient, we went eastward toward that part of the Occident which Americans call "the East."

Our trip from Honolulu to New Haven took nearly two months, which was a rather short time for attending an international conference, visiting a national park, and seeing two world fairs, in addition to traveling all that distance.

Having come to San Francisco from Honolulu, I had the illusion that summer was over. But it was summer again as soon as we left the bay region. It was 120 degrees in the shade when we drove past Death Valley and the wind blowing on my face felt like the air from an oven. As Yuenren was the only driver of the family, he was more affected by the heat than the rest of us. We rested a few days in the

Yosemite National Park. After having twice visited the Yellow Mountains of southern Anhwei, Yosemite was something of an anticlimax to me. Perhaps I would not have found it so if I had not been concerned about Yuenren's health. For I was never sure, until a year later, of his complete recovery from the effects of the malignant malaria he had had in 1937.

In order to ease the job of the driver, we took the shortest route across the continent at a leisurely pace.

"You've come a long way," was a common greeting by people who noticed Li Fangkuei's license tag of "CONN YU 879," which we were still using. Then Yuenren would go to great lengths explaining that we had just arrived in America, that a friend of ours from Connecticut had left the car for us at San Francisco, and that we were driving from there back to Connecticut. But that form of greeting was so frequent that Yuenren got tired of explaining everything each time. Besides, it seemed a little incongruous to stop a fellow who only said "How do you do?" to you and make him wait until you finished a whole long paragraph in reply. So, after a while, whenever anybody said, "You've come a long way," we simply answered "yes." Which was of course perfectly true—in fact, truer than the original remark was meant.

Strange how little insignificant things get attached to certain memories with more vivid feelings than things that you can name and describe. In both our driving trips across the continent, it was the children who "set the tone" of the journey. In our trip from Washington to Seattle in 1933, they sang *Lazy Bones* and *Stormy Weather* all the way. Silly words and silly tunes, those. But then there came a time when they ceased to be boring. After that they became a center of feelings always connected with that trip.

This time, it was a still sillier song: *The Three Little Fishes*, which the four silly little children kept singing all over the place. Then, when we stopped in a nice three-room cabin at the foot of the mountain where Brigham Young had said, "This is the place," the children started something else. They invented an artificial language. *Z-blah* means means "want," *ngécou-ngécou* means "eat," *ngahme'r* means "good," with tones and all. Not that I wasn't often annoyed with the noise they were constantly making, especially when I was busy packing and unpacking or when Yuenren was trying to pass a truck on a hill. Although the children have long forgotten most of the vocabulary of some one hundred words of their artificial language, and I never learned it, the sound of *The Three Little Fishes* still gives back the flavor of those days of driving across the country.

It was getting more and more to be like returning to America when we reached "the East" and started seeing old American friends. Well, we did not find each other so old after these years, the W. P. Daveys, the R. W. Kings, or the Y. R. Chaos, but where do these big children all come from? When they met last, they had exchanged paper dolls. Now they were exchanging notes about high school life and about movie stars.

We wound up our grand tour by a visit to the New York World's Fair. I found the outside effect more like that of the Chicago World's Fair of 1933 and did not like it so well as the San Francisco Fair we had just come from. I am a conservative in architecture.[1] Buildings have to look like buildings in order to be judged as buildings. The big halls and courts of the San Francisco Fair looked and felt big because they were of the more conventional forms of buildings but very much bigger. Walking among them made you feel that the great palaces of fairy stories had come to life. But with those geometrical shapes representing nothing in particular, the moment you stood a little distance away from them, they began to look quite small because of perspective, and you couldn't distinguish them in your mind from those toy models of spheres and spires.

For that same reason, I enjoyed very much the General Motors show called the "Futurama." It was so popular that people had to

---

[1] Except in the construction of mezzanines! —Y.R.C.

stand in line for two or three hours to see it. It was a dream of a show. In fact, the good thing about it was that you didn't have to wake up from the dream. You went into a darkish room to see some preliminary views of the future of highways in America on a big map, to get your eyes adapted. Then you sat down in a row of slowly moving chairs and began to feel that you were looking out from the windows of a bus or a train, passing miles and miles of highways and cities of the future. You were not conscious of the fact that the scale of the models became larger and larger. Instead, you felt that you were getting a closer and closer view of the same sizes of things. As you entered the city of the future, you noticed a nice and neat street corner, with elevated sidewalks, so proportioned as to look like about a block away. The "bus" stopped. You stepped out from your chairs and found yourselves on the elevated sidewalks of the "same" street corner you had just seen a moment ago. You could not recall exactly how you began to enter and form a part of that show. But there was no getting out of it. For this part was continuous with the rest of the World's Fair and thence with the rest of the world.

As a child, I used to hate to see the end of a party, with everybody dispersing and going away. That clever arrangement of the GM show made the ending so gentle that you could not draw the line between the dream city and the real world, between the future of a few minutes ago and the present to which you had just returned.

Yuenren was of course enthusiastic about such tricks of time and space. He said that it was a clever philosophical idea.

"If that can be called a philosophical idea," I said, "then I take back what I said against philosophy. I didn't know that philosophy built highways and cities."

It was time to get settled in New Haven, and we drove in confidently like an old-timer, as we had visited there twice in 1933. Arriving at the busiest center of the city, Yuenren tried to make a left turn at the intersection of Chapel and Church Streets, and was bawled out by the traffic officer. "No left turn," I supposed.

When we came to the same corner later, Yuenren tried to make a right turn. He was bawled out again.

"Can't you read, man?" the officer asked, more angry than ever, as he pointed at the sign overhead. It said, in big red letters: "NO TURNS."

"I'm sorry, officer, we are strangers here. You see, we've come a long w—," Yuenren checked himself. For he remembered that the tag we were carrying was not only that of Connecticut, but that the letters "YU" identified him as from Yale University.

57

NEW HAVEN, CONNECTICUT

THOSE WORDS of the traffic officer at the corner of Chapel and Church Streets were the only harsh words addressed to me during my whole two years' stay in New Haven. No, they were not, either. For they were addressed to the absent-minded professor, and not to the absent-minded professor's wife.

I soon found myself a natural part of the community with surprisingly little self-consciousness. So far as social life went, Yale might as well be a Tsing Hua University or an Academia Sinica, and the Department of Oriental Studies might as well be an Institute of History and Philology. When I watched Leonard Bloomfield think on his feet, which he did by tilting his head and looking at the left front corner of the ceiling, I immediately recalled Li Fangkuei doing exactly the same thing when he lectured in Nanking. And no wonder, since Li had been Bloomfield's pupil at Chicago.

One of the social functions I attended quite regularly was the Yale Linguistic Club, which met about once a month. Strictly, it was a professional gathering of linguists. But many wives of the members attended. Society began usually late Monday afternoon, when out-of-town members would arrive from Providence, New York, Philadelphia, etc. If I happened to drop in at the Hall of Graduate Studies, I would hear the resonant voice of Franklin D.[1] Edgerton echoing through the corridor. The party would begin with a dinner, at which no speech was made, since everybody spoke at the same time. One of the members would go around to collect payment for the dinner.

---

[1]Some of his correspondents refuse to believe that he has no middle name.

Once, I opened my handbag to pay for Yuenren and myself and I remarked that in China it was often the wife who loosened the purse string. At this, some of the wives present also loosened their purse strings, or started to. We would then retire to another place for the meeting proper, when some of the ladies would take out their knitting. I soon learned to do that, too, since I could not understand what the paper was all about most of the time. I did not have to sit through all that but for the fact that a midnight supper was still in store, usually in the basement of the Hofbrau. Here the arguments would continue along less scientific and more intelligible lines, until we felt that we were keeping the place from closing up for the night.

My contact was, of course, not limited to Yuenren's immediate associates. The F. W. Cokers, the Bert Andersons, the Triple-initial Northrops—you must pardon me for stopping trying beyond two initials! —what do they mean: "Yale is full of isolationists," when it has such world-minded people as those, not to speak of Wilsonian Seymour?

One reason that living in New Haven was more like living in an American community was the relative scarcity of Chinese there. There have always been few Chinese students at Yale, not more than a dozen usually. Occasionally, we got some live news from China when recent arrivals stayed with us for a short visit. One of our visitors was our old Cambridge and Peiping friend Dr. C.H. Hu, who had just come from Peiping. No sooner had he arrived than he at once made himself at home, as if it had been 3 Sacramento Place, Cambridge, Massachusetts, 1921.

"Let's roast a duck, Yuenren!" he said, as casually as "Let's make some tea!"

"All right," Yuenren said. "I'll help with the eating."

I bought and prepared the duck and Dr. Hu held it in front of the fireplace, rotating it continually Peiping fashion, so that the skin would not be flaky but shiny and crisp. The roast duck was a great success, making us all homesick for China. But the great pathologist from Peiping Union Medical College forgot that it was unhealthy to sit too near the fire. He got a terribly sore throat from holding that duck.

Another visitor of ours was also a doctor, who had come from Chungking for an operation at the New Haven hospital. After the operation, the responsibility fell on me, a doctor out of practice, to feed the convalescent doctor back to health. As our first floor flat on Orange Street was already full, I asked the Todds on the second floor whether they had rooms for a doctor friend of ours. They had. When Dr. F.C. Yen arrived, the Todds showed great surprise. Mrs. Todd took me to one side and said: "Excuse me, Mrs. Chao, but I thought it was a woman doctor."

"Did I say that he was a woman?" I asked.

"It's all right," Mrs. Todd said. "I'll take the makeup things off the dresser, and fix the room so that it will be suitable for a gentleman."

The incident was claimed to be a victory by my linguistic husband. For years he had been correcting my pronunciation of "he" and "she." I could distinguish the two words when I put my mind to it. But ordinarily, like the word "*t'a*" in the Liu-Chao song "How Can I Help Thinking of '*T'a*?" "he" and "she" in my pronunciation sound quite alike. I pronounce both words something like "hse," which Yuenren describes as consisting of two parts of "she" to one part of "he." That was what misled Mrs. Todd into thinking that I was talking about a woman. That was what gave Yuenren a chance to say, "Ha, I told you!" My reply was that if I had to wait for twenty years before it made any practical difference whether I said "he" or "she," then the difference wasn't worth waiting for. So, when later I wrote my cookbook, I continued to use my undifferentiated "hse."

We felt settled enough in New Haven to want a cat in the house. Yuenren and the children love cats by playing with them. I never play with cats. I love them by remembering to feed them and call them in when it's a cold night. But we all agree with William Lyon

Phelps in loving cats at least four times more than dogs; for he devotes, in his *Autobiography with Letters*, eight uncritical pages to cats and two critical pages to dogs.

We had not had a cat since we left our two kitties in Nanking, which Sixth Brother had given us. This time, it was Yuenren's Cornell classmate Leon Hausman who presented us with a tailless black cat. Kitty soon learned that Lensey was her chief moral support, but that I was the one to see to her wants. She liked to order you about, leading you to the kitchen or to the door, looking and meowing back to see that you followed her. You wouldn't dare not to do as you were told for fear of consequences, especially if you refused to follow her to the door. Yuenren spoiled her even further. If she happened to be purring comfortably on some of his papers, he would rather change to some other work than remove the cat. For, he said, once you disturbed a cat, it might be quite a long time before she would start purring again, or she might even be offended and would not stay in the room any more.

The tranquillity of our life with a purring cat was broken by two exciting incidents in the winter of 1939-40. One was a blizzard and the other was a fire.

There was a series of lectures on Chinese culture in New York, at which Yuenren was to give a lecture on Chinese music, to be assisted by Iris and Nova, who were going to sing the illustrations. The lecture was scheduled for the evening of February 14. The radio and the papers had warned motorists to keep off the highways, because a blizzard was coming. Earlier in the day, when Yuenren drove home from the office with Mr. E.H. Sturtevant, he had already made a perfect O-turn on the street.

"This-is-not-so-good," Mr. Sturtevant remarked, in his usual deliberate, professorial manner.

But Yuenren thought that he knew the Merritt Parkway so well that he could hold his course even if all landmarks had been obliterated. We four started out in the early afternoon to allow for delays.

As we got out of the city onto U.S. Highway No. 1, the snow drifts were piling up higher and higher. We passed a few abandoned cars. But that was no new sight in winter. A snowplow was standing still. Why doesn't the man get busy and clear up the highway? There was nobody at the wheel.

Then, to his consternation, Yuenren discovered that he had left his lecture notes and all his music at home! We turned back and got home, almost by "instrument driving." We were able to catch a train for New York because it was one hour late. We reached New York just in time for the lecture. With practically all surface transportation tied up, there was a good turn out of forty people to the lecture.

For once, it paid to be absent-minded.

The fire in our house was a more serious matter, because three gas-meters had burst into fame and a hole had already been burned in Lensey and Bella's bedroom when the fire was discovered. New Haven High School had very early classes, and Iris and Nova had already gone to school. I was awakened by Lensey's voice from the kitchen.

"Aiya! So much smoke!"

She had been trying to stop the smoke from issuing through the cracks in the kitchen floor and found that she hadn't enough feet.

I got up and noticed smoke coming out of the closet. "There is a fire," I said to Yuenren. I did not mean to be calm and articulate, but that was what I said.

Yuenren tried to turn on the light, as it was a dark winter morning, but the lights were already out of commission. I pulled Bella out of her bed, where she had covered herself in a quilt to keep the smoke out. She had thought that it was only something burning—which it was, too. Groping through the smoke-filled hallway, we were soon all on the street. I yelled, "Fire!" and a clanging fire-engine arrived in two seconds. Five more engines followed—our neighbors had already turned in the alarm when they noticed smoke coming out of our basement.

"Well! This the first time I have heard 'Fire!' that wasn't a mere illustration of the exclamatory sentence," Yuenren said to me with satisfaction.

Lensey acted quietly and rationally, and did exactly as I told her. I noticed a worried look on her face.

"It'll be all right, dear," I said to her repeatedly.

We were asked in by our neighbors the Dolans, from whose house we watched the firemen bring the fire under control. Food and other help were also offered by several other neighbors, whom we often passed on the street without a nod unless we should chance to meet them in a distant city or country.

When Iris and Nova returned from school, we were picnicking on the floor of our cold and smoky living room. They were very disappointed to have missed the show.

Lensey continued to have a worried look. I tried my best to make light of the whole incident, especially as we suffered no damage, apart from some scorched clothes and linen. By supper time, Lensey had gotten over her scare and worry and was quite herself again.

Several years later, Lensey wrote a theme on the story of that fire. "Where is the cat?" she asked herself, as soon as she found all the family was safely outside. "Where is the cat?" she repeated in paragraph after paragraph. The story ended happily with her discovery of the cat blinking miserably under the bed. She had been afraid to ask the question aloud until she was sure that the answer was the right one, after which there was no need to ask it.

As for me, I had been quite sure that animals could take care of themselves.

One cat was quite enough to keep me busy. Why should the children want to buy another? Besides, the big cat might not take kindly to the kitten. I studied the great big box, as we drove back from New York and tried to guess what surprise the children had brought for

Daddy and Mammy. I insisted on cutting holes in the box in order to give the pet some air, but the children only laughed. So I concluded that it was not a pet. Arriving home, the children shut us out of the dining room and kitchen for a long time.

Finally, twenty years to the hour after Hu Shih and Sister Hsiang came to supper with us in Peiping, the doors of our New Haven dining room swung open, and the children started a chorus of "Happy Wedding," as they escorted Daddy and Mammy to the feast they had "secretly" prepared. On a table, at one end of the gaily decorated room, was an enormous Swedish glass bowl, filled with a miniature landscape garden. That was the "pet."

New Haven was a good home for a home away from home. When we left for Cambridge in the summer of 1941, we said to our friends on our "P. P. C." cards:

"Thanks for everything, and thank you for having added for us one more place in the world returning to which will always be like returning home."

58

LOOKING AT YESTERDAY

CAMBRIDGE IS DIFFERENT. Cambridge doesn't count. Cambridge is almost yesterday, and it is hard to tell about yesterday and make it sound like autobiography. It is too near one to have any perspective.

As I sit here writing, trying to think of 9 T'ienyin An, Nanking, as my home, and wondering where I can find another bathtub to replace the one the Japanese took away from my house, my mind is still full of the little worries and trivial pleasures of life in Cambridge. I am unable to sort out what is worth remembering from what is not. How did I live, and what did I do while living in the Walker Street house? As I start telling about it, what I say gets to be more and more like the gossips and complaints I am in the habit of making when I write to Niece Lucy or Sixth Brother in Nanking. Of what general interest is it that my children never learned to return the kitchen things to their places after using them? What does it matter if I had trouble with my eyeglasses because, the doctor said, my astigmatism had gone and I didn't need glasses any more? Besides, where would such an isolated incident fit in?

The feel of yesterday's happenings is like the feel of that afternoon coming out of the "Futurama" show at the New York World's Fair. It was clever of its designers to make you step out of the scenes of reduced models onto the life-size street corner in the city of the future and walk from there continuously to the rest of the world. But in a few moments you were bound to reach the unromantic sight of crowded buses into the humdrum city of the present.

And yet, a near-sighted perspective is a perspective. Preoccupation with the smaller things of life seems to crowd out things that matter, just because the smaller things, for me, do matter. Though I was "Little Master Three" for the first twelve years of my life, and still show the effects of him, I have been a woman ever since I put on the dress of "Little Miss Three." As a woman, I am very much concerned with the smaller things of life. I may not like some of them as well as some others. Kindly time will usually fraction-distill it into a richer reminiscence, but that does not make the forgotten parts any less really lived. So I will not try to conclude this autobiography with a "larger view of things." I will not try to think up conclusions on the meaning of life. Instead, I will go on telling my story of the day's work. I will go on talking about kitchen things and eyeglasses. I will gossip and complain. My Cambridge won't mind.

59

TROUBLES AND COMPLAINTS IN CAMBRIDGE, MASSACHUSETTS

MY SECOND SOJOURN in Cambridge started with a bang. My car ran into a telephone pole. Nova had just learned to drive and had a brand-new license for driving our brand-new car. She had learned to take the little jerk out of a full stop and to match engine speed with car speed while shifting gears For Daddy would be satisfied with nothing less than perfect technique. He warned her that her first accident would mean the end of her driving.

We moved house by one of those big moving vans, but took the more important things with us in our family car, such as the big glass bowl and Kitty. After we got safely settled in an apartment on Lee Street, we still had to make another trip to New Haven to finish some business there and pick up the last odds and ends. Yuenren had already started work at Harvard and Iris had to enter summer school. So Nova and I went, with Nova at the wheel, as I had no driving license. We started out in the early morning. Nova was extra careful this time. If I told her to open or shut the window, she would bring the car to a full stop before doing so, since she had not yet learned to wind the handle of the window with one hand without also winding the car on the highway with the other. We were making better time than expected, and I thought we might get to New Haven before lunch. Thanks to my backseat driving habits, I always liked to call out the traffic signs I saw. As we were nearing Hartford, and the road was getting narrower and more crooked, I read out my soundings: "Slow!" "Twenty-five miles an hour!" It was just before a sharp right turn.

"What time is it, Nova?" I asked, as I thought of lunch in New Haven.

Nova crossed her left hand over to the right in order to show me her wrist watch. . . .

When Yuenren got my telegram in the afternoon, saying, "Safely arrived," he was puzzled. Why was it necessary to send a telegram about it? He called me up.

"Everything's all right now," I told him, before telling him that everything was once all wrong. I told him that nobody had been hurt, except for some slight bruises, and that the car had been in good enough condition for us to drive to New Haven under its own steam from the radiator.

The first thing Nova said after the collision was: "Daddy won't let me drive anymore!" When the garage asked one hundred dollars for repairs, she was for agreeing at once, in order to have a one-piece car to show Daddy. But I told her to wait. When I told Yuenren about it over the telephone, he said: "Tell Nova, since she drove that broken car safely from Hartford to New Haven, she may continue to drive. But wait for me to drive it back to Cambridge."

The damage was repaired, at another garage, for only a fraction of the first estimate.

Then we had trouble with our landlord, or rather the bank which managed the apartment. In China, a visitor will stay at your house almost as casually as a caller drops in for dinner. But the bank considered our visitors subtenants and wanted us to cut down on visitors. I hated to capitulate but also hated the idea of another house-hunting and house-moving in mid-July. Finally, Kitty decided it for us. There were two dogs in two other apartments in the same building. They kept barking. Kitty would go to the window nervously, and the sight of her would make the dogs bark more loudly. Moreover, she could not or would not learn the way in and out of our third-floor apartment. So we found a house on Bowdoin Street, paid a deposit on it, forfeited the deposit, moved into the Walker Street house, and lived in it for six years. It was Mrs. Woods, widow of Yuenren's teacher, Professor J. H. Woods, who happened to have seen the "For Rent" sign on the house and happened to have met me on the street later and told me about it. Things happen just like that.

A ten-room house with coal heating makes good and heavy housekeeping for anybody. With children in school and husband in office, it served the housewife right if she insisted on keeping the house tidy. When I had nothing to write when writing, the subject of household drudgery always came in handy as a filler. It also eased my conscience about living in a land of comparative war plenty when folks at home lived in a land of extreme war scarcity. I knew they had a much harder time in Chungking or Kunming, and it made me feel superior when, once in a while, I heard that so-and-so over there still had a servant while I had none.

Our more comfortable house also provided more comfortable guest rooms, this time without anybody to tell us who could live in our house. When Chinese came to Cambridge, the Chaos' home was almost as much a "must" as the glass flowers of Agassiz Museum. When the hotels were full, as they usually were, our guest rooms were full, too. If friends from China did not look us up when they came to America, we would feel disappointed. If they looked us up without having a meal or staying with us, we would feel disappointed. But if they did stay, we would complain about having to have too much entertainment. I would complain because of overwork. Yuenren would complain because he had no time to work. Our guests would, probably, complain because we kept them up late when staying with us—we had so much to ask them and so much to gossip about.

Not only did old friends come to see us, young friends also came all the time. If we had not known them before, we had probably known their parents anyway. It seemed that everybody was either somebody's son or somebody's daughter. Some came to bring news from their parents, such as Chang Ting (son of Y. S. Djang), who had accompanied our bus driver's singing with his mouth organ on our way to Kunming. Some came because they had no news from home, such as Miss Kuan Shuchuang, whose home was in Manchuria. Some came because of our daughters, such as Pian Hsuehhuang, who married Iris later, and Huang P'eiyung, who married Nova a little earlier. Some just came. I welcomed and entertained all. If I liked to be addressed by everybody as "Aunt Chao," I had to earn the title by acting like one. Even Ginnie Heffernan, Nova's classmate, came in and out of the house and got fed and scolded, like one of the daughters.

A frequent complaint Yuenren and I made to each other was that we never called on our American friends often enough. When Pearl Buck said to me that Chinese residents in America did not mix enough with the Americans, I immediately felt guilty myself. Time and again, I would make resolutions and schedules for calling on old neighbors, new neighbors, first-time Cambridge friends, and second-time Cambridge friends. Especially rewarding it was to call on those who had been teachers to two generations of Chaos, since it made time do double duty. Both Iris and Daddy studied under E.G. Boring, "Doc" Davison, and Edward Ballantine. Both Nova and Daddy studied under George Sarton.[1] But, in spite of all my time-saving schemes and schedules, I never had enough time to carry out my resolutions. I gave up making dinner calls. In fact, I had never learned to do it properly. In return to hospitalities, I often had to resort to buffet meals, and that was neither Chinese in taste nor Chinese in manners.

I felt I had no time for anything. Didn't it take time to write this book? Well, I wrote it practically in no time. When a memory came to me as I was at my dishes, I would just wipe my hands and jot it down on my kitchen pad. If I found the car locked and didn't have the key with me and had to wait for my husband to come out of the office, I would use the hood for a desk and write on it. That was how I found time in no time.

---

[1] Mrs. Sarton had laughed at me when I inquired about Shady Hill School, where she was teaching, when Iris was only two years old.

"No time, no time," seemed to be the constant theme of complaint during my second stay in Cambridge. Maybe it has been the constant theme of every period of my life. Maybe, as no time goes on, it will sound fainter and fainter, until some other theme or themes will ring out more clearly and true.

But surely Yuenren, who never washed dishes,[2] could not complain of having "no time." Surely Yuenren, who had no routine classes to teach, could work all he wanted during office hours. Yes, but he did not call that his work. He was called to Harvard to join the staff of the dictionary project. No, it was not the idea of the dictionary he had left behind when Professor J.H. Woods told him in 1924: "Chao, now you can write your *Dictionary of Modern Chinese*." It was a much larger project. It was to be a Chinese-English Dictionary based on cuttings from fifteen Chinese dictionaries and two foreign dictionaries of Chinese, pasted on one and a quarter million cards. As an *hors d'oeuvre* to that, a smaller dictionary, of four to six thousand pages, was to be prepared and published first. Yuenren estimated that the smaller dictionary would take about forty man-years, which, with the size of the staff available, would take about twelve years, not counting interruptions by war work. There was a current conception that it was Chao Yuenren's dictionary. It was not. It was a project of Harvard-Yenching Institute, under the direction of the eminent scholar Serge Elisséeff, who disapproves of the use of superfluous adjectives.

Yuenren's office was the best room in the building, a big, bright room, converted from a lecture room, in Boylston Hall, from which he could see both the Appelton Chapel and old John Harvard. Yuenren did not appreciate the privilege of having the best desk in the best room of the building, commanding the best view of the "Yard." He has a peculiar liking for small rooms a sort of intellectual agoraphobia, as it were. He says that the degree of his concentration is

---

[2]What, never?—Y.R.C.
Well, hardly ever.—B.Y.C.

inversely proportional to the size of the room. To him, Havelock Ellis's liking for doing his writing outdoors is quite incomprehensible. Even at home, he likes to stand bookcases and things in the middle of the room to make it look smaller. As a matter of fact, the four hundred odd filing cases containing the million-odd dictionary cards did break up the big office room a little. But he still complained that he could not concentrate. He claimed that that was why he wrote only three books in six years—and a large part of the work was done at home.

But when I come to think of it, that third-floor southeastern room of his in Academia Sinica in Nanking was not really such a tiny room, as rooms go. His study in that Lanchia Chuang home, the room that had had to be raised by five feet, was even bigger. From the way he often talked about those rooms, I don't think that his was a case of agoraphobia. I think his real "complaint" was a case of nostalgia.

60

WAR AND COOKING

"IT HAS BEEN a long time since you went away. We all miss you. We often talk about you. When are you coming back to China?"

In this vein, since we left Kunming, my friends and relatives wrote to me, Yuenren's friends wrote to Yuenren, and the children's schoolmates wrote to the children. Each time we received such a letter, conversation around the family table would take on a characteristic tone. Should we go back? Had we better go back? How were we going to go back? Most of the time, these questions would drift into aimless reminiscences and soon be forgotten. But if it was winter or early spring, when our plans for the next year were usually made, the questions would take a more practical turn, and occupy our minds for a longer time than in other seasons of the year. Pearl Harbor put an end to these sentimental gestures to ourselves. Whether I was glad or troubled—probably I was both—there was nothing further to do about it. A family like ours would have to remain abroad for the duration.

We were at one of those faculty teas that Sunday afternoon. The radio was on, an unusual thing at such a function, but a most natural thing on such a day.

"For further developments," the announcer said, "we take you now to Pearl Harbor. Go ahead, Pearl Harbor!"

There was silence. Then he tried to get Manila.

"Go ahead, Manila!"

Again, there was silence.

As I thanked the lady who handed me the tea, I overheard Yuenren say to the president: "Don't you think, Mr. Conant, that the Japanese were rather foolish to run such a great political risk by this action?"

"I am fearful," he replied, "that the next report may prove that they considered their military gain as far outweighing their political loss."

As everybody knows, the Japanese certainly did think so for almost three years.

My moods of that day alternated between tension and relief, tension when I talked with Americans, and relief when I talked with Chinese. Hu Shih had been saying all along that the only thing that China could do was to sustain the bitter struggle and wait for the change. The change, I thought, had come at last. "Japan's feet of clay" would soon crumble under her.

The next day, in a mood of ignorant light-heartedness, Yuenren drove with me to New Haven to attend the meeting of the Yale Linguistic Club. Turning from the Worcester Turnpike into U.S. Route 20, we were stopped by a traffic officer for passing a car by crossing the white line. Yuenren had done that more than once before. But several wrongs did not make one right. After looking at Yuenren's license, the officer asked: "Where were you born?"

"Tientsin."

"Tientsin, China? Why, that's where my wife was born."

Having ascertained that we were friends and not enemies, he kept us a little longer for the sociable part of the detention and sent us on without a ticket.

Passing Stafford Springs, Connecticut, we asked another policeman whether war had been declared. He thought so, and we identified our nationality by saying, "Hooray!" to that.

My New Haven friends were surprised to find me glad that war had come. Yuenren, on his part, was surprised that the discussion following his paper on the Foochow dialect did not branch off into the Japanese or the Hawaiian language. It was just like any other of those meetings.

Only gradually did I realize that, as the saying goes, things had to be much worse before they were better, that hard and desperate times were still to come.

I kept myself busy with wartime activities, not because I was any more patriotic[1] than others, but because I always like to keep myself busy. I like to talk about my activities, not because I am more boastful than others, but because I like to talk. Anyway, I did not have much to boast of. Being a back number of a doctor, I did little that any housewife in my place could not have done. The most I had to do with medicine was to buy new drugs and vitamins from time to time and send them by airmail to my friends and relatives. I did go to meetings of neighborhood first-aid groups and was made one of the doctors for Shepard and Walker Streets in case of air raids, but was fortunate in never having been needed.

But I kept running around just the same. You see, in all the relief agencies, such as the Red Cross knitting circles, European reliefs, the United China Relief, etc., many nationals of the beneficiary countries took active parts themselves. If older ladies—pardon my Chinese courtesy!—like Mrs. A.W. Hartt, Mrs. A.N. Holcombe, Mrs. A.M. Schlesinger, and others, tired themselves out from working for China, I felt I had no business to remain fresh and rested.

I thought at first that the war would take me farther away from the kitchen. But exactly the opposite happened. With all the difficulties of rationing, I had never had so much to do with cooking in my life. I already spoke of having to entertain friends that passed by. Then I had to cook for the China Relief luncheon once a week for several months. It is really as simple to cook for one hundred people

---

[1] There is need of a word which should combine the overtones of the word "patriotic" and the idea of "loyalty to the United Nations."—Y.R.C.

as for six, just as it is as simple to draw a map of the world as it is to draw a map of a city or simpler, in the case of Boston. I only needed to apply the method of increasing the quantity without increasing the variety.

On one occasion, when there was a church meeting in New Haven for raising funds for a college in China, I cooked a meal for over four hundred people, with the aid of only one Chinese and one American lady. Ten minutes before the dinner was to be served, when everybody was already seated, I discovered that the rice had been burned. Fortunately, there was extra rice and several gas fires, with as many extra pots. The subscribers to the funds were served after no more than the usual delay for such occasions.

After this, it was nothing to cook snacks for twenty people. Yuenren had a corps of young people to help him teach some 150 American soldiers, who had to learn Chinese in a hurry. His assistants, or "informants," as they were called, often met at our house for conferences. It was more convenient for Yuenren. But it was more inconvenient for the informants, and I felt that everybody ought to have a little something before they dispersed. For, if the meeting dragged on into a sort of Linguistic Club, as it often did, intellectual hunger was sure to become non-intellectual in the end.

A much more strenuous kind of entertaining was to stay up late to feed another group, night after night, for several weeks. Yuenren had a piece of map work to do, which involved a lot of translation of languages and dialects, and had to be rushed through by a certain date. So he got together a number of assistants and worked until the small hours of the night, sometimes until the small hours grew big again. Now it is a physiological fact that, to a considerable extent, sleep and food can compensate for each other, especially for healthy young people. Having no facility in doing any language work, I contributed to the common effort by providing midnight suppers for the workers—not just little bedtime snacks this time, but substantial meals that still had to last for several hours. When finally the papers came out with news of such and such places being bombed by the

Allies, one of the members of the team would say: "Why, that's my section of the map!" To me it meant the night of shrimp noodles.

Well, that was as much cooking as I ever cared to do. So, in order to have done with it once for all, I wrote a book, addressed to Americans, on *How to Cook and Eat in Chinese*. After that, I should look for my best Chinese meals in American homes, that is, if I did succeed in saying my say.

An unhappy, though by some standards trivial, incident occurred to us during the war years, which affected the tone of our home for quite some time. We lost our cat. We had missed her for two days. Nobody worried over much about her, as she had taken even longer trips away before. But this time a neighbor reported having seen a dead black cat under a tree that had recently been sprayed with poison. She wondered whether by any chance it was . . .

And I had said, after that New Haven fire, that animals could take care of themselves!

We buried her by a lilac bush in our backyard. We avoided mentioning cats in our conversation for weeks, especially in front of Lensey. After a few months, mice began to invade our kitchen. Some less sensitive members of the family suggested getting another cat.[2] I said no. I never play with cats, as I have said. But to me knowing a cat is like knowing a person. I still feel bad about having to leave our two cats behind at Lanchia Chuang when we left Nanking as refugees in 1937. We had better not have another cat until we knew where we were going to settle down.

---

[2] Not me.— *Iris.*
 Not me either.—*Nova.*
 I didn't.—*Bella.*
 Well, I thought perhaps we. . . .—*Daddy.*

61

V-J DAY

THEN THINGS HAPPENED fast. Between the spring and the winter of 1945, more seems to have happened than I remember during any similar period before. The United Nations was born—my first book was published—Germany surrendered—Nova was married—Japan surrendered—Iris was married. My mind shifted between public and personal events. V-Days alternated with Wedding Days. They presented a sort of pointilist effect, exciting and bright.

We missed the V-J Day crowds, because we were guests of the R.W. Kings at their quiet cottage in Greensboro, Vermont. Yuenren had not had a vacation for three years, and thought that a month in the Green Mountains would take off of the staleness of mind he felt was coming over him. Between bathing in the Caspian Lake and eating raw peas, fresh from the vine, he thought he could put my autobiography into English in one month. No, he didn't write the way I did, leaning on my elbow on the lawn, or lounging more comfortably in the big sitting room. He would coop himself up in the smallest bedroom in the house, with thick-growing pines shading the sun from his windows. He was making good progress at the rate of two years a day, and I had a hard time trying to maintain a lead of twenty or thirty years with my writing in Chinese.

One morning, I heard him start typing earlier than usual.

"Have you reached the 1911 Revolution, Yuenren?" I called from the kitchen.

"I have reached August 5, 1945! Let's congratulate ourselves that we are still alive, Yunch'ing!"

He had just heard the first news of the atomic bomb over the radio and was typing feverishly a letter to *The New York Times*. Since, he wrote, the explosion had not yet spread from Hiroshima to Greensboro, Vermont, by this time, the danger of the world blowing up by atomic energy was at least temporarily over. Secondly, he said, America had not wanted to boss the world because it was wrong and because it could not be done. Now, only because it was wrong. Finally, if the benefits of atomic energy that were sure to come could be distributed sensibly, there would be no need of anybody wanting to boss anybody else.

I could not absorb so much atomic energy in one morning, but, from the way Yuenren began to neglect my autobiography, it must have been very important.

Four days later, as you all know, was the false alarm about the surrender. When we heard the report, we tried to start a celebration. But houses were hundreds of yards apart and our yelling was not very impressive. Yuenren took a cowbell from the mantelpiece and rang it on the lawn as hard as he could. But one professor ringing a cowbell did not make a celebrating crowd. A girl of a neighboring family, who was rowing on the lake, thought that it meant "supper was ready," and immediately rowed back to her home for supper.

We had been outside the house for only about one minute. When we went in again, we heard the radio say: "Hold that! . . . There is no surrender . . . There was a mistake . . . All is confusion! . . ."

It repeated, "All is confusion" several times and concluded with "The war goes on."

It did so for two more days. When the real surrender came, we celebrated in a slightly more sober manner. While we made very little use of wine, we made much use of the now unrationed gasoline. We could not resist the temptation of saying again, "Fill 'er up!"

We felt like driving clear across to China. But instead, we drove to New York to see T'ao Mengho and Hu Shih to celebrate "the change." Then we went on to Washington, D. C., where F. Chang,

Yuenren's schoolmate at Harvard, had recently arrived from Chungking. Chang was no stranger there, but we showed him around a different Washington from the one he knew.

This, as we pointed out a house on Kalorama Road, was the earlier Chinese Educational Mission, from which Yuenren used to receive his monthly checks as a Tsing Hua scholarship student. This, as we passed a hat shop on Connecticut Avenue near Calvert Street, was the later Chinese Educational Mission, from which Yuenren used to send out checks to Tsing Hua scholarship students . . . Haven't you ever noticed the difference in expression between the two profiles of the Lincoln Memorial? Just walk a little this way, please, right behind here. You see, the northern profile contains a faint smile . . . Now you see the difference, the sadder face, from this other side?

Then, of course, I always visited the open-air Amphitheater behind the Unknown Soldier, no matter how briefly I visited Washington. For it reminded me of the open-air Amphitheater in front of the Sun Yatsen Mausoleum of Nanking. The children gathered on the stage and sang a three-part chorus I don't remember the name of[1] and drew an applause from an audience of about a dozen visitors, including ourselves. The girls were not so good at the vigorous song *Ch'i Cheng P'iap'iao* ("Banners are Streaming") by the late Huang Tzu. Though I don't understand singing, I knew it would take something like that big Chinese chorus we had heard in the Nanking Amphitheater to do that song:

The sun had set. . . . The wind had fallen to a light breeze. . . . The moon was sailing idly through one transparent strip of cloud after another without getting anywhere. It was very quiet and peaceful. There was something familiar about the whole scene.

"Let's go home," one of us said, meaning our hotel in Washington.

---

[1] It was *Glorious Apollo*, by Samuel Webbe.—*Iris.*

"Let's go home," said another, thinking of Walker Street and the fall term.

"Yes, let's go home," said still another, dreaming of Lanchia Chuang and Yenling Hsiang.

Then we all became as quiet as the scene around us. Yuenren must be thinking of his plans to resume his dialect survey in China. But no, I think he wants to write his *Fourth Green Letter*, and perhaps publish his translation of *Through the Looking Glass*, before taking up anything more serious. For I know that he always puts pleasure before work.

What am I going to do when I go back? Well, as a Chinese woman, I do appreciate the common desire of retiring to a life of serene contentment, with all children and grandchildren gathered around oneself. But, as Buwei Yang Chao, I hate to sit around while everybody else is busy. Now that the job of raising a family is nearly done, I should be able to take a more active part in things than I have been for years. I want my father to win his point about educating his daughter just like a son.

When mail from Nanking came through again after an interruption of four years, I got word from Cousine Chinghua at 1 T'ienyin An that our house—not the Lanchia Chuang home that had been burned, but a much smaller one at 9 T'ienyin An—was still intact, and we found ourselves millionaires in Chinese money.

So Yuenren resigned from Harvard. We packed up our things in wooden boxes to ship to China. But at our silver wedding, nearly ten months after V-J Day, we were still having our family picture taken in a Boston studio. Traveling is never so slow in these days of "fast travel," you know. But Nova and Peiyung are already in Yellowstone Park on their way to China. We'll follow along, sometime soon, I hope.

Till we meet again, I will say all my friends: *"Tsai chien!"*

APPENDICES

APPENDIX I

NOTES ON CHINESE NAMES AND TERMS OF ADDRESS

The normal order of Chinese names is last name first, as in a telephone directory. But you say the whole thing smoothly, without pausing for a comma in between. Thus, while I am Buwei Yang in America, I am Yang Buwei in China. When a woman marries, she adds her husband's family name to hers. When I sign my name in English, it is Buwei Yang Chao, but in China, I am Chao Yang Buwei. A general term of address follows the proper name. Thus, while I give my social address in English as Mrs. Y.R. Chao, I am Chao Yuenren T'ait'ai in China. In conversation, I am addressed or mentioned as Chao T'ait'ai.

A Chinese usually has a family name (same as his father's), a pet name, a formal name, and a *hao*, which means "appellation," but usually translated as "style" or "courtesy name."

The formal name is used in school, at law, and in your work. The courtesy name is used among friends, between husband and wife (often in abbreviated form), and in the salutation or on the envelope of a letter. Not knowing a person's courtesy name when you have to write to him is something like not knowing his initials.

My family name is Yang; my pet names are Lansien, Ch'uanti and Ch'uan'er; my formal name was Yunch'ing, then changed to Buwei, after which I decided to use Yunch'ing as my courtesy name.

There is a fashion now to use one name for both formal name and *hao*. My husband used to have a *hao*, but has long discarded it in favor of one personal name "Yuenren" for all purposes. Once, when he was addressed by (family name and) *hao* in an invitation, he accepted the invitation, but noted that the person under that name had "deceased."

The family name is never used alone, but must be prefixed to the formal name to form a full legal name, or to the courtesy name to form a full social name. It can also be prefixed to Hsiensheng (Mr.), T'ait'ai (Mrs.), Hsiaochieh (Miss), etc.

Relatives do not call each other by name, but by relationship, such as "First Aunt" or "Third Brother." But a person may call a relative younger than himself by pet name or, if the latter is grown up, by courtesy name.

The use of the pronoun *ni* ("you") is not polite to strangers or respectful toward relatives older than oneself. There is a word *nin* in the Peiping dialect for polite or respectful use, but in most parts of China, the general practice is to repeat the proper term of address without using any pronoun. For example, I would say: "Great-grandma, will Great-grandma let me play in Great-grandma's room a little longer?"

APPENDIX II

MY GENEALOGICAL TREE

Scale of Generations:

| 2 Up | 1 Up | Own | 1 Down | 2 Down |

Grandfather Wenhui (*tzu*[1] Jenshan)
    Big Uncle Tzu-hsin (*tzu* Hsiaoyuan) and Auntie, née Lang
        First born, boy[2]
            Second born, boy
            Big Sister
            Second Sister
            Third Sister
            Big Brother Fusheng and Sister-in-law, née Hsü
                Four girls
                → (**Shihfeng**, adopted from Second Brother)
            Second Brother Tsaisheng (*tzu* Yungch'ang) and Sister-in-law, née P'ing
                Shihfeng and wife, née Chin
                      Girl Naidey
                      Boy Chiachen
                      Boy
                      Boy
                Shihchung (died at 10)
                Johua and husband **Ho**
                Chaoho and husband **Kao**
                      Girl
                Twin boys
                Girl

---

[1] Tzu is the biographical term for *hao*, or courtesy name.
[2] Italics type means "died in infancy." Bold face means "now living."

Shihhao

Scale of Generations:

| 1 Up | Own | 1 Down |

        Third Brother Lisheng (*tzu* Hofu) and Sister-in-law, née Hsü
            Twin boys
            Girl Jo-yin (died at 6)
            Jo-hsien ("Lucy")
            Boy
            Boy
            Jo-ying
            Boy
            Jolan and husband
        Buwei (*tzu* Yunch'ing) and **husband Chao**
            Rulan ("Iris") and husband Pian
            Shinna ("Nova") and husband Huang
            Girl Lensey
            Girl Hsiaochung ("Bella")
Father Tzuch'ao (*tzu* K'ueiyuan) and Mother, née Hsiao
    (**Buwei**, adopted from Big Uncle and Auntie)
    → (**Sixth Brother**, adopted from Fifth Uncle and Aunt)
First Aunt and Uncle Ch'eng
    First Cousine Ch'eng and husband
        Boy
    Second Cousine and husband
        Nine children
        Two children
    First Cousin and **wife**
        Five boys
    Second Cousin (my ex-fiancé) and his wife
        Two boys
        Two girls
    Third Cousine
    Fourth Cousine Chinghua
Second Aunt (became nun, died at 53)
Third Uncle (died at 11)

Fourth Uncle (died at 10)

Scale of Generations:

| 1 Up | Own | 1 Down |

Fifth Uncle Fuyen (*tzu* Chihyuan) and Aunt, née Li
        Fourth Cousin and wife
            Girl
        Fifth Cousin Chungying and wife
            Girl and **husband**
            Four girls
            Five boys
            Boy
        Sixth Brother Yüsheng and **wife**, née Li
            Three boys
            Five girls
            Girl
        Fourth Cousine and husband Pao
            Boy Chengku
            Boy Chengp'eng
        Fifth Cousine
        Seventh Cousin and wife
            Eight children

APPENDIX III

GLOSSARY

Following is a list of special words and expressions used in this book. Where no definition is given, the meaning can be found from the text on the page indicated. For names of persons and places see Genealogical Tree and Maps.

Academia Sinica, "the Chinese Academy," a group of thirteen research institutes,
Buwei, "stride-great," my formal name, given to me by my schoolmate Lin Kuanhung,
chen bang, how smart!
Chang Three, Lee Four, used like "John Smith," and "Tom Brown," i.e. anybody, so-and-so,
civil service examinations,
cousine (pron. same as "cousin"), form used in this book for female cousines,
dollar (of Chinese money), worth about 40 cents in American money at par,
double-hour, one of the twelve divisions of the day, starting from midnight, in the old Chinese system of reckoning time,
"glazed,"
greeting, form of,
Han people, Chinese race in the narrower sense,
Hao le! "That's good!" "That's fine!"
haole (pron. *how lay*), Hawaiian word for the white people,
homohomonukunukuapua,
hsien, an administrative unit similar to a township or county in the United States,
Huap'ailou, street in central Nanking,
Lanchia Chuang, residential district in Nanking; short for "24 Lanchia Chuang," where I lived from 1935 to 1937,
leave taking, form of, 125
Lee Four, see Chang Three

li, Chinese unit of distance, equal to about one-third of a mile,
lungt'ang-style houses, tenement houses arranged in *lungt'ang* or lanes (Shanghai),
Mei, "younger sister," "I"
Nankai University, famous private university, situated at Tientsin, Hopeh,
National Peiping University,
National University of Peking,
o,
Lansien, "Orchid Fairy," my first pet name, given to me by Auntie,
pailou, decorative gateway or arch,
riding coat, half-length coat, usually black, worn over a long gown, constituting a man's full formal dress,
seiyō ryōri, "Occidental catering," Japanese term for Occidental meals or restaurants,
Shihtai, a *hsien* in southern Anhwei, where my own family came from,
singsong girls, "high-class" prostitutes, whose main activities consist in selling songs or sitting behind stag parties,
South, the,
t'a, Chinese pronoun for "he, she, it,"
tael, unit of silver money worth about half a dollar in American money at par,
Taip'ing uprising, the,
t'aitai, Mrs., (married) lady,
Tsai chien! "Till we meet again!" "Goodbye!"
Tsing Hua University, National,
Tsinghua Yuan, northwestern suburb of Peiping, seat of Tsing Hua University,
unveiling of the bride,
Western, i.e. Occidental,
"winds and waters," geomancy, i.e. system of choosing propitious sites for houses or tombs,
yen, unit of Japanese money, worth about half a dollar in American money at par,
Yenling Hsiang, street in central Nanking, 41; short for "house at 49 Yenling Hsiang," built by my grandfather,
Yunch'ing, "person with rhyme," name given to me by my grandfather,

APPENDIX IV

Map of Nanking

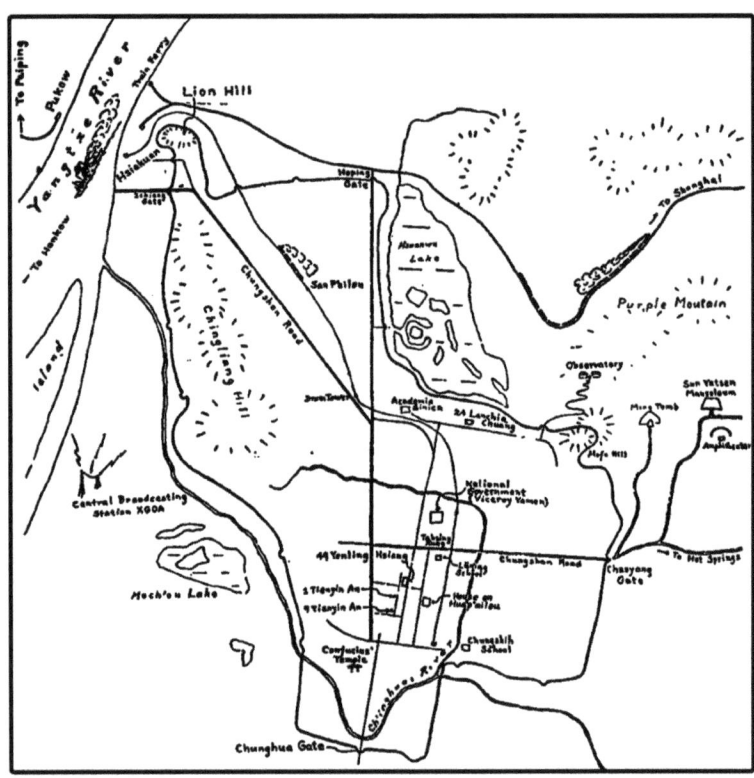

NANKING

APPENDIX V

Map of China

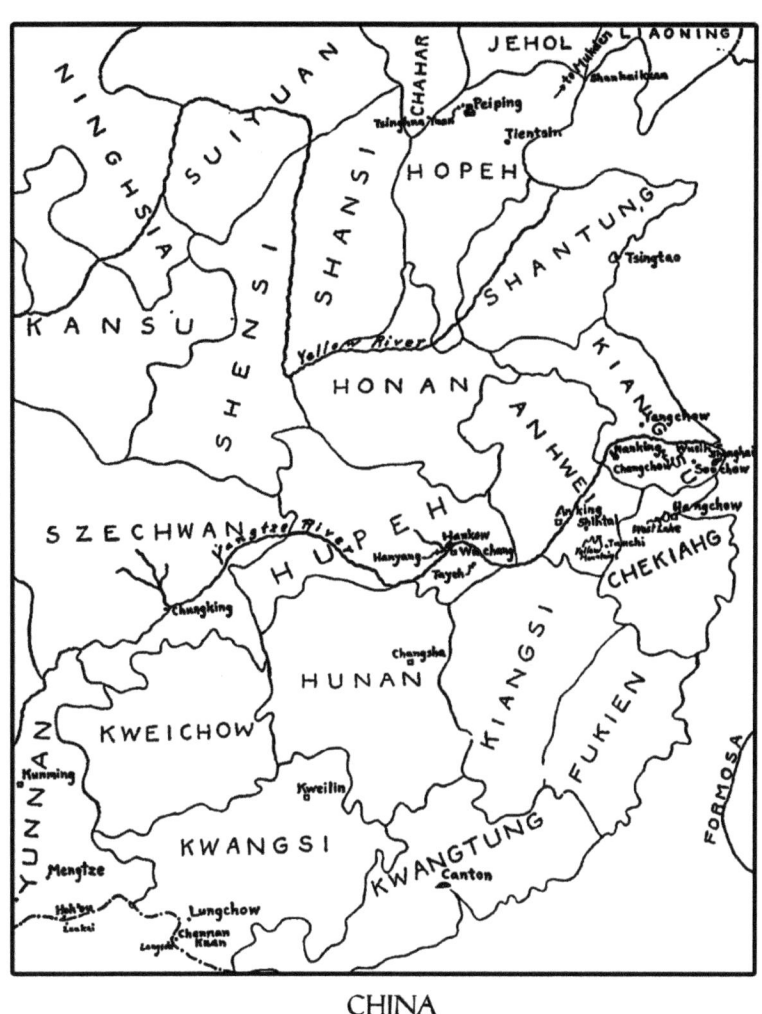

CHINA